CHRIST'S

At the very heart of Christian doctrine and late medieval practice was the image of the crucified Christ. In *Christ's Body*, Sarah Beckwith describes and explains the uses of the extraordinary iconography of this imagery, its social function and imaginative effects in a range of key devotional vernacular English writings.

In a fascinating and challenging series of readings, Beckwith develops a hermeneutic by which significant texts in the medieval Christian tradition – such as *The Book of Margery Kempe* – can be read as social texts for the first time. Criticizing the idealist underpinnings of much of the critical tradition surrounding the texts, *Christ's Body* develops a materialistic analysis of religious texts, showing the vital cultural work they do.

Sarah Beckwith is Assistant Professor of English at the University of Pittsburgh.

CHRIST'S BODY

Identity, culture and society
in late medieval writings

Sarah Beckwith

London and New York

First published 1993
by Routledge
First published in paperback 1996
by Routledge
11 New Fetter Lane, London EC4P 4EE

Simultaneously published in the USA and Canada
by Routledge
29 West 35th Street, New York, NY 10001

Routledge is an International Thomson Publishing company

© 1993, 1996 Sarah Beckwith

Typeset in Times by Intype, London
Printed and bound in Great Britain by
TJ Press (Padstow) Ltd, Padstow, Cornwall

British Library Cataloguing in Publication Data
A catalogue record for this book is available from the British Library

Library of Congress Cataloguing in Publication Data
A catalogue record for this book has been requested

ISBN 0-415-14426-4

To my mother and father

Why are ye troubled? and why do thoughts arise in your hearts?
Behold my hands and my feet, that it is I myself: handle me,
and see; for a spirit hath not flesh and bones, as ye see me here.

(Luke 24:39)

CONTENTS

CONTENTS

ACKNOWLEDGEMENTS

I would first of all like to thank the superviser of the dissertation on which this study is based, Janet Cowan, and my two meticulous and helpful examiners, Rosamund Allen and Peter Travis, whose own studies of and conversations about 'the body of Christ' have been as inspiring as they have been rich.

Each year of the incompletion of this book has certainly left me with richer and greater debts of gratitude to friends and colleagues both old and new. I would like to thank my colleagues in the School of English and American Studies at the University of East Anglia, especially David Aers who gave me detailed commentary on the first two chapters, and read this project from its very earliest stages with insight and more generosity than it then deserved. Also thanks to Jon Cook, Tony Gash, Roger Sales, Su Kappeler, Vic Sage, Andrew Higson and Peter Womack for being the gifted writers and teachers that they all, in their different ways, are, and for contributing towards the distinctive milieu which helped shape so much of what this book attempts to do. I would also like to thank Lisa Jardine.

Regina Schwartz gave me support and comments, especially on the first chapter. Thanks too to Elizabeth Robertson, Toril Moi and Lee Patterson, who carefully and responsively read the manuscript in its entirety.

I dislike making my thanks to the students who have worked with me over the years anonymous, for they are not anonymous to me. But I hope this thanks will be a gesture towards recognizing the humour, scepticism, intelligence and work that has helped and enriched as well as unconscionably frustrated the completion of this work.

My debts of course are not just scholarly. Simon Pummell and

Carol Sagar alone know, I hope, the extent of what they contributed towards this book; to them both my debt is personal and significant and I have not forgotten it. I would like to thank my parents, Thelma Thomasine Dawes and Arthur John Beckwith, for all their love, support, spirit and recognition over the years, my much-missed friends Sue Rankin and Shaun Hargreaves-Heap, and last, but as they say, by no means least, John Twyning, who was brave or stupid enough to step across the Atlantic with me in 1989, and who, luckily for me, has not yet regretted it.

It remains for me to thank Julia Hall, Talia Rodgers and Sarah-Jane Woolley for their careful, thoughtful and invaluable shepherding of the process from manuscript to book.

INTRODUCTION

Man is
the symbol using (symbol making, symbol misusing) animal
inventor of the negative (or moralized by the negative)
separated from his natural condition by instruments of his
own making
goaded by the spirit of hierarchy (or moved by a sense of
order)
and rotten with perfection.

(Kenneth Burke)

This book deals with an organizing metaphor in some late medieval devotional writings – the metaphor of Christ's body – and
examines its intertwined social functions and imaginative effects.
In particular I seek to analyse the image of Christ as physical,
suffering and embodied, in a range of Middle English texts which
may be identified by their very focus on such an image. Deriving
their meaning from the image which they so centrally figure,
such texts are often defined as belonging to a tradition of 'Christocentric' or 'crucifixion piety'. These texts, as I define them,
are extraordinary for the way in which they are shaped by the
requirements of their readership – the emergent lay readership in
the vernacular of the late Middle Ages. I am particularly interested
here in exploring the way in which Christocentric devotion
becomes a medium for the production of identity. Who, I ask,
is involved in such a production? What is at stake? What kinds
of historical agencies may be inferred from it? How can these
devotional texts be read in terms of the social practices to which
they refer and in which they participate?

What do I mean when I refer, as I will frequently in the course
of this study, to 'Christ's body'? It is perhaps better to start off
by saying what I do *not* mean or what is not implied by that
recurrent phrase. I am not attempting an analysis of the late
medieval theology of incarnation: that is, although some

1

theological issues are encountered and discussed, these are by no means the principal focus of analysis. Indeed in many ways, this book constitutes an attempt to move away from some of the idealist underpinnings of studies of medieval theology. It is precisely because the mechanisms for the transmission of 'theology' were expanding, and conventionally theological questions, or questions hitherto restricted to a clerical milieu, were being disseminated beyond the clergy in the vernacular, and hence understood and received in different ways, that we need terms of reference beyond the theological. Neither am I tracing a merely rhetorical or imagistic pattern through a series of texts which feature it, although such a movement of *topoi* will be a part of my analysis. Thus, in many senses, this study moves away from the two dominant and traditional arenas which have shaped the analysis of medieval devotional texts – the disciplines respectively of theology and philology. Rather this book examines the image of 'Christ's body' as a *symbol* shaping and shaped by the *social vision* of the *religious culture* of the late Middle Ages in England. Each of these terms requires some glossing.

My usage of the term *symbol* is informed by the perspective of cultural anthropology. Seeing the social world as always pre-interpreted, and therefore always already imbued with meaning, such a perspective sees symbols as the signifying devices which provide the communiciative context through which social worlds are imagined, invented and changed. Thus, men and women are viewed as creative agents in a world of their own active making and re-making, and symbolic forms are seen as indispensable to such making. Symbols then are intrinsically and definitionally bound to imply a *social perspective or vision*. That is, they are themselves unimaginable outside the context of social relations. As soon as symbols are placed in this analytical context, it becomes clear that the analysis of symbolic form is always to some extent the analysis of meaning in the context of specific social and political relations; what follows inevitably from this perception is that symbolic forms sometimes mobilize meaning in the service of power, that symbols, in other words, have an ideological dimension. Symbolic forms, then, need to be analysed in terms of the *cultures* of which they are a part. If *symbols* may be defined as 'tangible formulations of notions, abstractions from experience fixed in perceptible forms, concrete embodiments of ideas, attitudes, judgements, longings or beliefs'[1] and *culture* as 'a

2

signifying system through which necessarily (though among other means) a social order is communicated, reproduced, experienced and explored',[2] then it may be seen how mutually intertwined and constitutive the concepts of 'symbol' and 'culture' really are. In this way a cultural analysis may be described as 'the study of the meaningful constitution and social contextualization of symbolic forms'.[3]

To examine 'Christ's body' as a symbol, then, rather than as a theological concept or a trope is to ask how such an image *makes meaning* for its practitioners and interlocutors. Given the centrality of the image of Christ's body to the political construction of a Christian culture imagined as a unity, it is all the more important to stress that the study of symbolic forms needs to be understood in the context of social and political differentiation, of unequal power. The inviolable unity of Christ's body as eucharist was asserted through the doctrine of concomitance which proclaimed that the body and the blood of Christ were present in each element. This (Aristotelian) understanding of the relationship between 'substance' and 'accident' formed the philosophical basis for the understanding of the presence of Christ's body after consecration. The doctrine was formulated in the official teaching of the church for the first time at the Council of Constance of 1415, although theologians had articulated the notion prior to this.[4] It was this understanding that helped legitimize the notion that the host on every altar was the *same* body of Christ. And it was this notion that informed the universalist claims of the ecclesiastical polity and made it possible for the host, as symbol, to bear the weight of those claims.[5] Indeed, if Christ's body in the form of the eucharist was where the integrity of an entire culture was most celebrated and consequently protested, if belief in transubstantiation could literally define your bona fide membership of that 'imaginary community',[6] then Christ's body as it was violated, eaten, transgressed and otherwise played with, was also the symbol which suffered from the most extreme degree of inner contestation and self-difference.[7] Indeed it is precisely by being able to give body to divergent notions, claims and practices that symbols can come to tell us much about the 'structures of feeling' of a particular culture, about that 'field of contradiction between a consciously held ideology and emergent experience'.[8] For it is the very imprecision of symbols, the way they do not so much express meaning as encourage the creative attribution of multiple meanings to themselves[9] that lead them to become the 'subject of political and social contestation'.[10] Such political and social contestation, very often evacuated from the very conceptualization of 'culture', will be a constitutive part of my understanding of the creative symbolization of Christ's body at work in the texts under analysis.[11]

The image-repertoire of 'Christ's body' has been analysed in some recent studies. It is explored in the discipline of art history for example, in James Marrow's book, *Passion Iconography in Northern Europe in the Late Middle Ages and Early Renaisssance;*[12] in the early Christian period it has been studied extensively by Peter Brown;[13] in the medieval period it has come under the compelling scrutiny of Caroline Walker Bynum in her recent book, *Holy Feast and Holy Fast: The Significance of Food to Medieval Women,*[14] and more recently still in Miri Rubin's analysis of Christ's body as manifested in eucharistic practice, *Corpus Christi: The Eucharist in Late Medieval Culture.*[15] But each of these books is attempting something different from the focus of my analysis, though each informs my own. James Marrow's book is exclusively art-historical; its argument is concerned to elucidate the impact on a series of paintings in late medieval Northern European art of a particular recontextualization of a medieval habit of interpretation. What happens, he asks, when interpretative schemes hitherto allied to a particular framework of allegorical exegesis are reoriented to a wider audience who do not share that framework? Caroline Bynum's book is interested in the centrality of Christ as food, especially in terms of its religious significance to women. She therefore deals with the image of Christ's body primarily in terms of eucharistic piety and food for medieval women. Rubin's book focuses on the political, cultural and social processes by which Christ's body as eucharist is made politic in medieval culture. My own study, although it deals in passing with eucharistic piety, is not centrally or exclusively concerned with Christ's body as eucharist. For there were all kinds of other ways in which, in the devotional literature of the late Middle Ages, Christ's body was the focus of a complex symbolics of identification and role-playing. Christ was eaten in the eucharist. He was also looked at, identified with, imitated, violated, played with in an almost alarming variety of shifting social roles. And these series of relationships, which relied on the concept of the personhood of God as man, were constantly suggesting that the most important, indeed the defining aspect of that personhood was embodiment. Christ was imagined as having a life, and this involved having a body. And the symbolics of his imagined embodiment encoded an extreme cultural ambivalence – for his body was loved and adored, but it was also violated repeatedly. That violation, always implicit in the very doctrine of incarnation, is re-enacted, rendered literal with a special imagination and vision, a special attention to pain and limit in its realization. I trace the representation of Christ's body through a series of late medieval devotional texts, trying first to relate those texts to the cultural practices from which they are never absolutely separated, and secondly trying, within the internal dynamics of those texts, to explore the cultural implications of that imaging. I have focused on a series of texts whose potentialities for cross-reading make them particularly illuminating. In choosing to examine texts such as *The Prickynge of Love*[16] and the *Mirrour of the Blessyd Lyf of Jesu Christ*,[17] I am not simply focusing on late medieval texts known to have been enormously influential in the late Middle Ages, though both these texts, as translations, were previously known in more exclusive contexts, but also on texts where we can trace the imagination of Christ's body in quite some detail – in, for example, their use and assimilation by the late medieval visionary of Bishop's Lynn, Margery Kempe. For it is in *The Book of Margery Kempe*,[18] that the two concerns of this study – the symbol of Christ's body and the production of identity – come together with the most pressing explanatory logic; this book, deemed the 'first autobiography' in the English language, and therefore very much concerned with the construction of subjectivity, could hardly conceive of its own subject without the simultaneous imaging of the body of Christ.[19]

The first chapter of this book is a ground-clearing exercise designed to show how the ascription of 'mystical' to many of the texts that are central to my analysis has distorted our understanding of them. It is necessary to see precisely how this has been effected, and the extent to which it is the product of a very late historical endeavour before it is possible to develop a reading practice of these texts as social texts. The second chapter outlines the way in which the image of Christ's body becomes the bearer of social, political and economic meanings in late fourteenth-century and early fifteenth-century England. If chapter 1, then, may be seen as a historicization of the generic and formal categor-ies of description and ascription with which late medieval devotional texts have been examined, then the second chapter aims to provide a 'social contextualization'[20] of the symbolic forms which the texts under analysis will continuously encode. Understanding in cultural terms why (and how, and through what means) 'Christ's body' accrued such iconic centrality will be vital in unpacking the particular usages of this image in the dramatic, identificatory literature of 'crucifixion piety'. My third chapter will look at the play of identification as it uses and abuses the image of Christ's body in a variety of late medieval devotional texts. How precisely is Christ's life imagined in these texts, and what kind of cultural *work* is such an image doing in the context of these texts? This book began as a study of *The Book of Margery Kempe* and the *Book* is the subject of the final chapter, an analysis of the use of the symbol of Christ's body in the text and world of Margery Kempe of Bishop's Lynn, Norfolk.

If we understand religion as a 'system of symbols', then the method I have outlined briefly here and enact through the length of this book should help us further understand the shape and texture of the religious culture of the late Middle Ages in England.[21] Given the enormous success of clerical culture in generating itself as the account of an entire culture – the culture of western Christendom – given, that is, the success of its hegemonic attempt to make one stand for the other, we need to be particularly aware of thinking about culture as a set of ideas, in this case clerical ideas, imposed from above.[22] Such a stricture is even more important given the marked idealist bent traditionally ascribed to medieval thinking. By conceiving religious culture in terms of the categories of symbol, practice and use, it may be possible to envisage not so much the internal logic of such symbolism, but at least some kind of restoration of its practical necessity in the real conditions of its genesis.[23] This is especially important in view of the potentialities of sheer bizarrerie in the material under consideration. The aim, then, throughout my analysis has been to expose the normalness of the deployment of the cultural symbol of Christ's body in the texts under review, without reducing its particularity.[24]

1

THE TRANSCENDENT
AND THE HISTORICAL
Inventing the discourse
of mysticism

Pure Spirit is pure lie.[1]

(Friedrich Nietzsche)

The secular intellectual works to show the absence of divine
originality and, on the other side, the complex presence of
historical actuality. The conversion of the absence of religion
into the presence of actuality is secular interpretation.[2]

(Edward Said)

MYSTICISM AND DISENCHANTMENT

Invisible, ineffable, unrepresentable: this is supposedly the God
of the mystics – a God who, in a devastating tautology, is simply
who He is.[3] It is the mystical project, according to the classical
commentators who have made it their theme, to represent this
unrepresentable One. And it is this project, in the classical
account, that unites all mystics of any time, or any place, writing
in any language under any religious or theological system into a
truly ecumenical, transhistorical community. For mysticism in
this version is precisely that which escapes the institutional,
linguistic, doctrinal, social and economic contingencies of an
embodied material world. Because of its supposedly transhistorical character, its constitutive transcendence of the merely
material, it can function in this account like the inwardness of
religion itself, the soul of a soulless world. It can be both the
ultimate validation of the sacred, and because of that very
extra–institutional dimension, the essence of the dissenting soul.

In William James' classic formulation: 'Mystical classics . . . have neither birthday nor native land. . . . Perpetually telling of the unity of man with God, their speech antedates languages, and they do not grow old.'[4] Or, as Ernst Troeltsch says: 'Everywhere already mysticism essentially represents the same phenomena: a religious experience based on direct and vital contact with God.'[5] Mysticism so defined is the very essence, the very spirit, of religion. It is possible to see, for example, from the following quotation from G. van der Leeuw, the extent to which the mystical and the 'religious' collapse in a definition whose aim might be to restore the very 'essence' of religiosity to the secularized, the disenchanted world:

> The religious sense of a thing leaves no room for any other wider or deeper sense. It is the sense of the whole. It is the last word. That sense is never understood: that word is never uttered. Both go always beyond us. The ultimate sense is a mystery, which again and again reveals itself and yet always remains hidden.[6]

Central to this definition is a construction of that which is whole, harmonious, integral, yet simultaneously esoteric, unutterably enigmatic; final, but always about to be revealed. Such a definition allows the construction of a hermeneutics of mysticism that renders it both democratically universal, whole and available to all in the innermost recesses of their spirits, whilst also allowing its esoteric qualities to function in mysteriously elitist ways. Moreover, mysticism, because it is 'essentially religious realism, claiming and emphasizing first hand intuitive experiences of those spiritual realities which theology describes',[7] can survive the erasure of mere external manifestations, which themselves become a veil concealing and distorting the expressive spirit:

> Thus mysticism becomes independent of concrete popular religion, timeless and non-historical, at most concealed under historical symbols, the only valid interpretation of the religious process, under whatever form it may be clothed.[8]

And because it can survive that erasure, because that erasure is constitutive of 'mysticism' as such, it becomes the repository of a profound nostalgia, a repository for the continuation of the sense of the sacred under a different guise. According to one recent theorist who reviews this 'classical' phase in the discourse

8

of mysticism (embodied in the works of Underhill, Stace, Rufus Jones, Huxley, Zaehner, Smart), this view is endemic to the study of mysticism from its very inception.[9] He regards these authors as having

> fashioned a rather romantic and reactionary view of mysticism in which mystics are seen to stand aloof from and independent of the religious traditions 'of the masses' and to comprise a universal religious elite, a transcultural aristocracy of *illuminati*.[10]

And what informed their view of mysticism was a 'widespread loss of confidence in, and in some cases disdain for, traditional, institutionalized religion'.[11] According to Katz in an introduction to a book which has been important in renegotiating some of the influential assumptions of the classical account, the literature on 'mysticism' was a 'cure for anomie':

> The cure for anomie created by our revolutionary contemporary awareness of man's finitude, mortality, and freedom was now sought in a renewed, immediate, non-critical, largely non-cognitive, contact with the mystical depths of Being itself (whatever that is!).[12]

The term 'anomie' is of course Emile Durkheim's, and it is central to his analysis of modernity.[13] For Durkheim 'anomie' was that state of meaninglessness which was part and parcel of a social breakdown that was for him both institutional and moral. According to Durkheim, such a breakdown was significantly tied up with the absence of meaningful symbolic systems. Durkheim, himself an ardent rationalist, despised the mystical irrationalities of spiritual revivalism, regarding them as a sort of 'mal de l'infini'.[14] In his view articulations of mysticism provided a compensation for 'anomie' which both restored continuity with a fantasized historical past regarded as fully sacred, and salved and cured the fragmentation of modernity. They redeemed the legacy of the evisceration of institutionalized religious forms by their emphasis on union, fusion and harmonization, a conjunction whose power derived from their transcendent evasion of mediating structures in a warm embrace of God and the soul. Both universalistic and individualistic then, locating the universal in the human spirit itself, the construction of mysticism could solve the divisions and problems of the social sphere by erasing all consideration of it whatsoever. Evelyn Underhill, for example, writing her influential *Mysticism* in 1909–11, describes mysticism as 'the expression of the innate tendency of the human spirit towards complete harmony with the transcendental order'.[15] Such a fusion was to replace knowledge by merger and assimilation, a union that may perhaps be said to perform the psychological function of dissolving the boundaries of the individual personality on whom this religiosity so relentlessly focuses, thus alleviating its loneliness: 'We know a thing only by uniting with it; by assimilating it; by an interpenetration of it and ourselves. It gives itself to us; just in so far as we give ourselves to it.'[16] This osmotic absorption, this quasi-erotic interpenetration of God and the soul was also, then, a thorough-going dissolution of the historical. As Inge, one of the classic architects of the mystical revival and Dean of St Paul's Cathedral from 1911 to 1934, said in his Bampton Lectures of 1899:

> Mysticism may be defined as the attempt to realise the presence of the living God in the soul and in nature or, more generally, as the attempt to realise, in thought and in feeling, the immanence of the temporal in the eternal and the eternal in the temporal.[17]

In her account of the work of Evelyn Underhill, Regina Bechtle describes her as one of the chief architects of the mystical revival along with Inge and von Hugel. In addition to William James in America these writers were involved in a common project. Mysticism was to be given legitimacy by separating it from obscurantist dabbling in the occult, and by studying its psychological and phenomenological aspects.[18] These writers had very different religious affiliations – Catholic, Anglican, Quaker, Lutheran and Jewish – but, as John Hoyle has observed in an article which attempts to theorize mysticism so that its relationship to literature can be investigated, all concur with the notion that '*mysticism can be identified, defined and protected from contamination*'.[19] Because of that privileged immunity it can supposedly escape from the ravages of the temporal, of merely historical contingency. But this evasion of historical contingency, both in its actual historical time, the time of the mystics under description, and in the time of its critical reconstruction, must itself be historicized. It must be seen to emerge out of the urgencies of its particular time and place.

The formulation, elaboration and development of a language

about mysticism can be seen as establishing itself on the basis of the perceived 'death' of traditional institutionalized religious forms in the West.[20] So for Weber, who along with Durkheim is one of the most influential sociologists of modernity, the 'deepest community' (with God) is henceforth 'found not in institutions or corporations or churches but in the secrets of a solitary heart.'[21] Weber formulates the relationship between mysticism and modernity quite explicitly:

> The fate of our times is characterized by rationalization and intellectualization, and above all, by the 'disenchantment of the world'. Precisely the ultimate and most sublime values have retreated from public life either into the transcendental realm of the mystic life or into the brotherliness of direct and personal relations.[22]

LaCapra, like Steven Katz, relates this Weberian story of the 'protestant ethic' to Durkheimian 'anomie':

> The conception of the religious situation of man as that of a solitary individual whose salvation has been decided by a totally transcendent, hidden divinity might be seen as a symbolic representation which simultaneously made sense of, and functioned to sustain, a sense of isolation and anomic anxiety in a period of historical transition.[23]

Far from being immune from history, this definition is itself symptomatic of precisely that historical transition.

In some senses, then, so-called mystics never therefore 'practised nor propagated mysticism',[24] because, as Szarmach has recently argued, 'mysticism is itself a construct'.[25] And it is a construct crucially tied up with a protestant (post-reformation) view of the spirit. Although mystical theology has had a history that goes back to Origen and the Pseudo-Dionysus, 'mysticism' as a word was only first used in 1736.[26] In the words of Troelstch, mysticism is a 'radical individualism':[27]

> 'Spiritual religion' of this kind does not admit the possibility of appropriating the benefits of redemption through worship, the sacraments, or through church organization.[28]

Indeed:

> All that is ecclesiastical, historic, dogmatic, objective and

11

authoritative, is changed into a mere means of stimulation, into that which arouses that personal experience which alone is really valuable.[29]

Conceptualized as radically individualistic, mysticism is often viewed as essentially protestant: essentially, one might say, dissident – or at least it posits religiosity as an intensely *personal* phenomenon. It concerns the unmediated inner self and its relationship to the unmediated transcendent God. Putatively asocial and transcendent, it is radically bound up with questions of authority and authorization, and is actually involved in an anguished argument about what belongs to God and what belongs to the world, and how this relationship may be conceived. Steven Ozment has described it as being the site of the revolutionary potentialities of the Christian religion for this very reason. And here is where the modern construction of mysticism is linked very closely to the medieval practice of mysticism, for Ozment locates medieval mysticism as the very origin of radical protestantism:

> . . . medieval mysticism was a challenge, always in theory if not in daily practice, to the regular, normative way of religious salvation. It fed on the *de facto* possibility of the exceptional, on God's freedom to communicate immediately with men, to speak more conclusively in the depths of the individual heart than through the official writings and ceremonies of even the most holy institution.[30]

Ozment sees an intimate connection between the 'magisterial dissenters of the sixteenth century' and the medieval mystics. But the very claims of mysticism to immediacy also render it potentially deeply conservative, deeply orthodox. For mysticism in these descriptions can function dialectically both as a continuation of the spirit of religion, and also a revolt against it.[31] Because the mystics are equated with the knowledge that theologians merely describe and therefore authenticate ecclesiastical dogma experientially, mysticism shores up ecclesiastical institutions; it may also strike at the core of those institutions' claims to mediate God, by the very resistance of its own experience to that dogma.[32] Or, as Steven Katz has said, the very radicalness of the mystical hermeneutic may itself be a conservative factor.[33]

What defines the conflictual position of the term 'mysticism' and why it cannot finally be laid to rest as either *essentially* ortho-dox or *essentially* dissident, is precisely its emergence at what has been termed the 'dawn of modernity'.[34] Though variously historically located – anywhere from the 'Middle Ages' to the 'Enlightenment', to the Darwinian refutation of a biblical scheme of creation – what is seen to be characteristic of modernity from this perspective is the separation of fact from value, of knowledge from belief systems.[35] Henceforth what we know will be rational and instrumental, and what we believe will have no foundation in knowledge, will therefore be anxiously ungrounded, yet also dizzyingly unfettered. The sacred, that authentic bond that links man to nature and supernature in inseparable feeling and thought, is no longer what orders, binds, or connects (organicist metaphors predominate in such accounts). This envisaging of a history of 'modernity' is tied up with the nostalgic longing of a post-Enlightenment western rationality for a forebear. Such yearning for a world where humanity has not yet been brutally sundered from the sacred is then deemed the very price of 'progress'.[36] According to a recent theorist of mysticism, what the mystics were experiencing, and what modern theorists of mysticism describe (and lament and re-enact), is 'the disintegration of the sacred world'.[37] The mystical text is born from a fundamental 'socio–political instability' and a 'fragmentation of frames of refer-ence'.[38]

> The project of constructing an order amidst the contingen-cies of history, and the quest to discern in our earthly fallen language the now inaudible words of God (the problem of the spiritual subject) arose simultaneously from the dissol-ution of cosmic language and the Divine Speaker.[39]

What is apparent, then, is that writings on mysticism are not simply in the business of decribing something already there. The discourse of mysticism is also constitutive, and this reaching out for a transcultural soul, a universal spirit, is as much a modern need, a modern construction as it is a medieval phenomenon. Thus the characteristic idealism with which mysticism is usually regarded (which is indeed in some respects the guarantor of an idealist dogmatics, an idealist aesthetics) extends not just to the object of study – mysticism – but the subjects of study. The framework is rendered invisible and is not seen to have anything to do with what it innocently merely describes. The embeddedness of the articulators of 'mysticism' in the social practices of their own times is then rendered just as invisible as the social practices of the texts for which they purport to account.

THE IDEALISM OF THE MYSTICAL DISCOURSE AND ITS IDEOLOGICAL EFFECTS

The claims of the discourse of mysticism have had a profound effect on the possibilities of our reading practice of late medieval 'mystical' texts. These effects need to be investigated before a more suitable interpretative practice can be outlined. For by its claims to immediacy the dominant account renders the crucially mediating effects of history, of social, bodily, and linguistic practice, irrelevant. Further, it makes consideration of subjectivity in the mystical practice irrelevant and a consideration of the anxieties around authorization immaterial. Interpretation becomes unserviceable, because interpretation in mysticism is, in the words of Robert Gimello, an 'extrinsic template of meaning which has no role to play in the experience itself'.[40]

Writers on Christian mysticism have traditionally juxtaposed two strands of mysticism, deemed the negative and the positive way.[41] The negative mystical way is categorized by its attempt to dispense with analogy, symbol, or other forms of mediation since it sees all such analogies as essentially limiting, defining and reducing the divinity which can only be described negatively, by what it is not, by a head and a heart emptied of all limiting and prejudicial concepts in a 'Cloud of Unknowing'. Influenced by Pseudo-Dionysian Christian Platonism, such a tradition insists on God's incomprehensibility and is therefore strictly suspicious of the ability of symbolism to mediate and intervene between hidden divinity and immanent humanity. One of the best-known late medieval examples of this tradition, *The Cloud of Unknowing*, displays this suspicion in an intense distrust of any form of physical location of divinity. Such a distrust makes its author highly sceptical about the possibilities of a linguistic mediation of divinity too:

> So take care not to interpret physically what is intended spiritually, even though material expressions are used, like 'up, down, in, out, behind, before, this side, that side.' The

14

most spiritual thing imaginable, if we are to speak of it at all – and speech is a physical action of the tongue which is part of the body – must always be spoken of in physical words. But what of it? Are we therefore to understand it physically? Indeed not, but spiritually.[42]

The other form of mysticism with which the negative way is juxtaposed, the method with which the *Cloud* author takes issue in the preceding quotation, is the positive mystical way which uses analogy and symbolism surrounding the humanity of God in Christ as its path to God. Both forms exist in the Middle Ages, but it would be true to say that the most influential and popular form was the one embodied in the widespread influence in the late Middle Ages of Franciscanism, which stressed devotion to the human Christ. Nevertheless, theorists of mysticism have stressed the negative as opposed to the positive way, seeing this as the definitive type of mystical experience. And it is this definition of mysticism which most preserves the ahistoricism of the mystical discourse, and its transcendence of the social sphere, for a God outside time and history is inviolable to change. Dom Knowles, in his book *The Religious Orders in England*, describes the interactions of the two traditions:

> This stream (of pure spirituality) continued to flow till the reign of Henry VIII but there is some evidence that from the beginning of the fifteenth century onwards it was contaminated by another current, that of a more emotional and idiosyncratic form of devotion manifesting itself in visions, revelations and unusual behaviour deriving partly from the influence of some of the woman saints of the fourteenth century, women such as Angela of Foligno, Dorothea of Prussia and Bridget of Sweden. The most familiar example of this type in England is Margery Kempe.[43]

Positive mysticism is seen to drag the world back in, and in its most insistently feminine of forms – in the aberrant idiosyncrasies of emotional women. The mobilization of these categories, the categories of negative and positive mysticism, tacitly enlists highly sexist categories too. Positive piety is usually associated with women; its 'sentimental', 'personalized' tropes are seen to be particularly appropriate for women.

   . . . the austere mystical theology of antiquity with its

15

negative way on the one hand and its platonism on the other did not lend itself to the feminine temperament which is by nature so much more attached to the sensible and the personal.[44]

Or as the entry in the *Dictionnaire de spiritualité* under 'Humanité du Christe' puts it: 'The medieval "familiaritas" necessarily takes on the hue of a certain femininity.'[45] It is not just that negative and positive mysticism, here associated with their appropriate genders, are deliberately polarized in the tradition that constructs this dichotomy. It is more that the superior mystical way which constitutes negative mysticism needs to project out its body onto the feminized body of positive mysticism so that it can itself be a disembodied (male) and therefore soulful voice.

It is clear, then, that the ideological effects of this polarization of negative and positive mysticism, and the gender bias associated with it, have had a powerful effect on marking out the entire discourse of mysticism. Knowles' casual aside about Margery Kempe is backed by a powerful epistemology.

The figure of Evelyn Underhill embodies the continuity of idealist theories of mysticism with those particular constructions of medieval mysticism which tend to endorse its idealism, rather than analyse it systematically and historically. She is an instructive and relevant example because, to a greater extent than many of her contemporaries, she works her definitions of mysticism through the writings of the mystics, and this involves her in a popularization of medieval mysticism. She is responsible, for example, for writing introductions to *The Cloud of Unknowing*, Rolle's *Fire of Love*, Ruysbroek's *Adornment of the Spiritual Marriage*, Hilton's *Scale of Perfection*, Nicholas of Cusa's *Vision of God*.[46] Her understanding of mysticism as a timeless encounter with God is mediated, in fact, largely, though not exclusively, through medieval religious texts. It is no wonder then, that she should find *The Book of Margery Kempe* so 'disconcerting to the students of mysticism,' because it flouts her own categories of analysis so insistently, crippling their historical explanatory power.[47] Lee Patterson has indicated in his analysis of the institution of medieval criticism that religious devotion underpins some of the critical traditions of the study of medieval literature through the influence of exegetics. Perhaps that influence is nowhere so tenacious or so dominant as in the study of specifically religious texts, and especially those texts whose function seems to perform so cathectic and redemptive a function for these critics of the mystical revival.[48]

It is not that the medieval mystical texts I have mentioned in this chapter are not working with versions of mystical theology; they are surely attempting a transcendence of the temporal in an unmediated union with God. However, the terms of analysis set up by the classical versions of mysticism take the texts at their word. They refuse to see how polemic and argumentative, how rooted in historical contingency such texts might actually be. It is no wonder, then, that such accounts have had so little to say about the crucial focus of late medieval mysticism, Christ the incarnate God, and more specifically Christ both as infant and as crucified (and of course these images are often coalesced in the infamous late medieval *pietà*), the two moments, respectively moments of birth and death, which insist on the claims of the body most emphatically and obviously.

Even where the late medieval obsession with incarnation has been registered, the platonizing framework of mystical dogmatics slants the consideration of this material. Huizinga argues that such imagistic embodiments are themselves a sign of the decadence of the spiritual. On the one hand he locates an especial 'spiritual wakefulness' in the late medieval period; and on the other hand, the dangers associated with just such absorption. This 'spiritual wakefulness'

> results in a dangerous state of tension, for the presupposed transcendental feelings are sometimes dormant, and whenever this is the case, all that is meant to stimulate consciousness is reduced to apalling commonplace profanity, to a startling worldliness in other-worldly guise.[49]

In a classically dualistic formulation he characterizes late medieval religious images thus: 'The spirit of the Middle Ages, still plastic and naive, longs to give concrete shape to every conception.'[50] The spirit in this platonizing formulation is threatened with the rigidity of external form, for the tendency to embodiment characteristic of the late Middle Ages calcifies into 'mere externalism'.[51] For Huizinga there is tension in the relation between spirit and flesh in late medieval images, but his idealism means that he can only locate this as decadence and decline.

The dominance of profoundly idealizing organizations of the

'spiritual', themselves products of particular socio-historic forms, have all but obliterated any consideration of what were after all the dominant forms of late medieval catholic religiosity – and most particularly the subject of this study, the imagery associated with the body of Christ.

TOWARDS A READING PRACTICE OF LATE MEDIEVAL DEVOTIONAL TEXTS

Recent historical work on medieval and early modern religion has informed a decisive reorientation in the way we can begin to think about late medieval religious texts. Instead of considering the history of 'spirituality', historians have been more recently concerned with the study of religious practice.[52] But what would it mean to counter the evasive tactics of transcendence, of the wordless language of mysticism, with a commitment to embodiedness? What would it mean to see the incarnation of religion as an insistently this-worldly activity, a set of structuring symbolic practices and processes in which human relationships, sexual, social, symbolic, are invested? Perhaps Michel de Certeau's words are again useful here:

> In the beginning it is best to limit oneself to the consider-
> ation of what goes on in texts whose status is labelled
> 'mystic', instead of wielding a ready-made definition
> (whether ideological or imaginary) of what it is that was
> inscribed in those texts by an operation of writing.[53]

If we are to consider mysticism as a practice, and as a specifically late medieval practice, then we will have to pay heed to manifestations which are not merely the husk, the externalities of a phenomenon that is already described without them, but exist as particular and specific utterances, oriented towards the world of their embodiment. It is not therefore appropriate to begin with a definition of medieval mysticism, for that would be to fall prey to exactly the kind of idealist account I have been criticizing.[54] But what it is possible to say emphatically is that any materialist account must restore the world, the body, and the text to 'mystical writings'. It must see the language of their utterance as a 'two-sided act', to restore in fact a constitutive dialogism to the writings which have been read as the mere transcriptions of the monologues, of God Himself speaking through the expressive

18

spirit. Volosinov has talked of the way in which the theory of the expressive spirit is deeply bound up with what he has termed 'individualistic subjectivism' and the 'monologic utterance'.[55]

> The theory of expression inevitably presupposes a certain dualism between the inner and the outer elements and the explicit primacy of the former, since each act of objectification (expression) goes from the inside out. Its sources are within. Not for nothing were *idealistic and spiritualistic* grounds the only grounds on which the theory of individualistic subjectivism and all theories of expression in general arose. Everything of real importance lies within; the outer element can take on real importance only by becoming a vessel for the inner, by becoming expression of spirit.[56]

Thus an individualistic subjectivist theory of expression underlies mystical writings in the discourse of mysticism and acts as their guarantor. The mystics in this account act as amanuenses for the limitlessness of God; they record His monologues; they ventriloquize for Him. And it may be seen that at the heart of this poetics of mystical utterance is a mystical view of language itself. In restoring 'dialogue' to the mystical text then, in asking that simplest but most vital of questions – who is saying what to whom? – we may begin also to restore a politics of utterance to the social texts and social practices which will be the subject of this investigation.

For if 'mysticism' as a word and as a discursive formation seems to be a very post-medieval phenomenon, that is not to say that the attempt to forge an unmediated relationship with God (our working definition of mysticism) was not a medieval phenomenon. Though it is clearly of little explanatory power to see the late Middle Ages as 'a flowering of the spirit',[57] we might look again at de Certeau's theory of the mystic text to see what kind of epistemological and socio-historic contradictions are written into the medieval mystical project. For undoubtedly the attempt on the behalf of a significant, or at least significantly articulate number of people in late medieval England to enter into an unmediated relationship with God has the effect of both underwriting and undermining dominant authoritative modes. De Certeau stresses the extent to which mysticism has a highly contradictory relation to the institutions which desire to monopolize the transmission of God:

The texts always define themselves as being entirely the product of inspiration, though that inspiration may operate in very different modes. In every case though, divine utterance is both what founds the text and what it must make manifest. That is why the text itself is at the same time *beside* the authorized institution, but *outside* it and *in* what authorizes that institution i.e. the word of God. In such a discourse which claims to speak on behalf of the Holy Spirit and attempts to impose that convention on the addressee, a particular assertion is at work, affirming that what is said in this *place*, different from the one of the magisterium language, is the *same* as what is said in the tradition, or else that these two places amount to the same.[58]

In a sense then mystic texts encode a profound conflict about their relation to authority.[59] They derive their authority, their claim to speak, by claiming originary force: that they are a transcription of the voice of God Himself. Yet because they add to that voice, because they supplement it, they also subtly suggest that it may not indeed be the last word that it must claim to be. And of course this is no mere formalist quirk of mystical texts, but generated at least in the late Middle Ages by endemic and very profound threats to institutional ecclesiastical power and its hegemonic ambitions over control and mediation of the voice of God on which that power rested its claims. Even if we were to accept the fiction of the superiority of the negative mystical way, we would have to acknowledge a conflict and a contradiction in the very heart of the mystical project – the alarming fact that in the very claim to be revealing unmediated truths, authority, in the guise of the last word of God, is being continuously supplemented and fractured through the mystical texts.

Indeed we would have to say that the establishment of that dichotomy between the negative and the positive mystical way does not so much transcend that conflict (though the success of its polemical claim lies in whether or not it might be perceived to have done so), but rather *is* part and parcel of that conflict over the representation of the word of God which is being fought out in late medieval arguments about the transmission and availability of sacred power. The debate about the use and abuse of symbols and images was no idle or merely aesthetic one.[60] It touched the very resources of medieval sacred power and its legitimation. Where was the sacred to be located? Who was to control it? Who was to have access to it? Who was to make money out of it? These were the questions, both philosophical and emphatically material, that informed the debate about the means and mechanisms of the representation of God. Was He to be sought and worshipped in the form of images? Could He be adored in human form? Was He to be worshipped in the image of other men and women?

For it is in this period that the clerical monopoly over the administration of the sacraments, over the transmission of the word of God, both central to the very idea of ecclesiastical function, was being eroded. Sacred power was fundamentally contested in the late Middle Ages. This is nowhere more so than in those ardently idealist claims to have evacuated by transcendent means the ineradicably social arena of contest.

2

CHRIST'S BODY AND THE IMAGING OF SOCIAL ORDER

> For as the body is one and hath many members, and all the members of that one body, being many, are one body; so also is Christ.
>
> (i Cor. 12:12)
>
> Shameful is the part that is not congruous to the whole.
>
> (Augustine, *Confessions*: 2,8)
>
> The body is a representation.
>
> (Bryan Turner)

V. A. Kolvé, whose book on the mystery plays, *The Play Called Corpus Christi*, did so much to initiate interest in the relationship between 'dramatic' texts and religious practices, gives us the following citation:

> A post-Reformation copy of the Banns to the Chester plays included in Roger's Breviary of 1609, advertises a performance very different from those of the Middle Ages. God will not be acted, it says; only a voice will be heard speaking His lines, for no man can 'proportion' to the Godhead.[1]

The Banns exemplify the separation of voice and body that is also a decisive separation marked by reformation sensibility – however that complex phenomenon is conceived or periodized.[2] For in the mystery plays, as Kolvé remarks, God appears played indeed by His own creatures. And by 1609 that staging is seen to be grossly inappropriate, a blasphemous profanation.[3] There could be no more fitting passage to mark the transition from a consideration of the significance of the absence of God's body in the discourse of mysticism to the ubiquitous presence of Christ's in the religious practices of the late Middle Ages; nor from my first chapter to my second. Nor a better example of how very difficult it might be for the mentality of the era that produces such a Banns to accommodate and account for an age which happily and frequently staged God.[4] This chapter will aim to locate Christ's body, the place where God materializes most insistently in this period, in its late medieval religious and social context, to indicate why, as I shall argue, Christ's body was the arena where social identity was negotiated, where the relationship of self and society, subjectivity and social process found a point of contact and conflict. I begin with three exempla of late medieval provenance which locate some of the central dynamics bound up in the representation of the body of Christ.

THE BODY POLITIC AND THE BODY AS POLITIC: THREE EXEMPLA

(1) In 1381, after he has brutally crushed the Peasants' Revolt in East Anglia, Bishop Henry Despenser commissions a five-sectioned painting of the scourging, procession to Calvary, crucifixion, deposition and resurrection of Christ, which is to act as a reredos in Norwich Cathedral Priory.[5] The peasants who had dared, albeit abortively, to contest their ordained position in the social hierarchy and whose revolutionary gestures were based on an identification with Christ, are once again shown a story, a story they already know very well. Christ in the reredos meekly and willingly embraces the suffering inflicted upon him, he carries his own cross, submits to his own chastisement voluntarily, for the benefit of others, for the salvation of their souls, and he is finally resurrected at his father's right hand.

This particular representation of Christ is hardly unique. It is in fact one instance of an almost obsessively repetitive phenomenon. Like all obsessive repetitions, the repetition is necessary, is repeated to enact endemic and insistent cultural tensions which can't at this stage find another formulation.[6] But the particular context of this representation renders it tellingly poignant. If Christ can be emblematic of resistance, he can also be emblematic of acceptance, of humility, of being a body not *acting*, but *acted upon*. It is a depiction which appropriates the revolutionary Christ back on the side of the church militant, and in doing so reveals the signification of Christ's body as a highly contested area, an area that is crucially related to the strained social relations of late

23

medieval English society, and an area that touches the very core of self-perception and identity as a means of social control.

(2)   On 7 October 1428, in the diocese of Norwich, Margery Baxter is brought to trial for Lollardy. In her testimonial she denies the doctrine of transubstantiation, the pivotal sacrament of the catholic church, in a peculiarly profanatory way:

> Et tunc dicta Margeria dixit isti iurate, 'tu male credis quia si quodlibet tale sacramentum esset Deus et verum corpus Christi, infiniti sunt dii, quia mille sacerdotes et plures omni die conficiunt mille tales deos et postea tales deos comedunt et commestos emittunt per posteriora in sepibus turpiter fetentibus, ubi potestis tales deos sufficientes invenire si volueritis perscrutari; ideoque sciatis pro firmo quod illud quod vos dicitis sacramentum altaris nunquam erit Deus meus per graciam Dei, quia tale sacramentum fuit falso et deceptorie ordinatum per presbiteros in Ecclesia ad inducendum populum simplicem ad ydolatriam, quia illud sacramentum est tantum panis materialis.'[7]

Here, the very centrepiece of the catholic sacraments which bound believing Christians together in the body of Christ is seen as a profanation of Christ's body. To ingest it in the form of the host is not to join in the body of Christ, but to defile and debase him by a passage through the most inward, the most profanely, and profoundly dissolving of the body's mediums. Baxter, here, appears to share the Wycliffite view that the church's teachings on the consecrated host, the doctrine of the Real Presence – that Christ's body was materially present in the blood and in the wine – rendered it abject, an object less of adoration than of debasement. In the words of one Lollard tract, it was more abject than horse bread, rat bread, rat's dung or a tortoise.[8] Incorporation *into* Christ's body, effected by means of incorporation *of* it in the act of swallowing the host, is seen as an abjection, a profanation of the spirit. A true spirituality will loosen the ties of the spirit from an idolatrous attachment to place, from a profaning confinement to, say, a particular shrine, site of pilgrimage, relic or church, and manifest itself most insistently in the soul of the good man or woman.[9] That soul, in order to constitute itself as such, must here distance itself from an immersion in the body that threatens to become a contamination.

24

Yet one of Margery Baxter's contemporaries, also arrested as a Lollard, Margery Kempe, whose *Book* was written *circa* 1436 and discovered in 1934, cannot take communion often enough. She goes on countless pilgrimages and is reminded at the smallest association of the body of Christ with whom she identifies so intensely. For Kempe, incorporation into the body of Christ is the very height of spiritual attainment, an incorporation which is simultaneously an ecstatic and enabling identification of herself as a woman of flesh. For as Christ says to her in her book: 'I am in þe and þow in me. And þei þat heryn þe þei heryn þe voys of God.'[10] The emphasis here appears to be on divinizing the material rather than materializing the divine. And indeed, if Christ's body is the place where God materializes, if it is the meeting place of finite and infinite, of flesh and spirit, of the material and the immaterial, of the sacred and the profane in the destabilizing hybridity, the intoxicating boundary-blurring ambiguity of Christ's body, then either pole of that meeting can be stressed at the expense of the other. The very divergent religiosity of the two Margerys indicates the extent to which the relationship of the sacred and the profane is subject to urgent questioning and revision in this period; and again as in Despenser's reredos, the focus of this conflict is played out around the representation of and response to the very medium of Christ's body which is simultaneously the most public and the most intimate arena.

(3)   In an early fifteenth-century series of poems staged as a debate between Jack Upland, a Lollard, and Friar Daw, Daw's reply to Upland's comprehensive and vituperative anti-fraternalism proceeds in the following way:

> For riȝt as in þi bodi, Iake, ben ordeyned þin hondis,
>   For þin heed, & for þi feet, & for þin eyen to wirken –
> Riȝt so þe comoun peple God haþ disposid,
>   To laboren for holi Chirche & lordshipis also.[11]

Just as in the body, the feet and the hands and the eyes are naturally subordinated to the head, so the common people are ordained to work for holy church. The reference draws on a conventional view of the body politic with its accompanying and inevitable version of hierarchy and subordination, here to justify the division of labour which allows the 'preestes' to 'syngen her

25

masses'.[12] But Jack's 'Rejoinder' invests the hands of the labourer with a newly subversive power:

> Me merueliþ of þi lewdnes Dawe – or of wilful lesynges –
> For Poule laborid with his hondes, & oþer postilles also –
> ȝee, oure gentil Iesu, as it is opunly knowe.
> And þes were þe best prestes þat euer rose on grounde,
> And þe best messes song, not lettyng hem her labour.[13]

It is an inversion of the typically abstract and hierarchical image of the body as the naturalization of social order, a replacement of an idea about the body, in fact, with a working practice invested in it, a materialism of the body as opposed to an idealization of it. The hands of the labourer become the indispensable parts without which the ruling elite would have no grasp on the world. And Christ's labour, specified as the hands of the body politic, is brought in to sanctify the reference. It is no accident that this debate is staged between a friar and a Lollard, for as my second exemplum indicates it is Lollardy which mounts the most aggressive attack on the church's mediation and control of Christ's body, through its awareness of the acute political significance of its modes of representation, through its attacks on relics, on pilgrimages, on the representation of Christ in the mystery plays, and on the doctrine of transubstantiation.[14] And it is no accident that the body linked to Christ's in this example should be the body of a labourer, invested in this period, as Rodney Hilton points out, with a new subversive volatility and power.[15] The static image employed by the friar draws upon an immobile, hierarchized image of the body. But we know from the Statutes of Labourers enacted in this period that the labourer, freed after the Black Death from manorial ties, was a dangerously mobile figure.[16]

These three divergent but crucially interrelated examples indicate that the signification of Christ's body is a contested social arena in late medieval English society, one that functions in complex and multivalent ways. Ostensibly an image of the unity of Christian society, the strain in the model, and the questioning to which it is put, the different, conflicting uses which agents use it for, are easily apparent. I wish to context these exempla, and allow them to say more than this initial and casual juxtaposition permits by placing them within the context of a more detailed analysis of the representation of Christ's body in late medieval society. For it is only by understanding the context of those representations that we will be able to find a meaning for the extraordinary iconography of Christ's body in late medieval devotional writings. Christ's body then needs, as I outlined in chapter 1, to be brought back from its exile, for it is a key focus for the relationship between identity and the social structure for which it so often figures as an emblem. In this chapter then, I will analyse the multi-faceted cultural signification of the representation of Christ's body. I look first at the commonplace notion of the body as an image of human ordering, seeing how this idea is understood by the medieval notions of 'corpus mysticum' and 'corpus christi'. I examine the eucharistic dimensions of the configuration of Christ's body before going on to show how the burgeoning vernacular literature of the late Middle Ages encourages different forms of reception which fracture the claims to unity of the ecclesiastical polity. I argue finally that the body, and the symbol of Christ's body in particular, is actually a basic metaphor for pre-modern theorizing about the social order, one nuanced through the specific articulations of that metaphor to consider the urgent question of who was to be included in that social order and on what terms. I shall explore how Christ's body, as an image of both the collective and personal body, becomes the the ideal site for exploring the interrelationship between the two.[17]

It is perhaps a commonplace of medieval political and social theory that the body is the image *par excellence* of human society. In an Aristotelian model that stresses the organic nature of society, medieval theorists commonly use the human body as an image which can accommodate difference within unity and give the metaphor the legitimation of the 'natural': 'For the whole must be prior to the parts. Separate the hand and foot from the body and they will no longer be hand and foot.'[18] The state is thus imaged as an organism and its citizens as the component members or limbs of the community. The human body becomes a useful image for such theorists because it stresses the subordination of the parts to the whole, and the inability of the parts to function as independent and self-sufficient units. At best a metaphor which stresses the relational nature of constituent parts of society and the inescapability of the social in that identity, it is also a potentially highly hierarchized image depending of course on how the parts and the whole of the body are identified, as medieval political theorists realized.[19] In other words, one of the crucial questions would be, who is to be represented by the head? Indeed, who is representing the head in this way? It is a metaphor, an analogy, whose aim is above all to unify the divergent, multiple, conflictual limbs of medieval society into an organically whole body. Those representing the body in this way of course recognize themselves as its head, or indeed, acting for, or else in some privileged relation to, that head. Hence it is no surprise that their representation should be so disembodied, so abstract and heuristic. For to actually embody the representation might be to enhance the body, the component parts at the expense of the head.[20] The representation's ideological function rests on such disembodiment. The function of such representations is, according to Barkan, to 'reconcile the desire for physical and ideological unity with the obvious diversity of man and society'.[21] A fifteenth-century poem continues the analogy:

> I likne a kingdome in good astate
> To stalworthe man, mighty in hele
> While non his lymes other hate
> He is myghty. with another to dele
> If eeth of his lymes with other debate,
> He waxeth syk, for flesch is frele.[22]

The healthy body is here explicitly associated with the body in 'good astate', which is conditional on the harmonious relations of the limbs and their attitudes towards each other. Characteristically the image of strength and unity is stressed in its display of power against another enemy: when the body is 'myghty', he can 'dele' with 'another'. Internal conflict ends up in internal war, and ill-health and civil war are seen as synonyms. The strength of the social grouping as a whole depends on the way in which the limbs articulate with each other. Mary Douglas, in a useful comment on the body as image of human society, has said:

> The physical body is a microcosm of society, facing the centre of power, contracting and expanding its claims in direct accordance with the increase and relaxation of social pressures. Its members, now riveted into attention, now abandoned to their private devices, represent the members of society and their obligations to the whole. At the same

time, the physical body by the purity rule, is *polarized concep-tually against the social body*. Its requirements are not only subordinated, they are contrasted with social requirements.[23]

The body can simultaneously be used as an image of subordi-nation, of ordering a social hierarchy, and as resistance to that ordering. Mikhail Bakhtin has outlined one form of such resis-tance most influentially in his conception of the 'lower bodily stratum' and its complex interrelationship with the 'lower social stratum'.[24] But of course just as it is not possible to naturalize the social order by reference to a 'natural' body, the naturalization of bodily/social resistance is just as problematic. For as Mary Douglas again has said: 'the human body is always treated as an image of society . . . there can be no natural way of considering the body that does not involve at the same time a social dimen-sion.'[25] And later: 'the social body constrains the way the physical body is conceived.'[26] But it is not a question of any simple opposition between the natural and the social, or any mere impos-ition of the social onto the natural. We may here talk of 'body' in three senses to clarify the complexity of interaction: first, the individual body by which we mean 'the phenomenological sense of the lived experience of the body-self', second, the social body in the sense that Douglas intends, to refer to the uses of the body as a 'natural symbol' with which to think the interrelations between nature, culture and society, and third, body in the sense of 'body politic' which encompasses the regulatory mechanisms by which the body is managed (sexuality, reproduction, work, sickness).[27] The relationship between bodily metaphors and social categories is, consequently, a multiply determined one, and ritual practices and social classifications tend to congregate symbolically around the (dis)continuities between social, natural and personal body to affirm or break their symbolic homologies and the social significations they bear. The fact that 'the body is actively pro-duced by the junction and disjunction of symbolic domains',[28] or, to put this statement in the context of the three categories of the body itemized earlier, the fact that the relationship of social, natural and personal body is one of cultural construction, means that the fashioning of the individual body to the requirements of the social body, and the contestation of those requirements at the level of symbolic incorporation, are areas of potent signification and cultural struggle. The imagery that I shall be discussing in the following pages, then, is an imagery that, despite the different usages and contexts which we will encounter, has in common an attempt to reorganize the relationship between social, personal and natural body.[29]

CORPUS MYSTICUM AND CORPUS CHRISTI

The body analogy is one that provides the focus for the competing interests of both church and state and each finds in the analogy a metaphor which legitimates their own political aspirations. Perhaps the most famous instance of this usage of the body as an appeal and call to unity is Boniface VIII's *Unam sanctam* of 1302 where the analogy is mobilized against Philip the Fair of France:

> That there is one holy Catholic and apostolic church we are bound to believe and to hold, our faith urging us, and this we do firmly believe and simply confess; and that outside this church there is no salvation or remission of sins, as her spouse proclaims in the Canticles, 'One is my dove, my perfect one. She is the only one of the mother, the chosen of her that bore her' (Canticles 6.8); which represents one mystical body whose head is Christ, while the head of Christ is God. In this church, there is one ark, symbolizing the one church. It was finished on one cubit, and had one helmsman and one captain, namely Noah, and we read that all things outside of it were destroyed. . . . Therefore there is one body and one head of this one and only church, not two heads as though it were a monster, namely Christ's vicar, Peter and Peter's successor.[30]

The emphatic insistence on unity and unification which is the ecclesiastical claim to hegemony actually paradoxically proliferates its own monstrous two-headed image of the body. For it is obvious on the one hand that the church is claiming its unitary sovereignty in the growing realization of the very necessity for a competition both ideological and actual for that very sovereignty. An observation of Peter Stallybrass and Allon White is relevant here: 'The very desire to achieve a singularity of collective identity is simultaneously productive of unconscious heterogeneity, with its variety of hybrid figures, competing sovereignties, and exorbitant demands.'[31]

The ecclesiastical use of the term 'corpus mysticum' originally referred to the consecrated host, not to the church or Christian society. However. in the mid-twelfth century its meaning changes, for the church needs a doctrinal formulation which will be of use against heretical doctrines which tended to dematerialize the sacrament of the altar. The 'corpus mysticum' becomes the phrase which expresses the doctrine that the church is the 'organized body of Christian society united in the sacrament of the altar'.[32] As Kantorowicz notes, there is a correlation between the ' "corpus mysticum" interpretation and the ecclesio-political and constitutional developments of the thirteenth century'.[33] The importance of these developments is that the formulation allows the church to function as a body politic, as a legal and political organism 'on a level with the secular bodies politic which were then beginning to assert themselves as self-sufficient entities'.[34] The formulation of the Fourth Lateran Council of 1215 crystallizes the mutually reinforcing notions of the sacramental 'corpus mysticum' and the 'corpus ecclesiae mysticum', the mystical body of the church itself:

> There is one universal church of the faithful outside of which absolutely none is saved, and in which Jesus Christ is himself at once both priest and sacrifice. His body and his blood are truly contained in the sacrament of the altar in the forms of the bread and the wine, the bread being transubstantiated into the body by divine power. . . . And no one can perform this sacrament except a priest ritually ordained according to the (authority of the) keys of the church.[35]

It is clear from this formulation why the sacraments are so central to ecclesiastical doctrine. For along with the formulation of the doctrine of Christ's sacramental body, the exclusive rights of the church in the form of the apostles' legitimate successors to administer that body are also consolidated. As Nancy Jay comments:

> [E]ucharistic practice and theology never changed without corresponding changes in social organization. The Eucharist as 'blood sacrifice,' the Christian clergy as a specific sacrificing priesthood, and the unilineal organization of that priesthood as exclusive inheritors of apostolic authority, all came into being together and developed together; and the rejection of one entailed the simultaneous rejection of the others.[36]

Thus the Aristotelian notion of the body as a representation of society is sacralized in the notion of Christ's body, simultaneously the consecrated host which emerges to consolidate the function of the priesthood, and Christian society.

It is apparent from the very beginning that the image which is concerned with the establishment of unity automatically figures discord, for in its very establishment the unity it seeks to create is an exclusive one. Recent medieval historians such as Robert Moore have stressed the extent to which the putative unity is indeed productive of vicious persecution.[37] As Jeremy Cohen has recently put it:

> In a society which was committed to an ideal of organic unity, which demanded of all its members a functional contribution to the achievement of that unity, which defined both its ideal and its mode of organization in terms of the mystical body of Christ, which operated (at least in theory) as the centralized monarchy of the earthly vicar of Christ, and which gave rise to intense feelings of patriotism on its own behalf, no room existed for infidels.[38]

But if Christ's body has been the focus and medium through which clerical control seeks to establish itself, setting up an image of unity out of its very sense of division, borrowing from an older language of the body as image of society, it is also clear that by the late Middle Ages Christ's body is also further destabilized. For his body is also the focus for the democratizing, lay tendencies of late medieval piety. Christ's body is the host handled by the priesthood which establishes their exclusivity over the sacraments, and yet it is also, putatively, *all* of Christian society. And the paradox of a symbol that is simultaneously so inclusive and yet so exclusive is deepened when clerical monopoly is challenged and fractured in the late Middle Ages. It is for this very reason by the late Middle Ages (if it hasn't always been) a fundamentally unstable image, a site of conflict where the clerical and the lay meet and fight it out, borrowing from each other's discourses. For the laicization of society, the transfer of conventual to lay models of piety, provides a different point of access to the body of Christ and inflects the way it is perceived.[39] This becomes most obvious in the development of eucharistic piety, which is one symptomatic model of the deployment of the central symbol of the mass, the body of Christ, outside its liturgical, ecclesiastical setting and into the urban landscape, a departure which constitutes simultaneously an appropriation and an expansion of the terms of reference of Christ's body, and which changes its orientation and the potentialities of its meanings.

CHRIST IN A CAKE[40]

The feast of Corpus Christi was inaugurated in the late thirteenth century.[41] But the embryonic processional element present in this feast was developed in the later fourteenth century when the Corpus Christi procession became the symbol and forum for a complex display of urban status, rank and wealth. And it is indeed interesting that the very language of integration and unity which we have seen at work in late medieval discourse is reiterated in the writings of anthropologically influenced historians who revive it in functional accounts of medieval communities and the means whereby they achieve integration.[42]

For in a now deservedly influential and widely read article, 'Ritual, Drama and Social Body in the Late Medieval English Town', Mervyn James examines the socio-symbolic significance of the feast of Corpus Christi which was celebrated annually sometime between the end of May and the end of June.[43] James views the rites and processions associated with Corpus Christi as acting as a means of articulating social integration and social difference – a religious rite which he claims was particularly suited to urban societies, where the 'alternative symbols and ties of lordship, lineage, and faithfulness available in countrysides were lacking'.[44]

> . . . the theme of Corpus Christi is society seen in terms of the body. . . . the concept of the body provided urban societies with a mythology and a ritual in terms of which the opposites of social wholeness and social differentiation could be both affirmed, and also brought into a creative tension, one with the other.[45]

The procession which formed after the mass, carrying the consecrated host, the body of Christ, consisted of clergy and layfolk, and municipal officials. It made its way through the town, often symbolically linking, say, the cathedral to the market-place, or the square, or the quarters of the city to each other, rank and status being defined by proximity to or distance from the body of Christ. The body of Christ thus serves as a symbol of the unity of the community. It also serves to reinforce social hierarchy, ritualizing it and sanctifying it. It is above all a collective form, a communal spectacle, or rather a spectacle which stages community, since as Phythian Adams has pointed out, about a fifth of the adult males and all unmarried females were excluded from processing, and in the Corpus Christi plays it was generally only men and boys who could assume parts. Such ceremonial occasions were about defining the boundaries of community; they were rituals of exclusion as much as rituals of inclusion. As Phythian Adams notes:

> To all those outside or on the edge of the community, therefore, [such] ceremonies must have been a constant reminder of its discrete and predominantly masculine identity. For those inside it, on the other hand, they were the visible means of relating individuals to the social structure.[46]

In a way that becomes even more apparent when we come to discuss the body as an image of community in religious practice, the body is never really collective. Although its ritual and ceremonial force was precisely to symbolize community, there was always an outside and an inside. And indeed, the obsession with the rituals of unity belies what historians of urban revolt have called a 'continuous political fissure' in late medieval town life, where the threat to unity came as much from the enemy within, the ecclesiatical community, and factions within the ruling elite, as it does from 'below'.[47]

Nelson gives an example of fierce rivalry and dissension during a Corpus Christi procession:

> To the Worshippe of God and in sustentacioun of the procession of Corpus Xpi in the Towne of Newcastle upon Tyne after the laudible and ancient custome of the same Towne and in avoideing of dissencion and discord that hath been among the crafts of the said Towne as of man slaughter and murder and other mischiefs in time comeing which hath been lately attempted amongst the fellowshipp of the said crafts of the Tailor of the same Towne and to induce love charity peace and right.[48]

John Bossy concurs with Mervyn James in an impressive article on the 'Mass as Social Institution' which sees the Eucharist as functioning in essentially integrative ways. For James the procession of Corpus Christi sanctions the union of larger groups within an overarching community.[49] For Bossy, the mass is a ritual of community and integration.[50] Mervyn James is heavily dependent on the influential anthropological theories of Mary Douglas. The body, he states, is a 'pre-eminent symbol in the way society was conceived'.[51] He goes on to say: 'Natural body and social body indeed reacted on each other with a closeness which comes to near-identity.'[52]

Yet it is arguable that Christ's body is less the forum for integration and social cohesion than the forum for social conflict, the very arena and medium of social argument. This is apparent in the arguments around transubstantiation in the late Middle Ages in England. Arguments about transubstantiation were not merely abstract theological debates. They touched the most frictional tensions in late medieval society, for they concerned the vexed issue of clerical monopoly over the handling of Christ's body, and access by the community of the body which it supposedly imaged.[53]

It is for this reason that the sacraments and the place of Christ's body become so important in the major form of late medieval English heresy, Lollardy. Even the Peasants' Revolt, an uprising which was very much a refusal of social ordering, is seen by some contemporary chronicles in relation to the body of Christ. As Walsingham puts it; 'Many believe that the Lord deliberately sent these sufferings at the time when the Holy Church was making a special issue of the transubstantiation of the Body of Christ.'[54] And as Aston and many others have commented: 'It has long been recognized that Wyclif's views on the eucharist were his undoing.'[55] Wyclif's views on the eucharist decisively turned ecclesiastical attitudes against him and made a heretic of him. His belief was that instead of the 'substance' of the bread actually disappearing, the presence of Christ enters into it spiritually, and the words of the priest spoken to consecrate the host in Wyclif's view no longer transubstantiate the body into bread and wine but are simply the sign of Christ's presence. Clearly the role afforded the priesthood in Wyclif's views is very different. Such a view removes the indispensable mediation of the priesthood in the miracle of transubstantiation and locates the power in a miracle of God's. According to Gordon Leff, Wyclif's views on the eucharist are the hallmark of his heresy and they move him inexorably toward a 'comprehensive anti-sacerdotalism'.[56]

The re-evaluation of the doctrine of transubstantiation is therefore an attack on the central mediating role of the priesthood, an attack on its rights to be the exclusive handlers of Christ's body. Christ's body in the form of the host is the object of intense fights for appropriation in late medieval society. According to the Lollards, any good man or woman could consecrate the host. If, as one recent commentator has put it, the sacred powers of the host 'were largely indistinguishable from the growing powers of the clergy',[57] then an attack on the consecration of the host is simultaneously an attack on the clerical monopoly of the sacraments.

There is much evidence that by the late Middle Ages the mass was becoming more and more of a spectacle and less and less of a communion. The emphasis was increasingly on watching Christ's body rather than being incorporated in it.[58] All the major historians of the late medieval liturgy stress the extent to which, in late medieval liturgical practice, the role of the laity is reduced from offering and communion to seeing and hearing. Christ's body, as an emblem of the ecclesiastical community as a whole, is appropriated to the clerical elite, whose exclusive handling of it becomes a sacred spectacle, a spectacle indeed which very often had to be imagined. For, as Bynum comments:

> As the role of the priest was exalted, the gap between priest and people widened. By the late Middle Ages in Northern Europe, elaborate screens were constructed to hide the priest and the altar. Thus, at the pivotal moment of his coming, Christ was separated and hidden from the congregation in a sanctuary that enclosed together priest and God.[59]

As one major historian of the Christian liturgy puts it: 'The old corporate worship of the eucharist is declining into a mere focus for the subjective devotion of each separate worshipper in the isolation of his own mind.'[60] In Langforde's *Meditation in the Time of the Mass*, the direction which occurs at the elevation of the chalice reads: 'Call to your remembrance and Imprinte Inwardly in your hart by holy meditation, the holl processe of the passyon from the maundy unto the poynt of Cryst's death.'[61] The offensive in this passage is on the very minds and hearts of the participants of the mass. The celebration of private masses, the movement of the host outside the church to perambulate the town, the arguments in the late medieval period about frequent communion, all testify to a polarization in the way in which it is possible for Christ's body to function. As one medieval historian puts it: 'It was a common characteristic to regard the eucharist as a supremely important focus of religious feeling: at once the gateway to an intensely private world of prayer, and an image of the church, a *corpus mysticum.*'[62] The host is thus the site of an intensified clerical control and, as lay piety assumes greater and greater significance, of an increasing laicization for it has become the place of opportunity for incorporation into the body of the church. Charles Zika stresses clerical defensiveness on precisely this issue:

> Emphasis on the host as Christ's sacramental presence focuses on the act of producing the host and the role of those responsible for its production. In other words, the host is decisively located within the context of priestly power and the locally approved church and liturgy.[63]

Teaching on the eucharist constantly stressed that sacramental theology was not for lay people; their function was simply to believe.[64] But this ecclesiastical model of one-way transmission from clergy to populace was always a (clerical) fantasy. The lay were never simply the passive recipients of the 'arcana eucharistie' handed down from on high. And the context of a growing lay piety, and increasing use of the vernacular, was both product and symptom of the increasingly evident collapse of that model.[65]

Indeed, it is apparent that the arguments about the eucharist in the late Middle Ages hinge very much around the issue of so-called 'popular piety,' or as its detractors called it, 'lay superstition'. Margaret Aston has written that the consideration of eucharistic heresy went hand in hand with the development and deployment of a vernacular vocabulary to discuss eucharistic doctrine, and this in itself constituted another attack on another virtual clerical monopoly: Latin.[66]

REPRESENTATION AND UNITY

It will be obvious, then, that Christ's body is the focus of competing and conflicting cultural tensions. His body is the mythic focus and disseminator of the relations between materiality and

37

spirituality, between the charged and changing configurations of the sacred and the profane. But it is also crucial to my argument that the *representation* of Christ's body is also transforming, for the conditions of its production, reproduction, and dissemination are under question. Late medieval piety was both the product and symptom of the drive towards vernacularity and this resulted in a fracturing of authority and the techniques of authorization. The mode of transmission crucially and inevitably affected what it was that was being transmitted. It became increasingly clear that a God in the vernacular was a different God from a God in Latin, as contemporaries were well aware. The transmission of the sacred scriptures in the mother tongue broke down the division between clerical and lay which had been so ideal and central a notion of the central Middle Ages. Contemporaries, for example, genuinely asked themselves the question whether God could address Birgitta in her native tongue.[67] At issue was the fracturing of the medieval monopoly of learning and its aspiration to be the sole mediator of scriptural and spiritual truths. The result of this fracturing of monopoly was that more evidently and more widely than previously there are two languages of transmission. This obvious but crucial point has been much underestimated in the literature on devotional writings, largely of course because, as I outlined in chapter 1, embodiment, including the embodiment of and in language, has been so studiously downgraded. It matters little to the expressive spirit what language it speaks, for the language is the mere vehicle of its message. And it matters little that the mystical text, like any other text, is dialogic, because it was thought to be the monologue, the *one voice* of God Himself. But in fact the increasing use of the vernacular has a crucial effect, a simple but powerful one, for it means precisely that there is a renewed attention to the way that language actually affects what is being expressed. And once this relationship is acknowledged, the monolithic claims to speak for an oracular authority become markedly less convincing.

It was one of Bakhtin's central insights that language is pulled in different directions by its centrifugal and its centripetal tendencies, whose precise interaction depends on the historical dynamic in which such struggles take place. The centralizing mode of language, the mode which tends towards the production of a unified, homogeneous language, a 'monoglossia', is constantly undercut by a centrifugal tendency towards 'heteroglossia', registering the intrinsic social diversity of those who utter it. The unifying, centralizing tendency attempts to establish a cultural monopoly and hegemony.[68] Thus the establishment of Latin as the language of scriptural truth was closely tied up with the centralizing, ecclesiastical ambitions of the ecclesiasts of the central Middle Ages. Bakhtin's comment is worth quoting here:

> Aristotelian poetics, the poetics of Augustine, the poetics of the medieval church, of the 'one language of truth,' the Cartesian poetics of neo-classicism, the abstract grammatical medievalism of Liebnitz (the idea of 'universal grammar'), Humboldt's insistence on the concrete, all these, whatever their differences in nuance, give expression to the same centripetal forces in sociolinguistic and ideological life.[69]

When, on the contrary, one language comes to compete with another, its claims to be *the* language, the only language, the universal and the true language are exploded. The 'mobility of context' makes such claims strange. It is a very difficult position for a sacred language to be in. For when two languages function within a cultural system the dominant language is relativized and so are its attendant claims to truth. As Bakhtin once again puts it:

> After all, it is possible to objectivize one's own particular language, its internal form from the peculiarities of its world view, its specific linguistic *habitus*, only in the light of another language belonging to someone else which is almost as much 'one's own' as one's native language.[70]

The claim to a monopoly of scriptural truth is shattered at the same time, then, as the unitary nature of that truth. As Bakhtin says: 'Two myths perish simultaneously: the myth of a language that presumes to be the only language, and the myth of a language that presumes to be completely unified.'[71] The possibilities and the potentialities for the 'Word' to become dialogic are opened in a way that was not previously perceivable. And this renewed attention to language betrays an awareness of language as the arena of human production at the expense of divine transcendence.

The second factor which indicates that the *representation* of Christ's body is under question, is one that is concerned with the Lollard attack on images. For, as the *Lanterne of Light* puts it:

The painter maketh an image forged with diverse colours till it seems in the eyes of fools like a living creature. This is set in the church in a solemn place, bound fast with bonds, for it should not fall. Priests of the temple beguile the people with the foul sin of Balaam in their open preaching. They say that God's power in working of his miracles descends into one image more than another, and therefore 'Come and offer to this, for here is showed much virtue.' Lord, how dare these fiends for dread thus blaspheme their God and use the sin of Balaam that God's law hath damned, since Christ and his saints forsook this world's wealth and lived a poor life, as our belief teaches.[72]

The late fourteenth century sees an extended attack on images as modes of representing God. Involved in Wyclif's attack on images was the whole question of what belonged to God and what belonged to the world, and how, indeed, to demarcate the boundary between. My argument here is not concerned to explore a trajectory bound up with reformation practice, but I wish to suggest merely that the very fact that there is argument about representing Christ testifies to the instability of the figure. Roy Haines quotes a late medieval sermon which testifies to the defensiveness of clerical claims to sacramental unity in relation to Lollard doubt. An orthodox preacher reminds his audience that on every altar Christ's body is the same; there are many hosts but one body. He then tells them the story of a Lollard who enters a church to watch a sacring. For each sacring he observes he places a pebble in the sleeves of his tunic, and on going outside the church, he says to his companion that he has seen fifteen gods. But as he reaches into his tunic to show the stones, he pulls out not fifteen, but one.[73] Once again the assertion of sacramental unity is in the face of proliferating reinterpretations of the meaning of that myth. Hardly an image which will shore up dissent and endemic social conflict, it is itself the very medium of far-reaching debates about representation which touch on the relations of the sacred and profane world.

SUBJECTIVITY, BODY, SOCIAL ORDER

Ostensibly then an image which should be the very symbol of unity, Christ's body, is in fact an arena for an intense struggle, an arena which provides a historic meeting ground for a relationship between identity and society, between agency and structure. Indeed, one of the problems with the functionalist accounts offered by James, Bossy etc., is that they cannot deal with the relationship between agency and structure. Their accounts of the body as image of society assume that the model is always an integrative one, but there is never an account of the interaction between agents (who acts, and in whose interests? etc.) and the structure which is meant to integrate those agents so cohesively. This failure to account for the relationship between agency and structure means that the picture they provide is ultimately a static one. In the end their model of society cannot account for change, for history, for the dynamics of conflict. But in the late medieval representations of Christ's body it is precisely the relationship between subjectivity and social process, between agent and structure that is at issue.[74] For if, as one social scientist has recently argued, the body as such is the 'incarnate bond between self and society', then Christ's body functions as this embodiment in a very marked and significant fashion.[75] If Christ's body is the medium through which social conflict is often worked out in social rite, ritual and drama, then his body has another significant role to play. It provides a language through which the relationship of self to society is articulated on an individualized basis. One response to, and attempt at containment of, the Lollard polemic was to authorize a series of vetted translations of texts which attempt to construct a form of lay piety based on identification with Christ. These texts, which I analyse in more detail in chapter 3, attempt to construct the reader/listener in a series of identificatory roles in relation to Christ. Christ's body is used as a very medium of identification, and the formation of identity becomes an arena for social control.[76] The focus of many of the authorized translations of the late medieval period was precisely to encourage not merely a detailed, anguished and acute observation of the humiliation of Christ, but, of course, such texts also constitute an invitation to *become* him. Thus we must look at Christ's body not simply as a social and communal rite, but as the site of a momentous and historically significant process of internalization, of social control through the very formation of identity. Indeed many of these texts consciously highlight the transfer of conventual to lay models of piety by referring to the necessity to make of the heart itself a monastery. As a late medieval manual for the

41

'mixed life' puts it: 'A Jesu, mercy! Where may thys abbey and this relygon best been ifounden? Sertus, never so weel no so semely as in a place that is clepud concyence.'[77]

After Arundel's 1407 Lambeth Constitutions, ownership of any vernacular books was enough to arouse suspicion, and possession of a vernacular manuscript was forbidden without prior permission of the diocesan bishop. That permission could only be given for translations which antedated Wyclif.[78] One such text is of course Nicholas Love's *Mirrour of the Blessyd Lyf of Jesu Christ*. It was one of the most popular texts of the late medieval period. Approved by Archbishop Arundel in 1410, it provided a whole series of identificatory roles centring around the holy family. The reader is given a detailed exposition of the life of Christ, descriptions based on the thirteenth century *Meditations on the Life of Christ* which are intended to work in highly dramatic and affective ways. It is a work of meditation but it is staged as a participatory drama: 'And if you wish to profit you must be present at the same things that it is related that Christ said and did, joyfully and rightfully, leaving behind all other cares and anxieties.'[79] Thus it may be said that Christ's body was the arena for a conflictual and contradictory symbolics. On the one hand his body becomes more exclusive, more of a stage-managed spectacle of community, and on the other hand it is the site of an intensive cultivation of identificatory and privatized practice. It is precisely because of the failure of Christ's body to function as an image of unity, the impossibility of that project, that in late medieval crucifixion piety it is the borders and boundaries of Christ's body (which, as we have seen, simultaneously include and exclude so paradoxically in nearly every model and manifestation of Christ's body that we have located) that become the object of obsessive interest and attention. Late medieval crucifixion piety is a curiously literal embodiment of a drama of exclusion and participation in that body. For affective piety is obsessed with belonging, with the fantasy of fusion and the bitter reality of separation, and so with the entrances to Christ's body. For 'the wounds are clearly an entrance,' as it says in the *Meditations on the Life of Christ*.[80] Late medieval crucifixion piety locates an extraordinary preoccupation with the wounds, an extensive medieval fantasy which Huizinga has called both 'ultra concrete' and 'ultra fantastic'.[81]

Historians of the late medieval period have frequently talked about the 'privatization' of piety, and linked that privatization with mysticism *per se*. Thus, for example, John Bossy talks about the 'asocial mysticism' of frequent communion outside the mass which threatens the unity of its integrating and cohering function as a social institution.[82] And Gordon Leff talks about the mysticism of the period as 'subjective, often to the point of being indistinguishable from histrionics'.[83] But in doing so they are making the automatic assumption that the realm of the 'subjective' and the realm of the 'mystical' are automatically asocial, and they are therefore in danger of making a very modern, post-Romantic opposition between self and society. Inasmuch as their comments reveal a symptomatic shift in the very organization of piety, in its production, transmission, its distribution, its reception, they tend to relinquish the whole arena of identity, and the formation of identity, as one which happens outside a social arena. As Norbert Elias has said in a book which deals with the interrelationship of history and sociological theory:

> The individual [in sociological theory] . . . or what the present concept of the individual refers to, appears again and again as something outside society. What the concept of society refers to appears again and again as something existing outside and beyond individuals. One seems to have the choice only between theoretical approaches which present the individual as the truly existent beyond society, the truly 'real' (society being seen as an abstraction, something not truly existing), and other theoretical approaches which posit society as a 'system,' a 'social fact sui generis' – a reality of a peculiar type beyond individuals.[84]

The body, as I have argued, is one arena where self and society are materially related. This is an idea that functions at many different and conflicting levels. For the body, as Merleau Ponty puts it, is 'our general medium for having a world'.[85] And as Foucault would want to say, it is also the way the world grasps us, imposes itself upon us in the most intimate way imaginable.[86] Imaging the body is therefore imaging the social order as it acts itself out at the level of identity, and simultaneously imaging that very identity as fully social. And it is for this reason, as Bryan Turner has said in his book, *The Body and Society*, that the symbolics of the body are intimately related to the question of social ordering. Further, he says that the body, its character, structure and development 'thus provides a basic metaphor of pre-modern

43

social theorizing in such notions as the body politic'.[87] It is also for this reason that he can claim that a sociology of the body is also a study of the problem of social ordering.[88] In the late Middle Ages it is Christ's body that features as that language. For Christ's body is both exclusive – in Bakhtin's terms a classical body – closed, hermetic, monumental, static, elevated, awesome, homogeneous, and simultaneously inclusive, warm, material, welcoming, heterogeneous, the very existential stuff of birth and death, the very stuff too of mortality and bodily change, open to the world through its welcoming wounds. And it is the very simultaneity of that exclusion and inclusion, that simultaneous classicism and grotesquerie, that make it such an alarmingly hybrid image. For if it is a closed body which measures power by proximity to itself, by nearness and incorporation, then it must be wrenched open, violently penetrated, marked over and over again in countless iconic mutilations. For if the body is closed, then how can fusion not be a violence done to that body? And if it is an open body, then just who exactly is to be let in? Is Margery Baxter? Is Margery Kempe? Is Jack Upland?

3

'DYVERSE IMAGINACIOUNS OF CRYSTES LYF'[1]
Subjectivity, embodiment and crucifixion piety

Practical belief is not a 'state of mind', still less a kind of arbritary adherence to a set of instituted dogmas and doctrines ('beliefs'), but rather a state of the body.

(Pierre Bourdieu)

In chapter 2 I examined the multivalent, condensed and ambiguating symbol of Christ's body as a forum for cultural conflict across a range of texts and social practices. I argued, in opposition both to clerical fantasy and to functionalist anthropology, that this body was not a unified or a unifying symbol. In examining Christ's body as an image of social ordering, I showed how the embodiment of Christ and the 'passion imagery' of the late Middle Ages entails and occasions a debate about the relations of sacred and social power. Among the terms of that debate, as I briefly noted in chapter 2, was an elaboration, unprecedented outside monastic or clerical circles, of Christ's body as a vocabulary for self-modelling, for the production of social identity. The 'dyverse imaginaciouns of Crystes lyf' which formed the late medieval *imitatio Christi*, forge a language of subjectivity to which Christ's body is axiomatic. In the literature which tutored and formed its audience in the image of Christ, his 'mixed life' became an image for theirs.

It is the relation of the 'mixed life' to crucifixion piety then, that I will examine in this chapter.[2] I will, in the first instance, explore some of the theological developments of the high Middle Ages which, changing the meaning of incarnation and crucifixion, were so central to the articulation of affective piety in the late Middle Ages. I will then look at their changing articulation in a climate where the audience for affective texts was constituted to a larger and larger extent by the laity. In the later sections of the chapter I will deal with two texts originally composed in the thirteenth century which were translated and revised for a later readership to become the most influential and popular texts of late medieval English vernacular piety: *The Prickynge of Love* and *The Mirrour of the Blessyd Lyf of Jesu Christ*.[3] It is through these works that I want to attempt to come to a closer understanding of how these texts used the embodiment of God in man, the incarnation and crucifixion, as the medium for the production of social identity. What kind of identities were such texts attempting to produce? What psychic and social tensions did they encode around their extravagant imaginations of passion? The *Prickynge of Love* provides us with an opportunity to understand some of the techniques and vocabulary of the construction of this identity, a construction that was always a social renegotiation rather than a merely individualistic reform. The *Mirrour*, because of the particularity with which we are able to position it, allows us to register and explore some of the political and theological risks taken by the invitation to identify with the culture's central sacred resource and icon. Finally this chapter examines some of the ostensibly subversive uses of crucifixion imagery as deployed in the polemical Lollard accounts of the trial of Oldcastle, and explores the shift in relationship of private devotion and public imaging, between church, laity and realm that the fight against Lollardy actually ironically enabled.

THEOLOGIA CORDIS: OXYMORONIC DOCTRINE

Quid est filius hominis, nisi nomen assumptae carnis?[4]

It is a commonplace of late medieval histories of spirituality that the late Middle Ages witness a new and extraordinary focus on the passion of Christ. James Marrow says of this 'inventive expansion of passion imagery': 'Few other phenomena are so characteristic of the relation between changing forms of spirituality and literary and artistic creativity in the period of transition from the Middle Ages to the Renaissance.'[5] Let us trace through in the broadest of outlines some of these developments.

An incarnational aesthetic and practice was implicit in the very earliest stages of Christianity and Christian theology. The potentialities of *imitatio* are outlined in Galatians in a passage that echoes through scholastic writings of mystical theology: 'With Christ I am nailed to the cross, yet I live now not I, but Christ in me.'[6] It was by means of God's incarnation in Christ, and Christ's sharing of human flesh, that the legacy of the fall – irreparable separation between matter and spirit – could be atoned for and redeemed. But Anselm's *Cur Deus homo* marks a decisive shift in the theology of redemption when it moves the focus of interest away from the cosmic battle of God and the devil, which makes of the human soul a mere battleground, to the figure of Christ, whose atonement took the form of participation in fallen earthly humanity.[7] Incarnation becomes the salvific centre of a story which now highlights the relationship of individual man to God, a relationship given new hope, vigour and importance through Christ's humanity. It is Christ as the human *imago dei* who can restore the hopeless figures of corporeality in the fallen state. As Hugh of St Victor argued:

> Now Scripture says: 'As rational soul and flesh are one, so God and man are one Christ.' See the likeness. I say rightly: Soul and flesh are man, again I say rightly: Man is person. And again I say rightly: Soul and flesh are one person.[8]

The union of God and man in Christ affirms the union of soul and flesh, spirit and matter, in humanity. Furthermore it allows one to be a bridgeway to the other: 'The body ascends by sense, the spirit descends by sensuality.'[9] In such repeated analogies Christ's body was imaged as a ladder, leading upwards towards God:

> Since then we mount Jacob's ladder before descending it, let us place the first rung of ascension in the depths, putting the whole sensible world before us as a mirror, by which ladder we shall mount up to God, the Supreme Creator that we may be true Hebrews crossing to the land promised to our Fathers.[10]

Thus, although Christ's body is the doctrinally authorized

meeting-place for the sensible and spiritual world, the image is clearly hierarchized, and one is used to ascend to the other which is superior both morally and spatially. The sensible world is instrumental for such an ascent – and in this sense such theology affirms the world of the senses, the world of *caro* – but only in so far as it is used as such an instrument. Underlying this notion of the world of the senses and its potential for leading to the world of the spirit is the concept of anagogy. All things referred upwards because they reflected God and bore His traces. Such a world view was essentially sacramental, and, as de Bruyne said, it implied a view of symbolism as 'ontological participation'.[11] Every symbol in the conception of this theology contained the reality it expressed. Richard of St Victor's formulation of this notion revealed the dynamic optimism implicit in this notion of dissimilar similitude:

> Every figure demonstrates the truth the more clearly in proportion as by dissimilar similitude it figures that it is itself the truth and does not prove the truth; in so doing, dissimilar similitudes lead the mind closer to truth by not allowing the mind to rest in the similitude alone.[12]

For Richard, following Augustine, the soul inhabits a *regio dissimilitudinis*, but its natural likeness to God can be restored in the incarnate word who is Christ (John 1.14). In the following Anselmian elaboration of this concept, the soul is a mirror of God which has become clouded and dirty through sin. What is needed is a clearing away of the debris so that the natural likeness that is already there can emerge:

> I praise you, Lord, and give you thanks, that you created me in your image, that, remembering you, I might think of you, and love you. But that image in me is so worn away by the friction of vices, so blackened with the smoke of sins, that it cannot do that for which it was made unless you renew it and form it again.[13]

The likeness, then, between man and God both required and inspired an awareness of sin and the reformation of the soul, but this elaboration nevertheless stressed a continuity of the soul with God.

In order for this confident sense of the incarnation as a bridge between God and man to have any valency, some sense of the sacramental nature of God's creation must be present. Articulate in this doctrine of the incarnation, in the notion of Christ as a 'daring plastic translation of the *imago dei*',[14] is the simultaneous understanding of the anagoge as both ascent and return, involving at once an acceptance of matter and its austere supersession. As Chenu stresses, this sacramental understanding of the relationship between sacred and profane involved an image of the transcendent not as 'some pleasant addition to their natures: rather rooted in the "dissimilar similitudes" of the hierarchical ladder, it was their very reality and reason for being.'[15] All of humankind strove to recognize, cultivate and restore the likeness to their creator that was always already there. These developments of the implications of the incarnation are then made on the basis of a Neoplatonizing Augustinianism which imagined the entire visible world as bearing the traces (*vestigia*) of God. Christ's willingness to be incarnated, his embodiment, is crucial because it is only this condescension to the flesh which will allow other images to signify. It is only his incarnation which, by symbolizing and embodying the union of image and exemplar, establishes for fallen man the possibility of a knowledge of God through His vestiges in nature. The world, then, as an image of God, is potent with signification. The material world becomes a text which may be interpreted, scrutinized, allegorized and investigated for the way it pointed to its exemplar and author: God. In this extraordinary renegotiation, whose outlines and complexities I can only hint at here, there are new possibilities for the body as text and instrumental medium. So in the words of St Bernard:

> But we live on after the body dies; still, there is no access open to us, except through the body, to those things whereby we live in happiness. He had perceived this who said: 'The invisible things of God are clearly seen, being understood by those things which are made' – that is, corporal and visible things – unless they be perceived by the instrumentality of the body, do not come to our knowledge at all. The spiritual creature, therefore, which we are, must necessarily have a body, without which, indeed, it can by no means obtain that knowledge which is the only means of attaining to those things, to know which constitutes blessedness.[16]

Part and parcel of this renegotiation of the role of the body in worship, was a new appreciation and re-evaluation of the role of experience, affectivity and emotion: 'Because we are carnal and born of the concupiscence of the flesh, it is necessary that our desire, our love, originate from the flesh.'[17] Flesh is what human-kind and Christ share; and so a reciprocity is established, for it was only by means of compassion with Christ that his compassion with man could be understood: 'for only through passion can compassion be learned.'[18] In Nietzsche's aphoristic formulation: 'So that love shall be possible, God has to be a person.'[19]

Christ then, as simultaneously flesh and spirit, God and man, image and exemplar, sign and signified, is the oxymoronic means by which a *theologia cordis* is licensed and propagated. The early architects of this affectivity were the reformist writers of the 'new' religious orders: Anselm and St Bernard, whose understanding of incarnation builds on the Victorine reformulation of sacramental-ism. Crucially entailed by this understanding of sense and spirit as articulated through these doctrines of the incarnation was a reformation of the relation of self to God. The affective theology of St Bernard involved not simply a different understanding of the role of Christ in a different economy of salvation, but a different kind of subjectivity constructed in relation to the re-formed Christ – a self whose *love* would be the basis and medium of reform. Henceforth knowledge of God will be bound up with knowledge of the self, with a radical reflexivity.[20] The first step of truth, opines Bernard in the fourth chapter of *De gradibus humilitatis*, is to know yourself.[21] Though it is quite beyond my scope here to effect a sociology of Bernardine devotion, it is worth remarking that the reformulation of the relation between senses and spirit, and the active deployment of love, desire and affect, to remould and shape self and soul, occurred within a changing pattern of recruitment in the Cistercian monasteries. The novices of the Cistercian order, as Leclerq informs us, had not necessarily inhabited a monastic institution from birth.[22] Rather the new recruits were now much more likely to be adults who had previously been active participants of secular society. It is this new pattern of recruitment that is the context of the Bernardine elaboration of desire; not so much repressed, or behaviourally constrained, desire is rather made the instrument of the modelling of a loving need for virtue. As Asad explains: 'The critical distinction here is therefore not simply between "love

for God" and human love, but between desire which is measured
by an authoritative law, and desire as the motive for exercising
virtue.'[23] In Bernard's influential rendering, concupiscence itself
can be the 'material for exercising virtue'.[24] The conditions for
experience will no longer have to be controlled if the structures of
memory are transformed.[25] So the conditions for an Augustinian
formation of the will are engineered as the production of loving
subjectivities.[26] Asad's description of the implications of this
mechanism are intricate and interesting. For Asad, the Cistercian
monastery models a subjectivity which must learn to love, and
it is because this learning is never a mechanical, simple, or even
successful project, because it meets with resistance from 'concupiscence itself' that the developing self is at once 'social and non-
unitary'.

> Thus for the Christian the virtue of obedience is built not
> on a simple *identification* with an authority figure, but on a
> *precarious distancing* within a fragmented self – which is one
> reason why the notion of 'socialization' as a transitive pro-
> cess does not adequately describe how virtue is achieved.[27]

His comments are usefully considered in relation to the kind of
loving subjectivity that is moulded by the centrality of passion
imagery to the Bernardine *affectus*. Identification with the figure
of Christ (hybridly man and God) will not so much resolve, as
serve to exacerbate a self-division, that then seeks a more urgent
resolution that is even more intensely denied. The self-modelling
that is established in this process is then extraordinarily dynamic,
working off its own circular energies and impossibilities. Its very
failures produce merely an intensification of its operation. As
Asad says, under such conditions the novice is 'thrust into ambiguity and contradiction and his fragmented self made the precondition of a virtuous reformation'.[28] Deriving from an ultimately
Augustinian, Neoplatonic notion whereby the moral condition of
the soul depends on what it attends to and loves – 'Everyone
becomes like what he loves. Dost thou love the earth? Thou shalt
be the earth. Dost thou love God? Then, I say, thou shalt be
God'[29] – the image of Christ as lover becomes the medium by
which lovers themselves are likened to Christ.

The reformist understandings of affective theology developed
a set of interpretative strategies which disciplined the way in
which they were utilized and understood within the institutional

setting of the monastery. But the influence of these texts was felt far beyond the walls of the monastery. What is articulated in such notions is an understanding of Christ's body which involves, affects and cathects the self's understanding of itself, inaugurating in such radical reflexivity a self-division which it will be its mission to both exacerbate and dissolve. As such, it is part of the development of a vocabulary that understands the body of Christ as the site of a set of disciplinary practices, rather than the kind of non-cognitive ritualized cohesion talked about by Mervyn James.[30] Moreover, this set of practices emerges within a context of a reconfiguration of the relation between sacred and profane, whereby Christ's body is redefined as a medium in which to love and be loved, using rather than abandoning the profane world in the service of the sacred.

'I WOLD BEN CLAD IN CRISTES SKIN': FRANCISCAN *AFFECTUS*[31]

Franciscanism described the gestural techniques of *affectus* in its development of imitative and meditational schema for the production of contrition. Like Bernardine piety, Franciscanism was a decisive reorientation of the relations between sacred and profane. Its violently inverting tactics replacing health with sickness, embracing the leprous and the maimed, the high with the low, its embrace of filth and flesh, its emphatic fetishizing of Christ's torn and bleeding body as the object, indeed subject, of compassion and passion, were simultaneously strategies of profanation and sacralization.[32] Christ's body was the symbol designed to effect such a startling interpenetration; that was where the sacred was profaned, as it was also resacralized by that very act of profaning. Replacing the composite, complete and universally inclusive host with its visible borders with the porous, fragmented, excessive body of Christ crucified with its permeable membrane, Franciscanism also introduces a complex language of identification whereby through the medium of Christ's body, identities are restored, transformed, revived, absorbed and submerged. If it is simultaneously a medium of critique and reform, it is also and always a medium of transformation.

In Franciscanism, then, Christ's body was the symbolic vehicle for an astonishing transference of sacrality. For Franciscan texts became the medium of self-reformation that ultimately affected

lay audiences. And it was a transference that could be effected on
the very body of the follower of Christ and Francis. It was this
link, this visceral connection, between Christ's body and human
flesh that was the intimate quickening resource of Franciscan
symbolic theatre. The impact on lay religion has been explored
elsewhere and I do not intend to give a history of Franciscanism
here.[33] But it is worth highlighting a few key factors that are
crucial for any tracing of the embodied subjectivity explored,
constructed and embraced in the Christocentric piety of the late
Middle Ages on which Franciscanism vitally impinges. First,
Franciscanism imagined in its livening reformism an end to 'glosing', to the elaborate exegetical mechanisms by which scriptural
authority was to be understood.[34] As such its reformism was
potentially populist in that it allowed and encouraged the bypassing of those shadows, letters, analogues, anagoges and figura, the
complex metaphorics through which God mediated Himself to
men in texts. Second – and a related point – the best life was to
be a life of *imitatio* encouraged through a proliferation of texts
which talked of the loving contemplation of the tortured Christ.
Third, such narratives involved the translation of the life of Christ
into linear time.

The doctrinal and pedagogic medium for these elaborations lies
in a series of devotional Latin works which circulated under
pseudonymous authors in the thirteenth century. These works –
such as the Pseudo-Bernardine *Liber de passione Christi et doloribus
et planctibus matris ejus* and the *Meditatio in passionem et resurrec-
tionem Domini*, the Pseudo-Anselmian *Dialogus beatae Mariae et
Anselmi de passione Domine* and the Pseudo-Bedean *De meditatione
passione Christis per septem diei horae tibellus* – were all distinguished
by their treatment of the passion as a narrative sequence.[35] Each
work in different ways converted the symbolist understanding of
incarnation into a linear narrative of Christ's life, with specific
emphasis on the passion of Christ. Deploying the form of dialogue, and using the device of dramatic identification and re-
enactment, the interlocutor is asked to contemplate the passion
as a first-hand witness. Lastly, the eventual and increasing address
of these texts was to those of 'mixed life', that is those who
wished to lead a holy life whilst still being active in the world.
Several Franciscan texts were translated into Middle English in
the fourteenth and fifteenth centuries.[36] And such texts were
hardly the monopoly of the Franciscan orders. Elizabeth Salter in

her studies of the late medieval Lives of Christ, makes it clear
that although many of the translations of devotional and homiletic
material were designed for the use and instruction of priests, by
the fourteenth and fifteenth centuries some of these texts were
clearly revised with a lay readership in mind.[37] In the six vernacular Lives of Christ that Salter explores, the narrative of Christ's
life is always the vehicle for moral instruction. These texts are
based on the devotion to Christ's humanity as encouraged
by Anselm and Bernard and popularized by the Franciscans.
They draw on this literature in addition to the bible and patristic
literature.[38]

Hilton in his *Epistle on the Mixed Life* defines for us the new
challenges and tensions enjoined on such a readership:

> þou shalt not uttirli folwen þi desire for to leuen occupaci-
> oun and bisynesse of þe world, whiche aren nedefull to usen
> in rulynge of þisiff and of alle othere þat aren undir þi
> kepynge, and ʒeue þee hoole to goostli occupaciouns of
> praiers and mediations, as it were a frere or a monk or an
> oþir man þat not bounden to þe worlde þi children and
> servantes as þou art, for it falleþ not to þee, and ʒif þou do
> soo, þou kepest not þe ordre of charite. . . . Also, ʒif þou
> woldest leuen uttirli goostli occupacioun, nameli now aftir
> þe grace þat God hath ʒeuen to þe, and sette þe hooli to þe
> bisynesse of þe world, to fulfillynge of werkes of actif liyf
> as fulli as an noþir man þat neuere feeled devocion, þou
> leuest þe ordre of charite, for þi staat asketh for to doo
> bothe, eche of hem in dyvers tyme. þou schalt meedele þe
> werkes of actif liyf wiþ goostli werkes of lif contemplatif,
> and þanne doost thou weel.[39]

'Meddling' the works of the active life with the works of the
contemplative life blurs the old distinctions between those who
work and those who pray. The mixed life concerns those who
work and those who pray and obliterates the surrogacy of devotion to which the estate model attested. Many other works of the
late Middle Ages also testify to a widening of audience. Hilton's
Scale of Perfection, for example, widens its address from a 'ghostly
sister' to all Christian souls.[40] In a recent study, Michael Sargent
has posited a second tier of readers of the devotional works of
the late medieval mystics, an expansion from a spiritual elite to
a much broader artisanal readership. As he points out, the works

originally written for a spiritual elite by Hilton, for example,
were 'within two decades of his death being copied for and
presumably read by devout, prosperous businessmen'.[41]

All these contexts of the new readership of the Lives of Christ,
from the Bernardine contexts to the Franciscan ones, to the new
lay readership of the late Middle Ages, bespeak an obsession with
the hybridity of the passion and experience of Christ as social
symbol which implies that each new readership entails a social
renegotiation. It will be necessary to examine the renegotiation
of the relations between sacred and profane implied by Christocentric piety before the complex formations of subjectivity
entailed by it can be fully appreciated.

LIMENS, BOUNDARIES AND WOUNDS: CORPUS CHRISTI AS RITE OF PASSAGE

Durkheim understood the sacred to found itself in an oppositional
way through its exclusion of the profane. This separation was
intrinsic to his understanding of religious phenomena:

> . . . the real characteristic of religious phenomena is that
> they always suppose a bipartite division of the whole uni-
> verse, known and knowable, into two classes which
> embrace all that exists, but which radically exclude each
> other. Sacred things are those which the interdictions protect
> and isolate; profane things, those to which these interdic-
> tions are applied and which must remain at a distance from
> the first.[42]

Such a definition sets up an essential and immediate ambiguity
in the very category of the sacred: it is only through profanation
that the sacred can be known – the sacred through this definition
is what can be profaned. Roger Callois expresses the relationship
in the following way:

> On the one hand, the contagiousness of the sacred causes it
> to spread instantaneously to the profane, and thus to risk
> destroying and dissipating itself uselessly. On the other
> hand, the profane always needs the sacred, is always pressed
> to possess it avidly, and thus to risk degrading the sacred
> or being annihilated by it.[43]

How would we know what the boundaries of the sacred were,

how could they be traced, unless they were delineated by their antithesis? No wonder then that profanations, such as that understood by Franciscanism, were also associated with spiritual reformism and renewal. Profanation, understood often as contamination and contagion of the sacred, discovers a simultaneous danger and purity. Profanation threatens the sacred as it empowers it. For as Mary Douglas explains, bodily margins are where the bounded system is both created and destroyed, made powerful and vulnerable.[44] But in displaying the very outlines of that body (through dislocation, rupture, entry, exit or traverse), and by so revealing the demarcations of the bounded system, that outline is made available for redrawing.[45]

The image of crucifixion, central to late medieval piety as nurtured by the Cistercian and Franciscan traditions, thematizes the interpenetration of sacred and profane. On the one hand Calvary and its late medieval reproductions and imitations *are* the very origin of sacrality; they are also, however, the place where divinity is systematically debased, humiliated and degraded, where the sacred, by lending itself to the humanity that degrades it, traduces its own nature in profanation. Through the condensed imagery of crucifixion, the dynamic interpenetration of sacred and profane can be explored; the passion *is* the metaphoric site of conversion and transference.[46] In a society where the social bases of the specifically ecclesiastical guardians of the sacred were under profound renegotiation, the arena of Christ's body, the very touchstone of sacerdotal authority, makes itself both closed and open through its wounds.[47]

It is for this reason that the entrances to Christ's body and the exits from it are both the most defiled and the most sacred aspects of the devotion to the cross and the passion. I will explore this idea, which I see to be central to the kind of social renegotiation entailed by passion imagery, through an examination of a text which surely has one of the most extensive and reflexive considerations of the limens of Christ's body in late medieval devotional prose: *The Prickynge of Love*. This text is described by Elizabeth Salter as having 'far-reaching influence on English religious thought and literature in the fourteenth and fifteenth centuries'.[48] Once attributed to Bonaventura, it has been re-ascribed by its Quaracchi editors as the work of James of Milan.[49] The Latin verson exists in two forms. A short text of twenty-three chapters concentrates on the means necessary to achieve the contemplative life, meditation on the cross and the passion, and the means to perfection. The long text puts the passion chapters at the beginning, and contains long meditative sections on the 'Paternoster' the 'Salve Regina' and the 'Ave Maria'.[50] The Middle English version uses the long text as its basis, and is itself extant in eleven complete or originally complete copies, four sets of extracts and one fragment.[51] This text is at once exemplary and extraordinary for the way it examines the construction and dissolution of identity in relation to the body of Christ.

The text helps introduce its addressee to 'be contemplatif'.[52] Its principal means to aid such a transformation is the inculcation of love. Initially love is enjoined through the stressing of a shared nature, a continuity of flesh: 'kynde so knitted he wolde be that neuer wolde from vs twinne. but ʒif we make hit our-self.'[53] At times this continuity of flesh is defined in terms of a concession to earthly weakness:

> . . . ʒif þou wolt al-gatis loue fleshli loue. I praie þe loue þou none þan þe flesh of ihesu criste . . . Forbeden be fro þe liikynge in any odir flesh but only in þe swete flesh of ihesu criste þat is clene withouten wemme of synne.[54]

The power of such flesh will derive from the way it alone is free from original sin. But its power also derives from its transforming properties: 'Gostli shal þi loue be ʒif þow kan loue þat swete fleshe.'[55] The love of Christ who is both man and God will inexorably entail a transformation in the quality of that love, from fleshly to spiritual, or 'goostli'. The hybridity of Christ allows alternately an ascent of flesh to spirit, a transformation from flesh to spirit, but also an incorporation of fleshly love: 'not only þi sowle but al-so þi body shal fynde in him selcouthe swetnesse and sufficiaunt ese.'[56] That the embrace of flesh seems to be necessary for the transformation of one to the other is evidenced by the very next line of the text, which reads: 'in so mikel þat þe reste of þe bodi þat semeth fleshli shal be turned to gostli dilite.'[57] The kind of love made possible by the hybrid figure of Christ is at its most intensely significant when it contemplates the passion. In the imagination of crucifixion the boundaries which delineate Christ's body are subject to pressure on both sides: that is, everything that traverses them, from the inside out to the outside in, is the intense preoccupation of this text. The spear of Longinus assumes a sacral quality because it enters Christ:

A blessid be þat spere & blessid be þo nailes that maden þis
openyng. A that I ne hadde be there in stede of þat spere.
Sotheli I wolde neuere haue goon ouȝt fro cristes side but
I schuld haue seyd þis is my reste & here shal i wone.[58]

The identity of the worshipper becomes labile in its desire to
merge with the spear, with the nails that enter Christ's body.
But the identification is also to the cross itself: 'a whi ne hadde
i ben þere in stede of the cros þat crist myȝht haue ben nayled
to myne hondes & to my feet.'[59] The psychic logic which inspires
such preoccupations means that the wounds of Christ – where
the outside and inside of the body become indistinguishable – are
densely elaborated. The wound is occasionally a breast to be
sucked: 'For this shal þou loue þat holy flesh & souke out of hit
at his woundes þat aren so wyde þe swetnesse of grace þat is hid
wiþinnne.'[60] This image is developed with a literally appetizing
relish:

> & I shal fonde to sowke with him with al þe feith that i
> haue & thus shal I tempore to-gidere þe swete mylke of
> marie the virgine with þe blood of ihesu and make to myself
> a drynke þat is ful of hele.[61]

As well as functioning as a breast, the wound at the side is also
a womb in the act of perpetual parturition:

> & him þat i eer fonde in his modres wombe I fele now how
> he voucheth-saf to bere my soule as his child with-inne his
> blessid sides. But I drede ouer-soone to be sperid ouȝt fro
> þo delites þat I now fele. Certeynli ȝif he caste me ouȝt he
> shal neuerþeles as my modir ȝef me sowke of his pappis &
> bere me in his armes or ellis ȝif he do not þus I wote wel
> þat his woundes are ai open & þerefore as ofte as i falle
> ouȝt als ofte shal i entre in aȝen un-tyl that I be unpartabelly
> to hym festened.[62]

Here the acknowledgement that Christ's body is welcomingly
open almost immediately sponsors the anxiety that the very open-
ness of the wounds will not allow them to provide a safe harbour-
ing place for the soul. If the wounds are too open they cannot
retain and protect the soul they sequester; if they are too closed
there would, in this scenario, be no point of entry for the soul
in the first place. The fantasy, then, that provides for this dilemma

is one of perpetual parturition, an ensured birthing and rebirthing which guarantees that the relationship between the inside and outside of Christ's body will permit the passage of its ardent soul. In James of Milan's *Stimulus amoris*, the original pun between *vulnus* and *vulva* makes the equation an even more grotesquely economical one.[63] The image is one of a parturition that can never be finished, so that the wounds can stay open around the infant soul, and the regression to a foetus-like comfort can keep open the boundaries between inside and outside.

We might say that one of the functions of the wounds in this text is to melt all dividing differences: 'a ʒe myʒhti woundes woundande stonen hertis frosen souleʒ flaumande into fire & meltande brestes of adamaunt in swetnesse of loue.'[64] The boundaries of Christ's body and the body of the devotee are made so soft and so continuous with each other that where one ends and where the other begins become indeterminable: 'At þe openynge of his side mai owre herte entre & be ioyned to his.'[65] The hardness of the heart is literally seen as an image of closure, one which can be brutally reopened:

> And ʒut ʒif þow fele þyn herte ay hard & dryʒe with-owten steryng of loue or of compassioun þou may thenne make ʒif þow wolt a sharpe schourge myche peynande and not mykel hertande and goo into a pryuey place and scourge thi body nobli wel.[66]

Such strategies allow a reborn identity for the soul who 'half out of himself' can be reborn and absorbed into Christ at the same time, so that the rebirth is not felt as a separation or a bereavement.

> For-wy his ʒow art wat þou is þer-fore gif þi-self to hym & to non odir. And ʒif þow be þus turned in-to hym thorouʒ helpe of grace I may nouʒt trowe but þat thow shalt be wounded with his woundes & ouer-helte wyth peynes of his passioun.[67]

Thus, what seems central to the symbolism of the passion in this text, in ways that are both peculiar to it and paradigmatic of other texts, is that it can both enact and resolve contradictory images: of death and life, of individual and group, etc.: 'A certis þis is a loueli & venerabel passion þat so a-cordith contraries & so ioyneth dysseuerid and so festeneth to shere kyndes with þe bonde of blessid loue, & onyth hem vn-partabli in blisse of endeles ioie.'[68] It is the unlikely fact that Christ unites two separate kinds that makes him a suitable symbolic object for such cultural work. He can function quite literally like a rite of passage: no man comes to God except through him:

> For-wy þou man turne to me ʒif þou fonde for to entre in-
> to the loue of cristes herte bi holis of his woundes not only
> þi sowle but also þi bodi shal fynde in him selcouthe swet-
> nesse and sufficiaunt ese.[69]

Going through Christ then is a means of redefinition of self, and it is the hybridity of Christ that allows him to function as such an effective symbol. As Roberto da Matta has explained, what we call 'symbols' often become so as a result of passage from one domain to another one that is quite removed and contradictory, and thus become the focus of strong allusions: 'The heart of the symbolizing process is thus the passage of an object or its appearance in a different domain.'[70] If a change of passage is, as da Matta argues 'a fundamental part of the process of symbolization', then Christ's body performs a double dislocation as a cultural symbol.[71] It removes that most ordinary of objects, the human body, into a sacred sphere. Conversely, it takes that most extraordinary of objects, divinity, and transposes it to the banal domain of the human body. As a symbol, then, its double dislocation makes it doubly effective. It becomes the vehicle of 'strong allusion' in its mobile and continuous dislocation of spheres and condensed interaction of incongruous, incommensurable domains.

This understanding of the symbolism of Christ's body activated by and in the *Prickynge of Love* should give us a much more complex sense of what is at stake in the late medieval identification with Christ. It is decidedly inadequate to talk about the kind of *imitatio* advocated by this text as an 'internalization', for this would imply that this process is merely a screening onto a passive mind, wholly constructed by an external stimulus. Furthermore, such an understanding traduces the polysemous uses of the symbol of Christ's body in the formation and deformation of identity. Our analysis of the *Prickynge of Love* should enable us to perceive the extent to which such a mimesis mobilizes both the active and the passive meanings of *imitatio*. The *imitatio* that is at once advocated, described and enacted in the *Prickynge* does not merely impersonate or counterfeit the gestures of crucifixion, it does not merely duplicate something already there, but is itself newly creative. The *Prickynge* does not merely encourage an impersonation of Christ. Rather, such an impersonation is the vehicle for the formation and imagining of a subjectivity unreachable but through this means. Just as Christ's body is imagined as both image and physical presence, so the body of the addressee of this text is reproduced as a representation of Christ not only inscribed on, but also felt by the body itself. To put it another way, it is the fact that the irreducible origin and accompaniment of imitation is the human body itself, which ambivalently codes the body as representative (body as vehicle) and experiential (body as agent).

In crucifixion piety then, the human body (Christ's body, and the body of the addressee) is both an image and a physical, experiential, felt presence. This is perhaps one reason why we return obsessively to the metaphor of theatre to describe this form of spirituality, for it is in the nature of the theatrical medium to foreground the human body through the mechanism of the actor as at once image and physical presence, at once representation and experience.[72]

The 'costume' of Franciscan theatre *is* the very skin and body of Christ. And it is the vision of Christ's body as a traverse between inside and outside that informs its dynamic coding – the striving towards an inside dynamically recodes what may be understood by the outside. Christ's body is both barrier and passage in a constant process of moving symbolization. 'I wolde ben clad in Cristes skin,' opines John of Grimestone in a late medieval lyric, articulating precisely the obsession with the motif of the traverse of inside and outside which we have seen at work in the *Prickynge*.[73] The metaphorization of the skin as a bodily costume indicates the way in which exteriority and interiority are outrageously inverted in such imagery. If, as Mary Douglas has said, 'it is only by exaggerating the difference between within and without, above and below, male and female, with and against, that a semblance of order is created',[74] then the ambiguating inversion of edges and boundaries surely casts doubt on the reigning classifications dependent on such differences. In this process, the skin, which constrains the body's contours and mediates the world outside, functioning then as both 'an organic and imaginary order',[75] can metaphorize the system which both protects a composite individuality and is the medium for interaction with others. In shifting the borders of the skin, then, the very structures of identity are put into psychic play – dissolved, reconfigured, fragmented and reunited.

Thus although the images of wounds, limens and boundaries are usefully explored in the text of the *Prickynge*, they are by no means peculiar to it. Richard Rolle, for example, articulates one of the most baroquely elaborate ornamentations of the wounds of Christ:

> þan was þy body lyk to hevyn. For as hevyn is ful of sterris, so was þy body full of woundes; bot, Lord, þy woundes bene bettyr þan sterris, for sterris shynen bot by nyght, and þy woundes ben ful of vertue day and night. . . . And yet Lord, þy body is lyk to a nette: for as a nette is ful of holys, so is þy body ful of woundys. Here, swet Jesu, I biseche þe, cache me into þis net of þy scourging, þat al my hert and love be to þe . . . efte, swet Jesu, þy body is lyk to a dufhouse. For a dufhouse is ful of holys, so is þy body ful of woundys. And as a dove pursued of an hauk, yf she now cache an hool in hir hous she is siker ynowe, so swete Jesu, in tempation þy woundys ben best refuyt to us. . . . Also swet Jesus þi body is lyk to a honeycombe. For hit is in euche a way ful of cellis, and euch celle is fulle of hony, so þat hit may not be touched of a clene soule withouten swetnesse of lyking . . . more yit, swet Jesu, þy body is lyke a boke writen with rede inke: so is þy body al written with rede woundes . . . And yit swet Jesus, þy body is lyk to a medow of swete flures and holsoume herbes: so is þy body ful of woundes. . . . swet savourynge to a devouryng soul, and holsome herbes to a synful man.[76]

Such a passage may be seen as exemplary for the extravagantly fertile imagery provoked by the contemplation of Christ's body as a dovehouse, stars in a night sky, net, honeycomb, book, meadow of sweet flowers. Thomas à Kempis, writing in the fifteenth century, inspired perhaps by benedictions of the Virgin's limbs, composed fourteen prayers to the different limbs of Christ, a prayer known as *Oratione ad membra Christi*.[77] The late medieval poem 'Symbols of the Passion', reprinted in *Legendys of the Holy Rood*, illustrates and itemizes everything that pierces or touches the surface of Christ's skin.[78] Itemized in this poem are the bloodstained clothes that are stripped from Christ, the scourges that whipped him, the nails that pierced him, the cross that bore him, the crown of thorns, the spear of Longinus, the sponge that wiped the sweat off his face. Described sometimes as the 'arma Christi', the very symbols of arms and armour are recoded as the very image of frailty.[79] It is not simply that these are images of inversion then, but what may better be described as images of hybridization, described by Peter Stallybrass and Allon White as a process that 'produces new combinations and strange instabilities in a given semiotic system. It therefore generates the possibility of shifting the very terms of the system itself . . . by erasing and interrogating the relations which constitute it.'[80] The cult of the five wounds articulated in *The Prickynge of Love* and celebrated in the newly created late medieval liturgical feasts can explore the body as a medium for the self, can manifest the latent potentialities of the body as outer manifestation and inner being. The duality of the body, overdetermined by the duality of Christ's body, can be the medium of an individual reform that is also a social reclassification, a reclassification that importantly involves the reorganization of sacred–profane relations. It is no surprise then, that those groups who propagate and develop most effectively and affectively the imagery of Christ's body are those groups who are both intensely reformist, and yet who also in their constitution and practice have to renegotiate a relationship between 'lay' and ecclesiastical society. It is no wonder that an imagery which maintains the sacrality of the social body of Christ, but expands its boundaries to let in 'new' recruits, would prefer an imagery that maintained the fiction of a body sacredly and simultaneously closed and open: open enough to let in newcomers, closed enough to maintain the integrity of a distinctive group. In articulating such a vocabulary of passion imagery, the body is formulated as the medium of the interrelationship of self and society.

LOVE'S *MIRROUR*

As I stressed in chapter 2, because Christ's body is also a special preserve which defines the clerical establishment as the exclusive transubstantiators of bread and wine, access to the body of Christ by other means was potentially subversive. Thus in the late Middle Ages, vernacular texts are felt to be deeply threatening because they made fragile the clerical monopoly of that body, as well as the language through which it was mediated.[81] It is interesting, then, to remark that the notion of Christ's body as a model of ascent, a means of passage, a way of making porous the relations between heaven and earth, is often counteracted by images of violent hierarchization. As Claire Kirchberger remarks in her translation of the *Prickynge*, those passages in the Latin version of the *Stimulus amoris* which talk about the conversion of man to God through the medium of Christ are regularly modified by an increasing emphasis on the humility of Christ. The Latin 'sic deificatus et transformatus' becomes 'so turned and transformed into God' and the term 'resolvat in Deum' becomes 'yield and relinquish all unto God'.[82] Kirchberger notes an increasing insistency in the references to the humanity of Christ and the words for God, 'deus' and 'creator' are turned systematically to 'Christ our Lord'.[83] The intoxicating licensing of the hybridity of Christ is thereby tempered, constrained into a model of ascent and descent.[84]

Some similar mechanisms can be seen to be at work in another translation of an early thirteenth-century work, Nicholas Love's *Mirrour of the Blessyd Life of Jesu Christ*. A translation of the *Mediationes vitae Christi*, originally written for a poor Clare around Siena at the end of the thirteenth century, this text was popularized throughout Europe.[85] Indeed it is hard to underestimate the importance of the *Meditationes*, for it was the text that literally translated the life of Christ for his followers, and itself became a work that was developed in several vernaculars.[86] Elizabeth Salter, in her study of the transmission of medieval Lives of Christ, locates seven separate versions of the passion section of the *Meditationes* during the fourteenth century alone, before Nicholas Love's translation of the fifteenth century.[87]

Michael Sargent's work on the *Mirrour* in the preparation of his critical edition has established the highly polemical contexts in which the *Meditationes* were translated for an English audience in the early fifteenth century. Authorized by Arundel after his Lambeth Constitutions which required all new biblical translations to be submitted to episcopal authority for approval before publication in an effort to combat Lollard heresy, it was approved for the edification of the faithful and the confutation of heretics.[88] Its entrenched and defensive combativism could hardly be more clearly stated.

The *Mirrour* is a Life of Christ which encourages the kind of identificatory practices that have by now come to seem familiar. But its mixture of the 'ghostli' and the 'bodily' is much more carefully adjudicated and manipulated, as if the dangers and difficulties of identificatory practice are by now apparent.[89] In Love's translation the interaction of 'ghostli' things and bodily things provoked by the imagining of Christ's life in such concretely literal terms instils an anxiety that is as much social as it is doctrinal. At the beginning of his translation, Love explains to us that lay people are like children. What they require, he says, is the milk of light doctrine, and 'not sadde mete of grete clergie and of hige contemplacioun'.[90] It is because of the putative 'simplicity' of some of his addressees that he will concentrate his instruction on the 'manhede' of Christ:

> And therefore to hem is principally to be sette in mynde the ymage of cristes incarnacioun, passioun and resurreccioun; so that a symple soule that kan not thenke bot bodies or bodily thynges mowe have somewhat accordynge unto his affeccioun wherewith he may fede and stire his devocioun.[91]

The incarnation of Christ then becomes a means of social and linguistic condescension, a model not so much of ascent as of descent. And this model of descent seems intent on limiting the creative damage that the hybridizing figure of Christ in its blurring and movement of categories might be in danger of introducing into social relations. The reader is enjoined to 'Now take hede and ymagine of goostly thing as it were bodily and thinke in thyn herte as thou were present.'[92] But this imagining must not confuse what is spiritual with what is bodily, what is high with what is low (the very effervescent mixing which the incarnational aesthetic licenses):

> But now be war that thou erre nought in ymaginacioun of God and of the holy trynite supposynge that thise thre persones the fader the sone and the holy gost ben as thre erthely men that thou seest with thy bodily eige: the whiche ben thre dyverse substances eche departyd from other so that none of hem is other.[93]

That the operations with which he is engaging are very destabilizing ones is something Love appears acutely aware of. Rather than the porousness of categories – symbolic and social – licensed by incarnational practice, he insists, contrarily, on a hierarchical model which erects a ladder of social and linguistic condescension.

The model of descent becomes one way for clerical orthodoxy to refute potentially socially subversive incarnation doctrine, licensed as it was by the wider availability of vernacular writings.

Let us trace through some of the further tensions unleashed by the social valency of the metaphor of the body of Christ, simultaneously inculcated and restrained by Love's text.

It is the systematic function of Nicholas Love's *Mirrour* literally to map the hours of Christ's passion onto the body of the individual worshipper.[94] This is done by a narrative elaboration of Christ's life which is orchestrated in Gail Gibson's phrase as a 'theatre of devotion'. Sometimes as Christ, sometimes as an onlooker, sometimes as one of the key characters in the passion story, the reader is besought to be present at the crucifixion. The language of exhortation is 'beholde', 'understande', 'give good intente', 'be stired,' 'take good hede', 'beholde we inwardly', 'ymagine' – all words which stress the intensely affective address of these passages. But the exhortation to the imagination of Christ's life is also effected by the means of the book's organization and construction. For the narrative of the life of Christ is divided into separate parts for regular meditation on separate days of the week. In doing this it enhances, refers to, and parallels, liturgical time which envisages the mass as a re-enactment of all the events of Christ's life. The meditations, then, like their counterparts, the Books of Hours, juxtapose ecclesiastical time with individual time, and attempt to make the one act in concert with the other:

> And for also moche as this book is deuyded and departyd in VII parties, after VII daies of the weke: every day one party or somme therof to ben in contemplacioun of hem that han therto desire and devoicioun. Therfore at the Moneday as the firste workeday of the weke bygynnyth this gostly werk tellynge of the devoute instaunce and desire of the holy aungelis in heuene for manis restorynge and his salvation; to stire man amonge other that day specially to worschippe hem; as holy chirche the same day maketh special mynde of hem. Also not onliche the mater of this book is pertynent and profitable to be had in contemplaci-

oun the forseide dayes to hem that wollen and mowen bot also as it longeth to the tymes of the yere.[95]

The crucifixion structures the time of everyday life. On the one hand, of course, this is a logical extension of the imaginative embodiment of the mass itself, an extension of the clerical mastery of the mystery, but on the other hand it is an anxiety-inducing blurring of the boundaries of clerical and lay worship.[96] For Love's translation of the *Meditationes* cannot avoid entertaining the interpretative licence it is commissioned to counteract. The problem of translation has for Love raised the question of authority and authorization in a peculiarly urgent way. For one thing, his own imaginative addition to the scriptural precedents for a Life of Christ, and his licensing of an interactive reinvention of that Life (a re-enactment that brings it into an impure and contaminating contact with the imaginations of others), needs to be legitimated within the project: 'holy writt may be expounded and understonden in dyvers maneres and to dyverse purposes so that it be not agens the belief of God's manere.'[97] This, indeed, is intended to be the means of a thoroughgoing reinscription of ecclesiastically ordained doctrine in the very hearts, minds and souls of the laity. He repeats the Pseudo-Bonaventuran citation of the exemplary St Cecilia to state the importance of this project:

> Among other vertues commendynges of the holy virgyne Cecile it is writen that sche bare alwey the gospel of crist hyd in hir brest; that may be understonde that of the blessyd lyf of oure lord Jesus Christ in the gospel sche ches certayne parties moste devoute in the whiche sche sette hir mediation and hir thought nyght and day with a clene and hole herte. . . . And so . . . in that manere the gospel of Christ sche sette and bare it euere in the priuite of her breste.[98]

But within its context, such a logic implicates a great deal of anxiety:

> And so what tyme or in what place in this book is writen that thus dide or thus spak our Lord Jesu or othere that ben spoken of and it may not be proved of holy writt or grounded in express seeing of holy doctoures – it shal be taken none other wise than as devoute meditacioun that it might be so spoken or doun.[99]

It is hardly any wonder then that Love should devote such a large proportion of his work – all of it entirely added to his Latin original – to reiterating the centrality of the sacrament, for it is precisely this aspect of Christ's body that was clerically administered – handled between clerical hands as one late medieval morality play suggested – rather than individually licensed and propagated.[100] According to Michael Sargent, currently preparing a critical edition of the *Mirrour*, Love's major additions to the *Meditationes* consist in a passage of 2,000 words on auricular confession and two additions on the sacrament of the altar. One of these insertions occurs in the Maundy Thursday section, where Love rehearses the events of the Last Supper, and the other is positioned at the end where he adds 10,000 words of a 'short tretys of the higest and moste worthy sacrament of cristes blessed body and the mervayles therof'.[101] This treatise is present in all but five of the numerous manuscript copies. It is therefore, in Sargent's considered opinion, not a mere afterthought but actually an integral part of the *Mirrour*.[102]

Significantly, in the Maundy Thursday passage, Love is acutely aware of both clerical and lay elements of his readership, and he makes a careful distinction between them. First, the Last Supper is used conventionally as a scriptural licensing for clerical power: 'And after he gaf hem power of that consecration and alle preostes in hem.'[103] After this reminder Love continues:

Take now good hede thou cristen man but specially thou preost how devoutly how diligently and trewely thy lorde Jesu Criste firste made this preciouse sacrament, and after with his blissed handes mynystred it and commmuned that blissed and his beloued meigne. And on the tother side take hede with what devoute wondre firste they sele him make that wonderfulle and excellent sacrament; and after with what drede and reuerance they toke it and receyved it of him. Sothely at this tyme they lefte al their kyndely resoun of man and onely restede in trewe byleue to alle that he seiden and didde beleuvynfge with oute eny dowte that he was god and myghte not erre. And so moste thou doo that wolt fele and have the vertue and the gostly swetnesse of this blissed sacrament.[104]

The clergy and the lay are differentiated as makers and receivers of the sacrament. After the indispensability of the cleric is reaffirmed, the lay are enjoined to abandon their reason and simply believe. Love seems to be acutely aware of the doubt that inheres in the reception of the sacrament especially as it pertains to the denial of the received understanding of the transubstantiation by the 'lewde lollardes'.[105]

In reiterating the centrality of the sacrament at such self-conscious length and making it so vital a component of his translation of the *Meditationes*, Love is not simply trying to counteract a potentiality that gnaws the text from within. In so ardently insisting on the host, the sacred body of Christ, he is returning the worshipper back to the collective body from which the very form and function of his own text, with the logic of its desire to inscribe the gospel within the privacy of the breast, had categorically removed him/her. The very means by which Christ's body has been made available endangers as it extends the clerical project. At some levels of the text, Love acknowledges the difficulty and risk of incorporation into the body of Christ.

The final few lines of the *Mirrour* are constituted by a 'shorte devoute prayer' to Christ in the sacrament, a prayer that again returns the worshipper to the mass, the public, clerically controlled means of manipulating Christ's body – for it is a prayer that is to be 'seide in the prescence of that holy sacrament at the masse with inward devocioun'.[106] The prayer is, of course, an elevation prayer, to be uttered when the priest raises the host aloft. It is, then, as I explored in chapter 2, an instance in the mass where Christ's body as a clerically administered spectacle, and as an act of 'inward devocioun' is simultaneously joined and separated, merged and divided. The prayer contains the desire that such outer devotion of the mass and the inner meditation that has been the central licensing and individualizing manoeuvre of the *Mirrour* will be welded rather than separated in Christ's body: 'My god, I beseke the that thou wille so graciously bowe the and from thi hye heuene nowe come downe to me that I knytte and ioyned to the be made oon spirit with the.'[107] Similar prayers are extant in late medieval 'lay folk's' mass books.[108] Unlike missals, these were designed for lay use. Generally containing instructions on how to behave at mass, what prayers to say at what moments, some of these late medieval materials, like the texts of the *Lay Folk's Mass Book* are books designed for private reading.[109]

Although Love's principal target was Lollardy, the *Mirrour* was by no means chiefly a doctrinal refutation of Lollard heresy, but rather, like the Bernardine piety that so pressured and informed it, an attempt to reimagine and invent the kinds of subjectivities, loving subjectivities who would ardently desire to be obedient to God's will, now made synonymous with clerical will. Ultimately this project was a very dangerous one for, by helping to introduce and expand the notion of the radical reflexivity of the human will, such piety ultimately gave an extraordinary dynamism to lay piety, whilst it subtly de-authorized clerical authority. Love's text, though authorized primarily to mitigate anti-clericalism and preference for the vernacular, had conceded the strength of some of its opponents' arguments in the very act of translation and authorization. Once again, the language of image and argumentation used Christ's body as its fundamental resource.

It should by now be apparent that the reformation of the human heart involved in such an imaging, and the articulation of its modes of loving, suffering and identification, were not simply individual issues, even when they were communicated in the most privatized forms. The radical and extraordinary focus on individual reformation that these texts articulated has perhaps entailed an unfortunate underestimation of the social and political currency of their usage. Perhaps nowhere is such a relation better articulated than in the trial of Sir John Oldcastle.

'WHERE IS THE CROSS CHRIST DIED ON?'[110]

One of the aims of this chapter has been to examine some of the uses to which 'passion imagery' (Lives of Christ, imagery of the wounds, etc.) is put in late medieval England. The lineage of passion imagery is traceable through a Latinate tradition dating from the tenth and eleventh centuries which moulds the body of Christ into the medium for producing devotees whose desire, love and affect can be the vehicles of transformation. Such a transformation entails redefining the resources of subjectivity. The two scholarly traditions that have been involved in the analysis of the imagery of Christ's body have mostly divided their considerations between the public, collective (often ritualized) versions of the body of Christ and the private, interiorized, individual versions. To a certain extent, although I have been attempting to break down this dichotomy in my own account, the very division of my chapters (2 and 3) in some cases underscores this division. But part of my argument is concerned to show that the 'private' uses to which passion imagery and crucifixion piety were put were themselves subject to public deployment and articulation, and that the 'public' constructions of Christ's body work through the somatic reach of the human body as the private unit of experience. The 'private' and 'public' articulations then are not so easily separable as we may have supposed. Moreoever, I claim, it is the specific symbolic signification of Christ's body to interweave collective and individual meanings, using one to validate the other. It is not, however, a simple question of mutual validation since one level of meaning can actually conflict with and undermine the other.

Victor Turner has said that what he calls dominant symbols are characterized by multivocality, and the unification of disparate signata, but most significantly for my purposes here, by 'polarization of meaning'.[111] In his account dominant symbols possess two distinguishable poles of meaning. There is an ideological pole around which are clustered significations deriving from modes of corporate grouping, principles of social organization, and the 'norms and values inherent in structured relationships'.[112] And there is a sensory or orectic pole around which are located signata which arouse somatic, gross and visceral desires and emotions. 'Sensory signata are also gross in that they are frankly, even flagrantly, physiological, and thus have links with the unconscious. They represent items of universal experience.'[113] In other words, to understand the imagery of Christ's body in such a way that it would be responsible to its meaning and function as *symbolic* form, we need to be able to see how inextricably interrelated, how utterly mutually implicated, symbolically speaking, are the ideological and sensory poles, which have too often been polarized in the critical traditions that account for this imagery.

In the last section of this chapter I will analyse a particular, and in my view pivotal (both symbolically and historically), instance of passion imagery which indicates how much our understanding of the context and substance of this imagery is stretched and illuminated if we can perceive the interpenetration of public and private, of ideological and sensory meanings in the use of Christ's body – the trial of Sir John Oldcastle.

Oldcastle was tried for the heresy of Lollardy in September of 1413, before Archbishop Arundel.[114] During the course of this trial he was condemned, then delivered to the secular arm to be burnt to death. In October he managed to escape from the Tower of London and masterminded and led a plot to seize the king in January 1414. He was eventually captured and executed in December 1417. A Lollard pamphlet made after his trial cites the following conversation purported to have taken place within it:

> 'Why sir,' said one of the clerks, 'will ye not worship images?' 'What worship?' said the Lord. . . . The friar said, 'I put case, Sir, that it were here before you!' The Lord said, 'This is a ready man! and to put to me a question of a thing, that they wot never where it is? And yet I ask you, what worship?' A clerk said, 'such worship as Paul speaketh of, that is this, God forbid me to joy, but in the cross of our Lord Jesus Christ.' 'Then,' said the Lord, and spread his arms abroad, 'this is a very cross.'[115]

Ecclesiastical authority used the doctrine of the incarnation to license and underscore its use of images. But here *imitatio* is being used as a dramatic counter-accusation to effect an identification with Christ that directly subverts the authority of the church. It is a technique that has been deployed during the course of the account of the trial. Oldcastle acerbically remarks to his judges that it was Annas and Caiaphias who sat and judged Christ, by this analogy placing himself in the position of Christ. Their response takes up the challenge on the very same terrain: Christ, they say, judged Judas, thus identifying themselves with Christ, and against his betrayer, John Oldcastle. But the dramatic reinscription of crucifixion in his own body, effected by the simple gesture of spreading his arms wide, emotively capitalizes on the full potentiality of the image of crucifixion whilst simultaneously abjuring the dissimulative mediation of an actual image:

> As to the adoration of the Holy Cross, he said that only the body of Christ which hung upon the cross ought to be adored, because that body alone was and is the cross to be adored. And being asked what honour he would do to the image of Christ on that Cross, he expressly replied that he would only do it the honour to clean it and put it in good custody.[116]

He efficiently invokes the Pauline script against its clerical invocation and his identification of Christ is economically effective because it is a gestural one, a rhetoric of the body, an image and a literal abjuration of image through its enactment, through the display of tenor and vehicle in one body.

Oldcastle's assumption of the posture of crucifixion at his trial is in many ways thoroughly in line with the *imitatio Christi* advocated by Love. Indeed, one reason why this battle was both so dense and so highly coded was because the subtext of Oldcastle's vision elucidated the sometimes repressed but always implicit agenda of lay piety. For Oldcastle, the true successors of St Peter's keys were formed not by sheer virtue of office, but by virtue of the *imitatio Christi*.

Oldcastle's trial is significant for many reasons. It marks, first of all, a genuine watershed in the treatment and consideration of heresy because it affected the secular realm as well as the ecclesiastical polity. Though derisory, the uprising performed by a respected and high-ranked man indicated the extent to which Lollardy could infect the upper echelons of the realm as well as the church. The years in which Oldcastle remained uncaptured were a period in which both the secular and ecclesiastical polities combined to survey and investigate the orthodoxy of parishioners. The Leicester Parliament of 1414 passed laws that necessitated the participation of royal officers, from judges to bailiffs and mayors of cities and towns, requesting that they swear an oath on entry to office that they would 'put out, cease and destroy all manner of heresies and errors, commonly called lollardies, and assist bishops and their officers when called upon to do so'.[117] In other words, as Peter Heath specifies, orthodoxy was made the subject of quite routine investigation on the part of the secular arm of the law, and secular governors of the realm. As he puts it: 'The definition of true faith was still in the hands of the professional theologians, the clergy, but the state could now on its own initiative compel observance and had elaborate machinery to do so.'[118] Chichele, in 1416, ordained that each deanery and parish was to make regular and diligent inquiry as to heresy. The defence of the realm and the faith were to be jointly articulated. Such an alliance is made clear in the address of the Prince of Wales to the parliament of 1406 in a petition against Lollardy. The petition was submitted on behalf of the temporal lords, for the argument was made that, since the church held land by as good a title as any lord in the land, to breach such a tenure would encourage a similar assault on the estates of secular lords. As landholders, then, the ecclesiastical establishment and the temporal lords could perceive serious interests in common, interests to which an articulation of the organicism of the medieval church and state was a necessary legitimizing cliché. As Heath expresses it in a telling metaphor: 'the bond of faith and politics was as intimate and fundamental as that of the soul to the body.'[119]

Jeremy Catto has emphasized the historic importance of the unification of church and state in the articulation of heresy:

> From the Leicester Parliament of 1414 until the triumph of toleration in the eighteenth century, religion was established and enforced by public authority, and dissentient voices subjected to the rigours of statutory felony. By contrast, before 1400 religion was outside the competence of the secular power, and after 1800 would become a matter of indifference to the cabinets of Europe. But between these dates, in England as in other countries, it would be a matter of the utmost importance to government, and a source of bitterest conflict, what the allegiance of its subjects was, what they believed, and how they expressed it in public worship.[120]

Henry V, dubbed 'princeps presbyterorum' by the St Albans Chronicle, and self-styled 'defender of the faith' was the architect of a different relationship between private religion and communal religion. The church needed the secular arm to deal with heresy; the king needed the church to grant legitimacy to its Lancastrian usurpation. This alliance was crucial to the reforms of Henry V, and they involved a fundamental renegotiation of the relationship between church and state and clergy and laity. Hughes has described this new alignment as a 'state-controlled, public religion . . . [which] embodied the ideals of the mixed life'.[121]

Henry V encouraged a sense of his personal devoutness and used piety for the purposes of propaganda. St John of Beverley's body distilled liquid for sixty-one days when Henry V's father landed at Ravenspur, for example. The entire church was encouraged, by means of indulgences, to pray for military victory. The national significance of the Sarum rite was increased and liturgical practice was homogenized at the same time as new feasts – St George, the Holy Name – were inaugurated.[122] The object of the liturgical reforms is not dissimilar to Love's. Chichele's reformed liturgy encouraged 'a liturgy in which personal devotions could be incorporated and the call of private conscience could be harmonized'.[123]

Arundel promoted Love to the charterhouse at Mount Grace, a house founded in the Carthusian order so strongly supported by Henry V.[124] Henry V founded the charterhouse of Sheen in 1415. Founded through the confiscation of alien priories, its endowment was an instance of the kind of nationalistic religious reinvestment which was such a hallmark of Henry V's reign.[125] For the Carthusian order encouraged a contemplative life in a monastic and therefore communal setting. It organized and propagated the dissemination of some of the principal texts of the devotional interest in crucifixion piety in the late Middle Ages. Henry used Sheen and Syon as a kind of 'gigantic powerhouse of prayer for the Lancastrian dynasty';[126] their hermits prayed for military victory. This relationship between public worship and private devotion is a hallmark not just of the religious accommodation of Henry V, but it is also central to the new religious foundations of the Carthusians.[127]

Such accommodations make it clear that we cannot talk about the piety of the late Middle Ages as part of a move which simply vulgarizes, internalizes or privatizes. All these terms are part of the language by means of which this piety is generally described. Such language polarizes the terms of reference and fundamentally depoliticizes them. It stops us from considering the interaction between piety and politics which is in fact a crucial demarcator of this historical period.

Images such as Christ's wounds were not simply subject to an intensely affective devotion of private religion – they were also symbols of political power: Oldcastle has the host and chalice on his banners during the attempted uprising in Lichfield.[128] Indeed, the Lancastrian dynasty may have been both particularly susceptible to, and capable of using, popular cults and religious devotions to gain a legitimacy which it had threatened in its very founding.[129] Henry V was known not simply for his renegotiation of the relation between the lay and ecclesiastical polity, but also for his personally austere piety.[130]

Perhaps the opposition of personal devotion and communal rite is exaggerated in the consideration of late medieval devotion. So much of the vitality and energy of late medieval devotion is said to emerge from its individualism. And yet such piety is not entirely understood within those terms. It is rather in the tension

and interrelationship of public cult and private devotion that crucifixion piety is best understood. The affective power and emotive
reach of the symbol of Christ's body lay in the way it could
function simultaneously as the most intimate experience and the
most public resource; and it was precisely through the connections
between these two realms that its political resourcefulness was
articulated – in the potentialities of the animation of the relationship between *esprit de corps* and *état de corps*. It could animate the
relationships between individual and group, between the sacred
and the profane, between representation and experience and it
could figure finally as an important vehicle for the establishment
of a historic relationship between state and citizen.

SACRAMENTALISM, BELIEF,
RELIGIOUS PRACTICE

The symbolic figure of Christ's body underpins the system of
sacramentalism in the late Middle Ages.[131] Recent critics have seen
the proliferating imagery of incarnation, passion and crucifixion as
an index of the extension of sacramental theology into the world.
'The fifteenth century commitment to the particularity of
religious experience' says Gail Gibson, 'is not so much . . . an
increasing secularization as much as a growing tendency to see
the world saturated with sacramental possibility and meaning and
to celebrate it.'[132] And in a lyric rendition, Travis, speaking here
of the body of Christ dramatized in the Corpus Christi cycles,
has similarly asserted that Christ's body 'blesses the material. It
bonds with the physicality of its torturers; it extends to the city
walls and gates. It is a natural symbol that embraces and is part
of the living body of the community.'[133] The direction of my
thought in this book has led me to rather different conclusions.
Christ's body in late medieval crucifixion piety and passion imagery is just as much about the undoing of sacramentalism as it
is its extension. The object of ritual cohesion, but also the resource
of specific disciplinary practices, it refers to the collectivity and
to new forms of individualism and it can use one to validate the
other, even as one actually undermines the other.

The notion of the sacrament of Christ's body as a form of
ritual cohesion depends on that division between the sacred and
profane that ritual techniques manipulate and monitor. But the
logic of the imitation of Christ, modelling Christ in the human

soul, entails a different understanding of sacred–profane relations. The denial of any special place or person (church, priest) is also a denial of the very distinction between sacred and profane, and an affirmation of their interpenetration. It is also an index of the redefinition of religious practice in terms less of rite, non-cognitive activity, than in terms of doctrine and belief. Christ's body is the material that can still integrate these realms that are moving, and historically will move, further and further apart. The violence and the difficulty of the imagery are a measure of how hard such a task had become.

4

THE USES OF CORPUS CHRISTI AND *THE BOOK OF MARGERY KEMPE*

Sche sey hyr Lord steyn up in-to Heuyn, for sche cowde not forberyn hym in erde.

(Margery Kempe)

In Rome, when God asks for Margery Kempe's hand in marriage – the apotheosis, surely, of any late medieval mystical career – she is on the brink of refusing Him. For she wants not the 'Godhede' but the 'manhode' of God:

> Also þe Fadyr seyd to þis creatur, 'Dowtyr, I wil han þe weddyd to my Godhede, for I schal schewyn þe my preuyteys & my cownselys, for þu xalt wonyn wyth me wythowtyn ende.' þan þe creatur kept sylens in hir sowle & answeryd not þerto, for sche was ful sor aferd of þe Godhed & sche cowde no skylle of þe dalyawns of þe Godhede, for al hir lofe & al hir affeccyon was set in þe manhode of Crist & þerof cowde sche good skylle & sche wolde no-thyng a partyd þerfro.[1]

It is a typical and ambivalent gesture which holds dialectically in tension the rejection of the Father with her own abasement before Him so that her preference for the Son can be reread as the measure of her humility rather than her megalomania. But it is nevertheless this refusal and all that it implies in the eyes of her commentators – her lack of a seriously vocational mystical career, her inability to release the son for the father, her need for the mediation of earthly roles, her preference for embodied relationships rather than heavenly transcendence – that have earned her considerable abuse as a mystical writer, a testimony to how deeply she has affronted her critics.[2] Rather than rehearse this attack and defence yet again, I propose in this chapter to look at the uses of the imaging of Christ's body in *The Book of Margery Kempe*, for this unique document in its belatedly discovered manuscript has provided us with the means to challenge some of the most dearly held pieties concerning late medieval religiosity. How does Margery Kempe respond to and creatively reconstruct her own cultural symbolic of crucifixion? How do contemplation of and identification with the incarnation and crucifixion of Christ allow her to renegotiate her position in her own society – late medieval Bishop's Lynn? How does it authorize her and what licence does it give her? How does Kempe's imitation of Christ relate to Christ's body as social body, clerical body and private body? These are some of the questions which we may address to *The Book of Margery Kempe* and that it may answer for us.

Kempe knows Love's *Mirrour* and is very influenced by the kind of identificatory practices it advocates.[3] Because of the unusually detailed contextualization in the *Book*, we are able to trace with some specificity her relations with the clergy, and her participation in the 'sacramental' life of her community. Accused of Lollardy, her form of piety, knowledge of scriptural texts and unlicensed preaching, though eventually pronounced orthodox, are an index of the uneasy relations between the clergy and the laity, when the circulation of vernacular texts was providing an alternative mechanism for access to the body of Christ. Accused of being 'Cobhamis dowtyr' at the very time when John Oldcastle, Lord Cobham, is in hiding in the countryside, she is more than metaphorically associated with his overt subversion.[4] Finally, the manuscript in which her book appears has associations with the Carthusians of Mount Grace priory, near Northallerton in Yorkshire, and with the Carthusian reformation of the early fifteenth century.[5] The fact that excerpts from Kempe's *Book* were printed by Wynkyn de Worde in 1501 indicates that Kempe's work forms part of the characteristic dissemination of texts to a broader and broader lay audience, to those who, like Margery herself, desired their own access to the body of Christ.[6] The *Book*, therefore, has intricate and complex relations with so many of those aspects of late medieval religious practice that I have explored in this book – the changing relations of clergy and laity, the ritualized sacramental administrations of the body of Christ as eucharist, its alternative pursuit through texts advocating the 'mixed life', the contestation over the body of Christ spearheaded by the Lollard movement, its relations to both the reformist, but resolutely orthodox, Carthusian order, and the wider society of an urban readership in London. Kempe seems to exhibit a religiosity that is increasingly inward at the same time as her extravagant externalization and display of the very signs of her special election have meant that she has often been associated with the very 'outward' aspects of religiosity that were at the core of later protestant critique and redefinition. The symbol of the body of Christ is central to the development, conflict and interrelationship of 'outward' and 'inward' practices. Repeatedly described or dismissed as a degraded hagiography, a bathetic attempt at the sublime by a woman who cannot get the smell of stockfish off her hands, or the manhood of Christ off her mind, it is precisely the insistent grating of the literal against the trancendent in the *Book* that offers us a way of understanding the cultural meaning of crucifixion piety and the imaging of Christ's body for one of its most ardent, erratic but representative practitioners.

MARGERY KEMPE'S *IMITATIO*

The licensing force of Kempe's religiosity is of course the figure of the incarnated God, Christ. The mimesis of Christ is at the very centre of Kempe's book. In a society which prohibited women from writing and preaching, from adjudicating the authoritative scriptural word, it was only the direct word of God and Christ, prophetically authorized, that could make a woman's words worth the listening or transcribing.[7] So in *The Book of Margery Kempe* Kempe can speak to those around her and get her book written only through an arduous apprenticeship in the discernment of spirits.[8] What licenses her piety is the accompanying apprenticeship in suffering enjoined by her imitation of Christ.

From the very beginning the figure of Christ in her book exists in complex relation to the clerical establishment. Her book, after all, begins with a refusal of the mediating counsel of the clergy. She refuses to confess a particularly heinous sin to a confessor after the birth of her first child. Christ's first 'visitation' to Kempe coincides in her narrative with that refusal. Christ enters 'in lyknesse of a man, most semly, most bewtyows, & most amyable þat euyr mygth be seen wyth mannys eye'.[9] Christ the man is juxtaposed with the institutional church as an alternative source of mercy, forgiveness and redemption. And he appears at his most familiar and speaks in a language to which she can respond. Although she understands the basics of Trinitarian doctrine, her interest is entirely in the Second Person. She talks about accompanying Mary and Joseph to visit Elizabeth to help her bear St John, and assists Mary at the nativity in the very same tone used to discuss her life in Lynn. It is a seamless rendition of the meditations enjoined by Nicholas Love in his *Mirrour of the Blessyd Lyf of Jesu Christ*, and bespeaks an extraordinary continuity of her life and Christ's.[10] That continuity is a continuity of shared fleshliness, for as Christ says to her: 'for þu hast so gret compassyon of my flesche I must nede haue compassyon of þi flesch.'[11] It is no surprise, then, that she should wish to concentrate on those parts of his life which emphasize that embodiedness most completely. Her text returns repeatedly to the moments of Christ's birth and death, and sometimes, as in her contemplation of the *pietà*, that image which depicts Christ dying in the arms of his mother, where birth and death coalesce. Having then been present at, indeed having aided in, the very parturition of Christ as baby, she becomes most interested in him at the moment of his death, his crucifixion. This is where her identification is at its most literal and empowered. So, when she goes to Calvary, the meditations of her mind assume an utterly literal actuality: 'Sche had so very contemplacyon in þe sygth of hir sowle as yf Crist had hangyn befor hir bodily eye in hys manhode.'[12] Similarly, as there is no difference for her between the sights of her soul and her bodily eye, so graphic are her imaginings, so there is no difference between a crucifix and the object of its memorial signification:

> & sumtyme, whan sche saw þe Crucyfyx, er yf sche sey a man had a wownde er a best wheþyr it wer, er yf a man bett a childe be-for hir er smet an hors er an-oþer best wyth a whippe, ȝyf sche myth sen it er heryn it, hir thowt sche saw owyr Lord be betyn er wowndyd.[13]

A priest, amazed at the cries she utters at the sight of a *pietà* tells her that 'Ihesu is ded long sithyn.' She replies, 'Sir, hys deth is as fresch to me as he had deyd þis same day.'[14]

Ultimately the concreteness of these imaginings is rooted in the visceral compassion with the passion of Christ as she *becomes* him on Calvary:

&, whan þei can up on-to þe Mownt of Caluarye, sche fel
down that sche mygth not stondyn ne knelyn but walwyd
& wrestyd wyth hir body, spredyng hir armys a-brode, &
cryed wyth a lowde voys as þow hir hert xulde a brostyn
a-sundyr, for in þe cite of hir sowle sche saw veryly and
freschly how owyr Lord was crucifyed.[15]

And it is these cries, uttered for the first time at this moment of
maximal identification, in the very pose of crucifixion on Calvary,
the historic point of Christ's death renewed in the culmination
of her pilgrimage, that reproduce and repeat that mimesis at every
utterance. They become, for Kempe at least, the proof of her
sanctity.[16]

But if this is the moment of most literal identification, Kempe's
imitatio Christi also consists in her willing assumption of suffering,
and the way she functions as an object of scorn to those around
her. Several times during the early parts of the book, she imagines
ways to die[17] for the love of God, but as her narrative continues,
it is no longer so necessary to invent or imagine her own persecution, for she has successfully constructed herself as the object
of scorn she craves to be. Thus, in an irritating, albeit Christ-
like fashion, she thanks people for the abuse they heap on her
head, and the book comes to read more and more like a trial, a
test of her sanctity where sanctity is proved by the act of testing
itself. She is of course tried as a Lollard, and catechized several
times, in Bristol, Leicester, York, and Hull,[18] and each of these
tests forms the occasion for an enforcement of her identification
with Christ as the object of persecution. These trials are an
important part of the fabric of her book and her life, but more
than the actual events themselves, they are organizing tropes for
a hagiography, whereby each act and event is an opportunity for
an enactment of virtue or resistance to temptation:

Than thys creatur þowt it was ful mery to be reprevyd for
Goddys lofe; it was to hir gret solas & cowmfort whan sche
was chedyn & fletyn for þe lofe of Ihesu for repreuyng of
synne, for spekyng of vertu, for comownyng in Scriptur
whech sche lernyd in sermownys & be comownyng wyth
clerkys. Sche ymagyned in hir-self what deth sche mygth
deyn for Crystys sake. Hyr þowt sche wold a be slayn for
Goddys lofe, but dred for þe poynt of deth, & þerfor sche
ymagyned hyr-self þe most soft deth, as hyr thowt, for

dred of inpacyens, þat was to be bowndyn hyr hed & hir fet to a stokke & hir hed to be smet of wyth a scharp ex for Goddys lofe.[19]

In this passage, for example, her torments from her reprovers and scolders immediately lead to an imagining of her own martyrdom. On one level, of course, this is an identification with Christ, but it is also characteristically a taking of his place, in a redemptive substitution, a replacement of his suffering.[20]

Kempe's prolonged identification with Christ also organizes the very timing of the events of her book, most of which, as Atkinson has pointed out, take place on a Friday, the day in which Christ's passion is commemorated in ecclesiastial ceremonial.[21] The rhythms and tempo of her life are governed by the time of the passion in just the kind of mixing of past and present time recommended by Nicholas Love.[22]

Margery Kempe's very identity is osmotically absorbed in Christ's. As she tells us at the very beginning of her treatise, her book will deal 'in parcel of hys wonderful werkys' and 'in party the leuyng' of his creature Margery Kempe.[23] And it will treat the one through the other, for, as Christ says to her: 'I am in þe and þow in me. And þei þat heryn þe þei heryn þe voys of God.'[24] The identification with Christ then engenders a porosity of identity, an exchange between Christ and Margery, and it also enjoins a remarkable lability of social roles created by this very porosity. Kempe renegotiates her own cultural position by means of such identification and role-playing.

HOLY FAMILY ROMANCE

Many critics have remarked on the variety of roles which Christ and Margery play in relation to each other.[25] Too often this is seen in terms of a static model of substitution and replacement. Goodman, for example makes the following statement:

[A]t the root of Margery's conversion to a lonely and prickly way may have lain the reactions against her marriage role of a forceful and determined woman, whose emotional patterns and physical constitution inhibited her from fulfilling it satisfactorily. Her new way, carried to extremes of perfection, assuaged her guilt at failing the expectations of father, husband and kinsfolk.[26]

Margery is seen here to be simply rejecting the 'earthly' expectations of her society rather than also critiquing them. Such a rejection is then read as a *personal* inadequacy rather than an implicit judgement on the institutions of the medieval family household. In describing such psychic transactions as a one-to-one replacement – 'Above all, Christ became the father who instructed the soul, the husband who embraced it, and the son who doted on it'[27] – Goodman radically underestimates the complex fluidity of Christ's positionality. For in Margery Kempe's 'theatre of devotion', God as the Second Person forces an imagination of the range of social roles he could play. Kempe, as we have seen, *is* Christ, but she also exists in a series of fluid, interchangeable relationships which license for her an extraordinary mobility and flexibility of identity.

There is no question that there are instances in the book where an almost embarrassingly blatant substitution of her newly espoused spiritual family is indeed at play, a substitution that *does* work along the lines Goodman suggests. When Christ asks who Margery would like to accompany her to heaven, her answer is her 'gostly fadyr Maystyr R',[28] i.e. her confessor Robert Spryngolde. But the very blatancy of her substitution is actually noticed and accommodated by Christ, for after asking Kempe why she should prefer 'mor hym þan thyn owyn fadyr er þin husbond', Christ says: 'I grawnt þe þi desyr of hym, & ʒet schal þi fadyr ben sauyd, & þi husbond also, & alle þi chylderyn.'[29] The model of substitution is then here explicitly rejected: heaven will not be preferred to earth but rather included in it; there will be no transcendence or supersession of familial roles, but there will be a decisive transformation of them. That this transformation is a social one, one which will allow her to change her life here on earth, is emphasized by Christ's repeated reiteration of his equal love for wives and virgins, the traditional brides of Christ.

Kempe is well aware that the manner of life that she has espoused, the life of a bride of Christ, is a life that has been especially reserved for virgins: 'þan seyd þe creatur, "Lord Ihesu, þis maner of leuyng longyth to þy holy maydens".'[30] But Christ negates the ecclesiastically sanctioned differences between wives and virgins, thereby licensing her own dangerous and transgressive form of piety:

ʒa, dowtyr, trow þow rygth wel þat I lofe wyfes also, and specyal þo wyfys whech woldyn levyn chast, ʒyf þei mygtyn haue her wyl, & don her besynes to plesyn me as þow dost, for, þow þe state of maydenhode be mor parfyte & mor holy þan þe state of wedewhode, & þe state of wedewhode mor parfyte þan þe state of wedlake, ʒet dowtyr I lofe þe as wel as any mayden in þe world.[31]

In validating wives on an equal footing with virgins, Kempe's Christ inverts a sanctioned hierarchy which made celibacy a precondition for sanctity. In the process he functions not so much as a substitute husband but a liberator from husbandry – an infinitely more subversive postioning:

Dowtyr, ʒyf þu knew how many wifys þer arn in þis worlde þat wolde louyn me & seruyn me ryth wel & dewly, ʒyf þei myght be as frely fro her husbondys as þu art fro þyn, þu woldist seyn þat þu wer ryght meche beheldyn onto me.[32]

That the relationship between Kempe's holy family and her earthly one is more than a simple substitution is effectively demonstrated by the bargain that Kempe strikes with her husband for a celibate marriage. It is the arrangement which allows her to become a bride of Christ in the first place. Within the tenets of medieval marriage law, the conjugal debt, sexual intercourse, was mutually owed, by the wife to the husband, and the husband to the wife as a condition of marital relations. Kempe cannot be a bride of Christ whilst she is still the bride of her husband. In chapter 11 of the *Book*, Kempe prays to Christ for help in arranging a celibate marriage. Christ allows Margery to stop fasting on Fridays, a concession which her husband has demanded and with which she is willing to comply to win what in her eyes is the greater concession of a chaste marriage:

þan þis creatur thankyd owyr Lord Ihesu Cryst of hys grace & hys goodnes, sythen ros up & went to hir husbond, seyng un-to hym, 'Sere, yf it lyke þow, ʒe schal grawnt me my desyr, & ʒe schal haue ʒowr desyr. Grawntyth me þat ʒe schal not komyn in my bed, & I grawnt ʒow to qwyte ʒowr dettys er I go to Jerusalem. & makyth my body fre to God so þat ʒe neuyr make no chalengyng in me to askyn no dett of matrimony aftyr this day whyl ʒe leuyn, & I

schal etyn & drynkyn on the Friday at зowr bydding.' þan
seyd hir husbond a-зen to hir, 'As fre mot зowr body ben
to God as it hath ben to me.'[33]

John Kempe's trade of his conjugal debts for the repayment of
his financial debts is a pragmatic substitution that licenses as it
commodifies Kempe. It indicates the interaction of earthly and
heavenly social roles at the most concrete material level – the
exchange of hard cash. Kempe literally buys the right of her own
body back from her husband (possibly with a bequest from her
recently deceased father) to be able to make it free for God.

In some sense this might again underwrite Antony Goodman's
claim that Margery substitutes Jesus Christ for John Kempe.
Christ certainly behaves like an indulgent bourgeois husband at
times:

> & dowtyr, þe mor schame, despite, & reprefe þat þu suffer-
> yst for my lofe, þe bettyr I lofe þe, for I far liche a man
> þat louyth wel hys wyf, þe mor enuye þat men han to hir
> þe bettyr he wyl arayn hir in despite of hir enmys. & ryth
> so, dowtyr, xal I faryn wyth þe.[34]

His love is likened to the way a bourgeois husband might clothe
his wife to give her a status which would make her and him the
envy of his neighbours, here placed in the position of competitors.
But Christ's role is nowhere near as static as this simple competitive substitution might imply. For this is merely one in an
extravagant overlapping series of roles that Christ plays for
Margery Kempe.

Sometimes Christ is Kempe's mother. Thus, one of Margery's
confessors says to her: ' "Dowtyr, зe sowkyn euyn on Crystys
brest." '[35] This figure, a conventional figure, evoking a eucharistic
piety and the image of Christ as mother popularized in Cistercian
writings, nevertheless belies the gender stability of Christ's role
as substitute husband. Sometimes in their holy family romance,
Kempe herself is imaged as Christ's father, a thought that escapes
blasphemy only through the sheer implicitness of its analogy. In
chapter 14, Christ says to her: 'Dowtyr, þer was neuyr chyld so
buxom to þe fadyr as I wyl be to þe to help þe and kepe þe.'[36]
Although this sentence claims the paternal role in its message that
Christ will help Kempe and look after her, Christ is nevertheless
clearly positing himself as child to Kempe as father. Christ and

Kempe try on a variety of social and familial roles in relation to each other:

> þerfor I preue þat þow art a very dowtyr to me & a modyr also, a syster, a wyfe, and a spowse, wytnessyng þe Gospel wher owyr Lord seyth to hys dyscyples, 'He that doth the wyl of my Fadyr in Heuyn he is bothyn modyr, broþyr, & syster un-to me.' Whan þow stodyst to plese me, þan aryt þu a very dowtyr; whan þu wepyst & mornyst for my peyn & for my Passyon, þan art þow a very modyr to haue compassyon of hyr chyld; whan þow wepyst for oþer mennys synnes and for adversytes, þan art þow a very syster; and, whan þow sorwyst for þow art so long fro þe blisse of Heuyn, þan art þu a very spowse & a wyfe, for it longyth to þe wyfe to be wyth hir husbond & no very joy to han tyl sche come to hys presens.[37]

Here they play Kempe as daughter to Christ as father, Kempe as mother to Christ as child, Kempe as sister to Christ and the world, and finally Kempe as spouse to her husband, Christ. But, as I have remarked elsewhere, whereas it is the separation and social fixity of these roles in a one-to-one identification that is encouraged for example in Love's *Mirrour*, here it is the simultaneity and lability of social roles, their complexly overlapping quality that melts the rigid separation of roles. Thus, Christ addresses Kempe in the following way:

> þerfore most I nedys be homly wyth þe & lyn in þi bed wyth þe. Dowtyr, þow desyrest gretly to se me, & þe mayst boldly, whan þu art in þi bed, take me to þe as for þi weddyd husbond, as þy derworthy derlyng, & as for þy swete sone, for I wyl be louyd as a sone schuld be louyd wyth þe modyr & wil þat þu loue me, dowtyr, as a good wife owyth to loue hir husbonde. & therfor þu mayst boldly take me in þe armys of þi sowle & kyssen my mowth, myn hed, & my fete as swetly as þow wylt. &, as often-tymes as þu thynkyst on me er woldyst don any good dede to me, þu schalt haue ȝe same mede in Heuyn as þyf þu dedist it to myn owyn precyows body whech is in Heuyn, for I aske no mor of þe but þin hert for to louyn me þat louyth þe, for my lofe is euyr redy to þe.[38]

Liberated from her role as wife, but also perfected in it, her interplay with the figure of Christ allows her a critique of that role and the ability to transform it. Such transformations take effect not just in her fantasy, but, as we shall now see, in her actual relations with the people around her. Because those fantasies are the shared domain of her audience, they are made persuasive and compelling through the mediating symbol of the body and personhood of Christ.

TEARS AND CRIES

. . . for I am an hyd God in þe. . . . [39]

Kempe's devotions are at once intimate, individualistic, internalized, ('an hayr in þin hert)'[40] and private, yet also flamboyantly and histrionically public. If God is hidden in her, it is a mystery that must be openly proclaimed. For if God's hiding in Margery Kempe is to perform its function, the display of the workings of grace in one of His creatures, then such grace must be manifest and visible:

> & so schal I ben worschepyd in erth for þi loue, dowtyr, for I wyl haue þe grace þat I haue schewyd to þe in erth knowyn to þe worlde þat þe pepil may wonderyn in my goodnes & meruelyn of my gret goodnes þat I haue schewyd to þe þat hast ben synful.[41]

It is across this paradox of a private piety and its public display that Kempe's *bodily* identification with Christ and therefore her iconic status become so important and significant. Central to this status are her tears and her cries; legitimizing symptoms of her compassion with Christ and the stages of her becoming Christ, they are also and simultaneously the signs of a rampantly competitive and quantified display. Kempe's tears and cries are worth considering in some detail for they are part of the conversion of body from text and to text that was so centrally licensed by crucifixion piety. That is, if crucifixion piety was an attempt to abjure the heavy machinery of scholasticism and to record immediately the meaning of crucifixion in the body of the worshipper, then one of the consequences of that manœuvre was a creation of the body itself as text. In the late Middle Ages the claims to sanctity, or to a 'singular grace'[42] from God, were accompanied by intense scrutiny because, as we have seen, those

claims were eroding the clerical monopoly of the
mediation of God. Tears of compassion had long beer
a special sign of grace, for they were a sign of the str
soul's love for God, and for the effectivenesss of pray
Sarum missal contains a votive mass for tears:

> All-powerful and merciful God, who brought forth a spr
> of living water from the earth for thirsting people, draw
> forth tears of compunction from the hardness of our hearts,
> so that we might be able to grieve for our sins and merit
> receiving their remission from your pity.[44]

The imagery introduced by the mass is then part of the development of techniques for softening the boundaries of the body, to
increase its porosity. In Kempe's book they prove to be a very
controversial sign. Clarissa Atkinson points out that they are
given the ratification of no less an authority than St Jerome, who
explains to her when she visits his tomb on pilgrimage in Rome,
that tears are a gift whereby she will save many people. They
are thus a further way of mimesis and identification with Christ
that allow her a parallel redemptive function – the saviour of
souls.[45] That Kempe's tears do not appear to perform their function, that is, to speak for themselves, is evident from their controversial reception. Kempe's bodily text of tears needs to be ratified
by clerical text. It is only, for example, when her scribe reads
about the salvific tears of Mary of Oignes that he will validate
her tears. And the chapter where this validation is recorded,
chapter 62, provides a plethora of authority and hence authenti-
cation for the validity of Kempe's tears – from *The Prickynge of
Love*, from Rolle's *Incendium amoris*, from the *vita* of Mary of
Oignes and from the *vita* of Elizabeth of Hungary.[46]

But it is perhaps not so surprising that clerical approval was
so miserly and grudging in that the claims made for her tears
make her a competitor to the very functional centrality of the
clergy in the saving of souls. For her tears are a veritable treasury
of merit. It is on the basis of her tears that Kempe makes Christ
the executor to her will. Half of her tears and half the good
works that Christ has effected in Margery are to be Spryngolde's
reward from her treasury.[47] Her cries too, first received on
Calvary, are also subject to the same quantification:

Fyrst whan sche had hir cryingys at Ierusalem, sche had

hem often-tymes, & in Rome also. &, whan sche had come hom in-to Inglonde, fyrst at hir coming hom it comyn but seldom as it wer onys in a moneth, sythen onys in þe weke, aftyrward cotidianly, & onys sche had xiiij on a day, & another day sche had vij, & so as God wolde visiten hir, sumtyme in þe cherch, sumtyme in þe strete, sumtym in þe chawmbre, sumtyme in þe felde whan God wold sendyn hem, for sche knew neuyr tyme ne owyr whan þei xulde come.[48]

And this is no idiosyncrasy on her part but a widespread late medieval practice which allowed the living literally to account for the dead. Thus, she is often given money to pray for other people. One of her donors is the Bishop of Lincoln who gives her money to buy her white clothes, and 'to prey for hym'.[49] In such a transaction she is receiving endorsement from one of the most powerful ecclesiasts in the country, whilst at the same time he is acknowledging her salvific potentialities.

One of Margery Kempe's ardent concerns as she describes her tears and cries is to communicate her lack of control over them, for many of those around her regarded them as pieces of fakery and attention-grabbing. A repeated accusation was that she produced them herself whenever she wanted to; thus, by implication, she cried for self-glorification. That is why she is concerned to describe the reception of her tears and cries when she is alone without a potential audience. Thus the incident described in chapter 61, where a visiting white friar refuses to have her in the same church in which he is preaching, ends in her being alone in one place when he preaches to other people in another place:

> Sche had so mech sorwe þat sche wist not what sche myth do, for sche was putte fro the sermown whech was to hir þe hyest comfort in erth whan sche myth heryn it, & ryth so þe contrary was to hir þe grettest peyne in erthe whan sche myth not heryn it. Whan sche was alone be hir-self in on cherch & he prechyng þe peple in an-oþir, sche had as lowde & as meuelyows cryis as whan sche was a-mongys þe pepil.[50]

Her acute awareness of audience is not only a response to the hostility and accusations of her environment, but also a registering of the acute contradictions between her form of piety, simultaneously internalized, personalized and made individually private to her (a singular grace) and extravagantly externalized. Thus, in place of the 'harmony of her inner and outer life' which Denise Despres has found in the book, I find rather a disjunction of inner and outer.[51] That inner and outer are not in such utter accord is also evidenced in the preoccupation with hypocrisy which reappears throughout the book – hypocrisy registering precisely a perceived difference between what is proclaimed, and what is actually done.[52] She is accused of being an actress, but that accusation may rather be seen to be structural to a form of piety whose grace relies on its hiddenness, yet whose hiddenness can only be proved through its display.

THINKING WITH YOUR MIND AND PRAYING WITH YOUR MOUTH

Margery Kempe's tears and cries, then, are part of her hyperbolically labile identification with Christ; they perform a central legitimizing role for her 'singular grace' and special status. Extravagantly externalized, they are there to be noticed, to be read, perused and marked as signs and wonders. But there is another side to Kempe's piety, namely, its drive to a greater inwardness, internalization, its move towards less collective or prescribed forms. The identification with Christ's body may be seen as a subversive and dynamic private appropriation of an imagery that at least in eucharistic piety, was subject to intense and jealous clerical control, made all the more intense as a result of the alarming effectiveness of the erosion of that control. But the *Book* also displays an insistent drive towards interiority which is as urgent and obvious as the manifest outwardness of the book's self–display, and is also, as I argued in chapter 3, a vital component of the dynamic of the imaging of Christ's body. As I have argued previously, the uses of crucifixion piety in Kempe cannot be understood without perceiving both sides of this process, a process in which Christ's body functions as the indispensable matrix. For Christ's body is meant to be the very means and mechanism of the journey from outer to inner. The vestiges of such a journey are traceable through Kempe's text. The beginning of her 'journey to God' is described in the proem, for example, as the embarking on a path of fasting and penitential practices.[53] But later on Christ informs her that 'Fastyng, dowtyr, is good for ʒong be-gynnars'.[54] And he says this not, I think, within the context of an agreed and harmonious consensus, but as a rivalrous, defensive and competitive bid for one way of life amongst others:

> And for to byddyn many bedys it is good to hem þat can no bettyr do, & ʒet it is not parfyte. But it is a good wey to-perfecyon-ward. For I telle þe, dowtyr, þei þat arn gret fastarys & gret doers of penawnce þei wold þat it schuld ben holdyn þe best lyfe; also þei þat ʒeuyn hem to sey many deuocyons þei wold han þat þe best lyfe; and þei þat ʒeuyn mech almes þei wold han þat þe best lyfe.[55]

But the way of life validated by Kempe's Christ is 'thynking, wepyng & hy contemplacyon': 'And þu xalt haue mor meryte in Heuyn for o ʒer of thynkyng in þi mende þan for an hundryd ʒer of preyng wyth þi mowth.'[56] The move described here is, then, a move from the prescribed devotions of prayer to the privileged meditations with God which constitute Kempe's visions, and it entails a greater degree of self-sufficiency and self-authorization.[57] In the earlier part of the book, Christ judiciously allocates a certain amount of time for prayer – until six o'clock, but then he requests that she 'ly stylle & speke to me be thowt, & I schal ʒefe to þe hey medytacyon and very contemplacyon'.[58] But later on in the *Book* he is more outspoken in his validation of inner thought and contemplation over other forms of worship:

> For, dowtyr, þis lyfe plesyth me mor þan weryng of þe haburion or of þe hayr or fastyng of bred & water, for, ʒyf þu seydest euery day a thowsand Pater Noster, þu xuldist not plesyn me so wel as þu dost whan þu art in silens & sufferyst me to speke in þy sowle.[59]

This transfer of pietistic modes from prayer to meditation is linked to the self-authorization that connects this way of life with the act of writing a life, her *vita*. In chapter 88, the substitution of 'meditation' for 'recitation' and its connection with the bold self-authorization of writing is made explicit:

> Whan þis booke was first in wrytyng, þe sayd creatur was mor at hom in hir chambre wyth hir writer & seyd fewer bedys for sped of wrytyng þan sche had don ʒerys be-forn. &, whan sche cam to chirche & xulde heryn Messe,

purposyng to seyn hir Mateyns & swech oþer deuocyons as
sche had vsed a-for-tyme, hir hert was drawyn a-wey fro
þe seying & set mech on meditacyon. Sche beyng aferd of
displesawns of owr Lord, he seyd to hir sowle, 'Drede þe
not, dowtyr, for as many bedys as þu woldist seyin I accepte
as þow þu seydist them, & þi stody þat þuh stodiist for to
do writyn þe grace þat I haue schewyd to þe plesith me
rygth meche & he that writith boþe. For, þow ȝe wer in
þe chirche & wept bothyn to-gedyr as sore as euyr þu
dedist, ȝet xulde ȝe not plesyn me mor þan ȝe don wyth
ȝowr writyng, for dowtyr, be þis boke many a man xal be
turnyd to me & beleuyn þerin.'[60]

Here there is a deliberate shift in the forms of religiosity to be
validated. Christ makes it clear that her recitation (matins and
beads) and her weeping are not as important to him as her writing
of the *Book*. Christ's words here have something in common
with the kind of sentiments expressed by Elizabeth Stamford, a
Chiltern Lollard, though they are expressed less polemically and
from a very different position:

. . . that Christ feedeth and fast nourisheth his church with
his own precious body, that is, the bread of life coming
down from heaven: this is the worthy word that is worthily
received, and joined unto men to be in one body with him.
Sooth it is that they both be one: they may not be parted:
this is the wisely deeming of the holy sacrament, Christ's
own body: this is not received by chewing of teeth but by
hearing with ears and understanding with your soul, and
wisely working thereafter.[61]

Sacramentality is being transferred in this quotation from the
eucharist itself to the word. Similarly the sentiments voiced by
Christ in Kempe's text authorize the word, moreover her word,
as much as his word, as the very mechanism of the distribution
of salvation, and the mechanism of incorporation.

Kempe's text, then, describes first a form of mimesis of Christ
which makes of her body a text, and a form of internalized
devotion that makes her written text itself the resource of sacramentality. Such an exchange can only operate through the symbol
of Christ's body, which is both body and word. Both forms of

religiosity, it may be noted, involve a paradoxical buttressing and undermining of the position of the clergy.

CLERICAL RELATIONS

In chapter 45 of *The Book of Margery Kempe* we are given a description of a Corpus Christi procession:

> On Corpus Cristi Day aftyr, as þe prestys born þe Sacrament a-bowte þe town wyth solempne processyon, wyth meche lyth & gret solempnyte, as was worthy to be do, þe forseyd creatur folwyd ful of terys & deuocyon, wyth holy thowtys & meditacyon, sor wepyng & boystows sobbyng. & þan cam a good woman be þis creatur & seyd, 'Damsel, God ȝef us grace to folwyn þe steppys of owr Lord Ihesu Crist.' þan þat worde wrowt so sor in hir herte & in hir mende þat sche myth not beryn it þat sche was fawyn to takyn an hows. & þer sche cryed, 'I dey, I dey,' & roryd also wondirfully þat þe pepil wonderyd up-on hir, heuyng gret meueyl what hir eyled.[62]

The host, the consecrated body of Christ, symbol and image of community is, as I have already remarked in my second chapter, the very centrepiece of the Corpus Christi procession, whereby it achieved a new and important status in the religious practices of late medieval Christianity. Charles Zika has remarked on the way the late medieval clergy desired to construct the host as the central relic, unique in relation to all the other relics which often had miracles attributed to them *without clerical participation*.[63] Yet Margery Kempe's form of devotion in the Corpus Christi procession is disruptive and separate, essentially non-participatory. Her roaring disrupts and astonishes the people around her; it is not part of the decorum of the procession. Margery Kempe's relation to the clerically administered body of Christ is to demand special treatment. During the procession she creates herself as the 'gret meruayle'.[64] And she ensures an increased access to the body of Christ by receiving special permission to be 'houseled' every Sunday, a dispensation that has to be ratified by the Archbishop of Canterbury.[65] She thus receives the host dramatically more frequently than would have been usual.[66] So in some senses it might be said that her keen aspirations towards eucharistic piety reinforce the clergy, who are necessary to transubstantiate the

94

material bread. And yet, her eucharistic piety is more a singling out, a mark of a special religiosity, rather than the collective ritual of mass. For it comes by special request from Christ, bypassing the clergy, who become the mere medium by which God is to work his special grace in her:

> And in-stede of þat flesch þow schalt etyn my flesch & my blod, þat is the very body of Crist in þe Sacrament of þe Awter. Thys is my wyl, dowtyr, þat þow receyue my body euery Sonday, and I schal flowe so myche grace in þe þat alle þe world xal meruelyn þerof.[67]

Her illiteracy means that she has no access herself to the texts that mediated the life of Christ, and she is generally dependent on the clergy for any access to scriptural texts – for the writing and the reading of them. She has great difficulty in persuading her scribe to take down her book. The scribe who eventually completes this task demands constant proof of her special validating relationship to God.[68] Her only access to the word is through having sermons and texts read to her. That this is a situation that she finds inadequate is made patently obvious by the following words:

> On a tyme, as þe forseyd creatur was in hir contemplacyon, sche hungryd ryth sor aftyr Goddys word & seyd, 'Alas, Lord, as many clerkys as þu hast in þis world, þat þu ne woldyst sendyn me on of hem þat myth fulfillyn my sowle wyth þi word & wyth redyng of Holy Scriptur, for alle þe clerkys þat prechyn may not fulfyllyn, for me thynkyth þat my sowle euyr a-lych hungry.[69]

But as usual this comment is double-edged, for characteristically it endorses clerical words in putatively lavish terms while also equivocally suggesting that they could never be sufficient.

Kempe of course can supersede the desires of the clergy by her relationship with Christ, and this appears to be her characteristic mode of operation. For Christ says to her: 'Drede þe nowt, dowtyr, for þow schalt haue þe vyctory of al þin enmys. I schal ȝeue the grace j-now to answer euery clerke in þe loue of God.'[70] And this of course is possible because God speaks through Margery Kempe so that their two voices are one and the same: 'I am in þe and þow in me. And þei þat heryn þe þei heryn þe voys of God.'[71] It is this extraordinary power that allows her to

95

strike such audacious bargains with powerful ecclesiasts like Philip Repyngdon with whom she argues about his refusal of her request to wear the white clothes that would allow her to be a bride of Christ: 'And, ȝf ȝe clothyn me in erth, owyr Lord Ihesu Cryst xal clothyn þow in Heuyn, as I vnderstond be reuelacyon.'[72] Thus she makes many overt criticisms of clerical life on the basis of the special insights granted by God.[73] And each time this is done on the basis of the insuperable superiority of the will of God:

> Now, dowtyr, I wyl þat þu ete flesch a-ȝen as þu wer won to don, & þat þu be buxom & bonowr to my wil & to my byddyng & leue þyn owyn wyl and bydde þy gostly fadyrs þat þei latyn þe don aftyr my wyl.[74]

So although Kempe appears to be dependent on the clergy for access to scripture, Christ is posited as the better teacher:

> þer is no clerk in al þis world þat can, dowtyr, leryn þe bettyr þan I can do. . . . þer is no clerk can spekyn a-ȝens þe lyfe wheche I teche þe, &, ȝyf he do, he is not Goddys clerk; he is þe Deuelys clerk.[75]

Sometimes there is even an overt anti-clericalism but it is always put in the mouth of Christ: 'Dowtyr, ȝyf þu sey þe wikkydnes þat is wrowt in þe werld as I do, þu schuldist haue gret wondyr þat I take not vtter veniawns on hem. But, dowtyr, I spar for thy lofe.'[76] In this manœuvre, it is Kempe herself who once again takes on the salvific role of Christ, in an identification that once again seeks to erode the position of the clergy.

Her unlicensed preaching, the sheer publicity of her behaviour, the very nature of her claims rendered her subject to intense scrutiny. Her visionary claims had to be proved, authenticated by clerical opinion, and her book describes numerous occasions where she has her spirits discerned:

> þan went þei forth to Brydlyngton-ward and also to many oþer contres & spokyn wyth Goddys seruawntys, boþen ankrys & reclusys & many oþer of owyr Lordys louerys, wyth many worthy clerkys, doctorys of dyuynyte, & bachelers also in many dyuers places. & þis creatur to dyuers of hem schewyd hir felyngys & hyr contemplacyons, as sche was comawndyd for to don, to wetyn yf any dysseyt were in hir felyngys.[77]

Margery Kempe averts the potential threat in her position by
drastically pluralizing the authorities she seeks. Whereas her mysticism might itself be said to be a decisive index of the fracturing
of authority, so too is her own expansion outside the confines of
her parish. She has numerous confessors, she travels on extensive
pilgrimages, one mode of worship which was felt by contemporaries to undermine strict local and parochial control.[78] It is little
wonder that Kempe prefers the pilgrimages she goes on to the
more tightly clerically administered Corpus Christi processions
within her immediate vicinity. Charles Zika has recently pointed
out the dangers of pilgrimage to local parishional jurisdiction:

> Procession emphasized the community's celebration of its
> objects throughout prescribed political space; pilgrimage
> signified a potentially uncontrollable journey beyond the
> borders of one's territory (or through one's territory) to
> a foreign location sanctified by the relics and wonders of
> others.[79]

In her book, her pilgrimages become the object of clerical jurisdiction in which God overrules the clergy everytime, leaving her
free to wander:

> & I am wel plesyd wyth þe, dowtyr, for þu stondist vnder
> obedyens of Holy Cherch & þat þu wylt obey þi confessowr
> & folwen hys cownsel, whech thorw auctorite of Holy
> Cherch hath asoyld þe of þi synnes & dispensyd wyth þe
> þat þu schuldist not go to Rome ne to Seynt Iamys les
> than þu wyl þin owyn selfe. Not-wythstondyng al this, I
> comawnde þe in þe name of Ihesu, dowtyr, þat þu go vysite
> þes holy placys & do as I bid þe, for I am aboue al Holy
> Cherch & I xal gon wyth þe & kepyn þe ryght wel.[80]

Amongst the many named authorities that Kempe seeks and cites
as her supporters in her book, there are five names that are repeated
as locally influential figures. They are Master Alan, that is, Alan of
Lynn, one of the white friars of Lynn; Wenslawe, the priest who
becomes her main confessor during her stay in Rome at St John
Lateran; William Southfield, the Carmelite from Norwich; Robert
Spryngolde, the parish priest of St Margaret's in Bishop's Lynn;
and Richard Caister, the Vicar of St Stephens, Norwich.[81] It is the
contention of Hope Emily Allen and a later commentator, Antony
Goodman, that these men, chiefly, as he notes, Benedictines,

Carmelites and Dominicans, functioned as a group of clerical radicals who fuelled a kind of counter-reformation of piety in their local environment. That is, they tried to

> back . . . what were to turn out to be losing modes of piety, too individual and unsocial to appeal widely within, and to regenerate spiritually, a tense fissured urban society looking for modes of religious expression which affirmed rather than threatened its secular values, and strengthened its fragile communal cohesiveness.[82]

So far in this chapter I have tended to concentrate on Kempe's anticlericalism, implicit and explicit. However, it is evident that Kempe's relations with the clergy can hardly be subsumed under such a rubric. What did these religious men find in their support of her? What could their motives have been? Goodman and Allen provide one answer to this question. But to explore the issue further we will have to begin to see Kempe as townswoman as well as the visionary she so ardently claimed to be, and to return to some of the contexts she found it impossible to transcend.

My claim is the following: relations between the rich burgess class of Bishop's Lynn and the ecclesiastical community were under endemic strain. Could the appropriation of the daughter of one of the most prominent burgesses of Lynn, her flamboyant 'subjugation' to clerical authority, be one way of sending a powerful message to that community of burgesses? Kempe after all gives us a long description of her failed entrepreneurial plans, with a suggestion of their inherent pride and sinfulness. Now obviously, we know how deeply, by the late Middle Ages, the monastic and ecclesiastical communities were immersed in the mercantile, trading, and sometimes industrial community, but their economic and political centrality was being eroded by the burgeoning energies of precisely the powerful class to which Kempe's father and, to a lesser extent, her husband belonged.

Kempe's father, John Brunham, was an unquestionably prominent member of the Bishop's Lynn community. He was jurat, chamberlain, member of parliament, coroner, justice of the peace, alderman of the Trinity guild which was central to the organization of political life in medieval Lynn, and mayor in 1370, 1377, 1378, 1385 and 1391.[83] Most historians have remarked upon the persistent and serious tensions, sometimes erupting into outright violence, between the community of elite burgesses and the

Bishop of Norwich. In this, Lynn is typical of conflicts being fought out in a great many other late medieval towns. Following the pattern of so many of these other towns, it is on the basis of royal charter (in this case in 1205) that immunity from monies and fealties owed to the seigneurial bishop was won.[84] But rivalries and tensions were hardly laid aside by this charter, which was subject to subsequent reinterpretation and dispute.[85] Brunham was engaged in many vicious disputes with the Bishop of Norwich. Some of these disputes involved outright violence, as when Despenser was attacked and assaulted by artisans supposedly defending the ancient honours of the city. Brunham himself had to preside over the trial. In the year following this altercation, the Hall book records the compensation paid to members of the community injured in the fracas, and it records too the conciliation to the bishop: 13 shillings and 5d. was paid for a huge wax candle, weighing about 21 pounds, which was offered in the church of the Holy Trinity, Norwich.[86] It is A. Green, historian of fifteenth-century town life, who sums up the core of these endemic disputes:

> The question which lay behind all minor struggles was that of the administration of justice in the town – the question whether it was the mayor or an ecclesiastical officer who could preside in the courts, and whether their profits, fines and forfeitures should go to enrich the treasury of the bishop or of the municipality.[87]

That these conflicts circulated with insistent symbolic particularity around the figure of the mayor and the figure of the bishop is demonstrated by the dispute about the tipstaff in 1376. Despenser, visiting Lynn in 1376, insists that he has the honour generally accorded the mayor of the town be paid to him, that is, to have his chief officer carry before him the tipstaff, signal of his authority. The incident is recorded in Foxe, and is an instance of the considerable importance attached to ritual precedent.[88] What the mayor replies, as recorded by Foxe in this instance, is that 'they durst not take in hand any such new alterations of ancient customs and liberties . . . least the populace . . . should fall upon them and drive them out of town.'[89] For one of the key points in the dispute between the mayor and the bishop is over the franchise of the city. That is, in order to relieve the burden of tallages, the mayor tries to compel strangers in Lynn to take up the franchise.

The bishop insists on the withdrawal of the mayoral decree. His reasons for doing so are clearly financial. Because he has such a lucrative interest in the Tolbooth, he was more than anxious to increase the trade of the port.[90] If wealthy strangers could be enticed into the town by the promise of exemption from the borough rate, his own interests would benefit. At issue, then, was the question as to who was to define and control the very contours of the city, who were its legal inhabitants, what they might owe to whom, and whether they were to be incorporated into the fabric and structure of the town.

Margery Kempe was acutely self-conscious about her status as the prominent daughter of a Lynn dignitary.[91] We know this, however, because the context in which she informs us of this is the context of its renunciation. Retrospectively read as pride, arrogance, worldly ambition and greed, she rewrites the significance of her worthy kindred, and rewrites her failed entrepreneurialism as the judgement of God on an entire way of life. David Aers has recently persuasively reminded us 'how important were the values she exhibited in these episodes, and how marginal the moralizing clerical grid she later applied'.[92] Her drive to accumulation, he informs us, was part of an intricate 'web of economic and social relationships organized around market transactions and values'.[93] In an earlier essay Sheila Delaney explored the extent of the continuity of this realm of fiscal and material values with the organization of the next.[94] Kempe's attempt to accept and impose a clerical interpretative grid on her own retrospectively viewed covetousness belies the evident continuity of fiscal values from the clerical to the lay worlds. Hillen's history of the borough of Lynn, Dorothy Owen's detailed local historical study of King's Lynn and Norman Tanner's study of the closely connected bishopric of Norwich, which had such intimate links with Bishop's Lynn, have given us enough material to see how utterly immersed the ecclesiastical community was in the world of market relations. Just outside the parish church of St Margaret's, Margery Kempe's parish church and the only parish church in Bishop's Lynn, for example, was a lucrative market which was controlled by the bishop himself.[95]

It would seem difficult to believe that Kempe was in any way an anonymous figure. Around the countryside she is recognized and famed as John Brunham's daughter of Lynn.[96] There is no question that this frequently acts in her interests and for her protection. Her very fame might have made her a much more visible symbol of the clerical appropriation and shaping of her religiosity. It certainly seems that she receives more hostility from her community of peers than she does from prominent ecclesiasts, some of whom offer her protection.[97] In 1415, she receives communion dressed all in white in Norwich Cathedral. For her, the occasion seems to be marked by an increase in the animosity towards her: 'And on þe Trinite Sunday next folwyng sche was howselyd al in white, & sithen hath sche sufferyd meche despyte & meche schame in many dyuers cuntreys, cyteys, & townys, thankyd be God of alle.'[98] Goodman points out that the dislike evinced for her amongst urban elites is perhaps at its strongest in her home town of Lynn. He states that the basis of their distrust is her rejection of bourgeois, mercantile and familial values.[99] What upsets them most, for example, is the fact that she goes on pilgrimages when she has no money to support herself, that she gives away other people's money, and that she wanders about on her own all across the country and in other people's countries as well.[100] The threat she posed was made all the worse in that she did not choose to adopt the life of a religious. When a monk in Canterbury wishes that she were enclosed so that she shouldn't speak with anyone, he is expressing the desire for her immolation and separation from her community, rather than suggesting that this would be a more suitable life for a religious woman. However even though we know of the existence of local communities of women which seemed similar to the béguinages abroad, Kempe had no intention of ever joining one.[101] She strove rather to live out the logic of the 'mixed life' and clearly there were enough prominent ecclesiasts who supported her in that decision as a way of extending (but also inevitably endangering) their clerical pedagogy. Inevitably she was perceived by some as an 'anti-social virus in the body-politic' for she was a flamboyant embodiment and living exposure of the difficulties and contradictions of the mixed life.[102]

Her book is then, both an attack on the clerical domination of religiosity and also, as Goodman has said, a 'clerical cry against bourgeois values'.[103] Kempe's espousing of an imitation of Christ can thus be seen as espousing a life of humility, of the willing and voluntary embrace of suffering, martyrdom, self-sacrifice. But anyone who knows the book of Margery Kempe also knows that, though that may have been part of the clerical ambition that informs the transcription and writing of the book, the book is as much a bourgeois cry against clerical values as it is a clerical cry against bourgeois ones. Or more subtly still, it can be considered a complex examination of the world of their interconnection across the body of a bourgeois religious woman, and the struggle for cultural hegemony by means of it.

GUILD, PARISH, LAITY

It is evidently to Kempe as a *lay* woman that her community, lay and clerical alike, responded. Despite the intensity of her religious aspirations, this was also part of the way she viewed herself and wanted to go on viewing herself. Let us look now at some of the other, lay, influences on Kempe's religiosity. In 1438, at the very time, as Gail Gibson remarks, that Kempe's priest begins to write Liber II of the *Book of Margery Kempe*, Kempe is admitted to the guild of the Trinity at Lynn.[104] Her membership marks an association with one of the most powerful and influential bodies in late medieval Lynn, an association moreover that indicates the complex extent to which religious and political affiliations were inseparable. Trinity guild was the 'Great Guild'. It was a religious fraternity, that is, a voluntary pious association whose nominal functions were the repair of parish churches, the organization of processions for saints' days and funerals, the holding of feasts on holy days, and perhaps above and beyond all this, the provision of prayers for dead fellow members to help them through purgatory.[105] The commercial and municipal activities of the Trinity guild, its vast wealth and influence, made it of central importance in the town.[106] The guild employed thirteen chaplains – six in St Margaret's, Margery's parish church, four in St Nicholas' and three in St James'.[107] And this stark economic fact indicates some of the tensions between clerical and lay interests that the structures of the guilds highlighted. The guilds represented increasing lay responsibility in parochial affairs. In the guilds chaplains were the paid employees of the guild.[108] Such lay control was sometimes resented by the clergy. The religious guilds proliferating mainly in the late fourteenth century were often associated with Corpus Christi.[109] Their formation is often associated with the period after the Black Death and the need to take some kind of communal control over the appalling devastation and wastage of life in the community. Guilds then are often associated with the saying of masses for the dead of their guild, and the establishment of chantries. Westlake describes the foundation of one such guild which links the death toll and communal loss to the depletion in the honouring of the sacrament:

> In the great pestilence which was at Lynn in 1349, in which the greater part of the people in the same town died, three men (seeing that) the venerated Sacrament of the Body of Christ was being carried through the town with only a single candle of poor wax burning in front of it, whereas two great candles of great wax are barely sufficient, deemed this so improper that they ordained certain lights for it when carried by night or day in the visitation of the sick.[110]

The host on its way to visit the sick and dying becomes a synecdoche for the entire devastated society that it seeks to salve and embrace. The expansion of the lay religious guilds and fraternities at this time is linked to the urgencies of redemption in a world where death was always imminent, and to the consequent imperative and desire for greater responsibility and power in the solicitation of the means of salvation.

Recent historians of late medieval guilds, noting their proliferation in the fourteenth and fifteenth century, have asked what the social and religious needs might have been which prompted them.[111] They have asked whether they were established as a religious unit that competed as a source and support of lay piety with the central unit of ecclesiastical control, the parish. For in some respects, as Gervase Rosser has pointed out, the 'critical element of choice in participation set the guild, like the dissenting church of a later period, apart from the undiscriminating, all-inclusive parish'.[112]

The guilds were great supporters of the cult and feast of Corpus Christi, and indeed of many of the devotional practices associated with the five wounds. Rosser mentions a guild at Great Yarmouth which met on a Friday after vespers to say together repeatedly five paternosters and five Ave Marias, 'in honour of the wounds of our Lord'.[113] Toulmin Smith's listings of the guilds reveal the number of them devoted to the name of Jesus, to Corpus Christi itself, or to the cult of the five wounds.[114] So the guilds often practised collectively what we know from Books of Hours etc. to have been practised privately. They also helped to mould in tangible material ways the very shape of late medieval religion –

that is, their funds influenced and reorganized the shape of the parish churches which they helped to sustain.

In the church of St Margaret, for example, Margery Kempe's local parish church, the organization of space reveals the literal, material control of a variety of influences on late medieval religiosity. The chancel of St Margaret's was maintained by the priory, except for its north side, where the Trinity guild had its chapel, the chapel in which it retained six guild priests. If, as Pamela Graves has recently shown in a fine article, the medieval parish was the unit through which the authority of the church operated and gained sanction locally, then that authority manifests itself not simply in the explicit precepts of dogma and dictum, but in the material organization of space, in material culture, in what Graves, following Bourdieu, calls the *habitus* of the medieval parish.[115] Bourdieu's concept of the *habitus* considerably extends and nuances the cultural meaning of symbolism, and Graves has applied this notion to the material space of the late medieval parish church. *Habitus* is what defines the world of social relations 'through the intermediary of the divisions and hierarchies it sets up between things, personas and practice, whereby it enforces taxonomic divisions which underlie the arbitrary provisions of the culture'.[116] Relations of power and authority are thus created and reproduced, modified, nuanced or altered through these discourses. The *habitus*, then, is a concept which allows us to extend our analysis of symbolism so that it can fully incorporate human practice and agency, and the play of and struggle for power. It understands symbols to be formed through their use: 'The meaning objectified in things or places is fully revealed only in the practices structured according to the same schemes which are organized in relation to them (and vice versa).'[117]

Graves points out that one central organizing means for the production of meaning in late medieval culture, a meaning with which we have been centrally concerned, is the making of Christ's body in the mass. But this ceremony, this ritual, although figured in liturgical books and doctrine, was subject to the minute contingencies of local practice. Thus, for example, during the procession that was a component of the mass, the prescribed path of proceeding was for the ministers and the choir to walk in ascending order of dignity succeeding the cross, the holy water, incense and candles, and to leave by the western gate of the chancel, go down by the south side, up the central part of the nave, down by the north aisle, and return up the central part of the nave again.[118] The liturgy, according to Graves, provides a formula for combining space, time and action. The organization of the liturgy was obviously monitored and monopolized by the clergy because of their control over literacy, and the liturgy organized the control of ecclesiastical space.[119] But Graves uses examples from late medieval East Anglia to show how secular control exercised through the patronage of guilds and private bequests helped change the material shape and meaning of the parish church and therefore the *habitus* of late medieval religion.

> In Norfolk great churches were financed by those benefiting from the cloth trade, and Norwich itself saw a plethora of mercantile rebuilding. In this we can see the challenge of an emergent political power through the practice of established discourse.[120]

Graves suggests that the additions and restructurings of churches by guild, corporation or private sponsorship may have 'dramatically altered the processional route to which people had previously grown accustomed. It would serve to create, or rearrange a hierarchy of altars within the visting order.' Although in the Corpus Christi processions, the clergy might have wanted a spectacle of their own centrality to the body of Christ, their transubstantiation of it, and closeness to it, the procession had to be forced to accommodate fluctuating secular interests. When merchants and profit-makers of the late Middle Ages built so many churches on such a lavish scale they were 'literally creating space'.[122] Graves cites a striking example from Norwich involving the material rearrangement of clerical spectacle. The church of St Peter Mancroft had been rebuilt, extending it so greatly in length that a tunnel had to be built under its east end to allow processions to pass beneath it. The eastern passage, she points out, gave access onto the central marketplace which it dominated. Thus the material rearrangement of space necessitated by mercantile sponsorship and rebuilding of churches actually shaped the social space of the inhabitants of medieval Norwich as it reshaped the hegemonic ambitions of the clergy.

The importance of these concerns may make the dispute recorded in *The Book of Margery Kempe* in chapter 25, concerning the ambitions of St Nicholas' church to become a parish church on a par with St Margaret's, seem less petty than it actually is.

105

CHRIST'S BODY

The issue here is whether there should be a font in the church of St Nicholas – hardly a matter of earth-shattering concern. But this was, as usual, more than a matter of bricks and mortar. For if this church were to be granted the font, then it would also be granted the right to have burials and churchings and so the right to erode substantially the profits of St Margaret's church through parochial offerings and other material benefits.[123] The Brunhams here align themselves with the interests of the priory against the rival claims of St Nicholas', for the guild of Trinity had its own chapel in St Margaret's which would suffer from the derogation of St Margaret's. Margery describes her version of the dispute in chapter 25, and it is interesting to notice that she explicitly mentions the fact that this is a material argument:

> þe paryschenys whech pursuyd weryn rygth strong and haddyn gret help of lordshyp, & also, þe most of alle, þei wer ryche men, worshepful marchawntys, & haddyn gold a-now, whech may spede in euery nede & þat is rewth þat mede xuld spede er than trewth.[124]

Ironically enough the claim to be above material matters in this instance merely strengthens the material claims of her party. In the end the dispute is resolved to the satisfaction of Margery and her supporters, and through the grace of God working through – Margery Kempe.

Graves points out that the addition of chapels as accretions to ecclesiastical buildings, and the division of interior space by enclosure to form chapels fundamentally reorganized liturgical and perceptual space. Such accretions could change the access, the point of view on the central clerical focus of the high altar, sometimes obscuring or obstructing the vital view of the elevated host, for example.[125]

A member of the centrally prominent Trinity guild, which had its own chapel in St Margaret's, Margery is houselled in the prior's own chapel in St Margaret's. Perhaps Margery Kempe is an exemplification of Gervase Rosser's claim that the piety of the guild and the piety fostered by the parish were not so inimical to each other, not so mutually exclusive as the earliest commentators on the guilds would like to imply.[126] However, Kempe's book – its polemical structure, its argumentative, defensive appeal – does seem to bear witness to the existence of clerical and bourgeois conflict that is not only scored throughout the book,

106

but also across the very person of Margery Kempe. She was, it seemed, cathectic for both clerical and bourgeois interests for she both combined and separated them, made a drama out of their conflict and coalescence.

And her cathexis of the clerical and bourgeois conflicts ultimately lay in her ability to embody that very conflict in her own person, in her own 'singular grace'. In the compulsive repetition of her singular grace, what is affirmed and reinforced is both her competitive superiority to all her peers (the informing trait of an acquisitive, accumulative bourgeoisie), and her saintly privilege of election as God's chosen (clerical language): 'þu art to me a synguler lofe, dowtyr, & therfor I behote þe þu schalt haue a synguler grace in Hevyn.'[127] And He repeats this gesture with insistence: 'I haue telde þe be-for-tyme þat þu art a synguler louer, & þerfor þu xalt haue a synguler loue in Heuyn, a synguler reward, & a synguler worshep.'[128] Margery Kempe's competitive individualism is striking. It is not enough that she is saintly. The very proofs of her sanctity must also competitively be seen as marks which display her superiority to St Birgitta or the Mary Magdalene.[129] But these are not signs of a particular pathology as has so often been hinted by so many writers, but evidence of the very complexity of the piety evolving.[130] Simultaneously private and public, simultaneously lay and devoted to the appropriation of forms of clerical practice, simultaneously utterly conformist and outrageously and parodically subversive, Kempe's ultimate ruse is to substitute her own body as icon for Christ's. For her imitation becomes a substitution in the inexorable logic of her piety. Producing signs and wonders, tears and cries – what her editor Hope Emily Allen tellingly calls her own 'supplementary liturgy'[131] – signs which establish the authenticity of her *imitatio Christi*, subject to the most lavish clerical scrutiny and speculation, these controversial insignia perform the function of establishing Margery Kempe herself as the object of piety, of the veneration of others, one to whom in fact, others might do well to do pilgrimage. Concerned to show the merits of a particular way of life, the book has, after all, to advertise the merits of that life. Occasionally the book makes it quite explicit that she expects to be honoured as a saint in her own parish church of St Margaret's, as in chapter 63, when Christ says to her:

In þis chirche þu hast suffyrd meche schame & reprefe for

þe ȝyftys that I haue ȝouyn þe & for þe grace and goodnes
þat I haue wrowt in þe, and þerfore in þis cherche & in þis
place I xal ben worschepyd in þe.[132]

If part of the informing support she received from the clerical
community attempted a clerical subjugation of bourgeois values,
it was an attempt that was short-circuited from the very beginning, for in the most material and complex of ways, Kempe's
book shows both the conflict between, and the imbrication of,
clerical and bourgeois values, their complicity as well as their
invincible hostility.

I have argued in previous chapters that the image of Christ's
body is a conflicted symbol where hierarchies of high and low
can be dynamically reformulated and subverted. Kempe refutes
utterly the hierarchies of high and low, the oppositions of trancen-
dence and immanence present in the logic of clerical condescension, and articulated in the most minute organizations of space
of parochial control. Though she subjects her own book to the
grid of clerical analysis: 'For sumtyme that sche vundirstod bodily
it was to ben vundirstondyn gostly',[133] she also provides the very
means of its contestation, reordering the hierarchical logic of high
and low, transcendence and immanence with the alternative logic
of crucifixion piety – the one that insists on their irremediable
imbrication.

What this analysis of Kempe's *habitus* has enabled us to see is
how clerical and bourgeois values are not simply oppositional,
but interrelated, and that interrelationship works through the
valuation, purchase, economic access to cultural symbols that
were also and inescapably religious symbols. It also enables us to
acknowledge the force of Bourdieu's analysis that moves beyond
any simple economism, which would make Kempe's piety a mere
economic epiphenomenon of her social and economic class. If her
social and economic values inform her manipulation of cultural
symbols, and their manipulation of her, and it is the insistent
drive of this chapter to argue, like Aers and like Delaney, that
they do, this is because those cultural and religious values have
already been subject to the marks of a thoroughgoing economic
calculation. Economistic thought often misunderstands symbolic
activity as empty affect, lacking material or concrete effect, in
short, gratuitous. i.e. disinterested, but also useless.[134] But cultural
symbols such as the body of Christ were themselves subject to

108

a very minute, material, precise and local form of economic calculation. This underscores Bourdieu's point, which is worth quoting in full:

> The only way to escape from the ethnocentric naïveties of economism, without falling into populist exaltation of the generous naïvety of earlier forms of society, is to carry out in full what economism does only partially and to extend economic calculation to *all* the goods, material and symbolic without distinction, that present themselves as *rare* and worthy of being sought after in a particular social formation – which may be fair words, or smiles, handshakes or shrugs, compliments or attention, challenges or insults, honour or honours, powers or pleasures, gossip or scientific information, distinction or distinctions, etc. [135]

It is undoubtedly true that the central symbolism with which this book deals, the body of Christ, has certainly been subject to explanations which, in generous and utopian fashion, exalt its universalist appeal.[136] And they have done so by making the reverse version of the separation that Bourdieu talks about in his next passage:

> Economic calculation has hitherto managed to appropriate the territory objectively surrendered to the remorseless logic of what Marx calls 'naked self-interest' only by setting aside a sacred island miraculously spared by the icy water of egotistical calculation and left as a sanctuary for the priceless and worthless things it cannot assess.[137]

That is, they have isolated the world of remorseless and egotistical calculation from the sacred island of religious symbolism so that that realm can be literally priceless. But this analysis will, I hope, have shown how intimately and ineradicably they conjoin as a form of calculative sacredness or sacred calculation around the figure of Christ.

Kempe's ambivalent fame as the object of vituperative critical hostility after the discovery of her book in 1934 is standing testimony to what is at stake in the coalescence of these schemes: the desecration of that sacred and priceless world, the world of medieval catholic and therefore universalistic religion, its immersion in the brassy world of muck and money, the blurring of categories which should be distinct. For what is blurred here is both the sense of the sacred, and also that which is most culturally sacred to modern western culture – egotistical, economic, rationalistic calculation: a world pure of the sacred. In Margery Kempe these worlds are incomprehensible other than through their mutual relation. Her *habitus* is one that readily converts symbolic capital into economic capital and economic capital back into cultural capital.[138] And it is a world that is not fully understandable by a conceptual apparatus that maintains the distinction between those two forms of capital.

Most critics of Margery Kempe, those that find the coalescence of these realms most offensive to their sensibilities, have taken the characteristic path of projecting what are problematics of culture and cultural shifts onto the personality through which they are embodied. The cultural manifestations of the inter-relationships of these worlds are therefore seen as erratic, neurotic and ardently individualistic deviations from normative and other-wise universally agreed values. This viewpoint is only reinforced by an excessive over-confidence in the homogeneity of late medi-eval ritual practice. That is, if the rules of the procession of Corpus Christi are to bind and unify a community, then Kempe's 'deviant' behaviour isolates her from the main body of the pro-cession. This, of course, is to forget that any analysis of behaviour based on rules, norms and models will always look on any prac-tice of a rule as either an empty conformism, or, if it does improvise from the prescription, as a form of cultural deviancy. Kempe has been accused of both errors: on the one hand a banality which makes of her the perfect reflector of her religious culture, and on the other hand an idiosyncrasy so spectacularly and peculi-arly egocentric that it is uniquely hers and hers alone, an erratic deviation and interpretative licence of otherwise collectively understood cultural rules and norms.[139] It is precisely this oppo-sition that Bourdieu is attempting to evaporate by his use of the concept of the *habitus*, and his elaboration of a theory of practice. As he says, 'it is practice which is annihilated when the scheme is identified with the model.'[140]

This discussion is particularly important for the examination of the *habitus* of Margery Kempe, for an analysis of the complexity and signification of her deployment, appropriation and creative use of the symbolic capital of the body of Christ. For the arena of Christ's body is an arena saturated with ritual practice, part and parcel of the sacramental institutionalization of grace. Such understandings attempted to maintain control of the sacred, through exclusive mediation, and so they transubstantiate bread into body, they hold it aloft for worship and wonder, they require penitence on its behalf and as a prerequisite for whole-hearted incorporation. Kempe participates in precisely such clerical administrations of Christ's body. She takes part in the Corpus Christi procession, she gazes in awe at the elevated host; she consults the very highest ecclesiasts in the English church. But she also has a much more intimate relationship to Christ's body which licenses her to by-pass the clergy as the sole ministers of grace. Far from confirming her in her social role as wife and mother, it allows her to take up a variety of overlapping social roles in relation to Christ. And she is finally able to write a book, a book which is acknowledged as her own if only through the repeated ascription of 'autobiography' to define it. That she can be paradoxically called both Lollard and mystic is a testimony to the complicity of both such forms in the fracturing of authority of her age. Like the Lollards, like certain mystical writers, and like certain ecclesiastical reformists, she is concerned as much with the production of *virtue* as the production of miracles and images. The production of virtue inevitably involved just the kind of self-scrutiny that would give the book the dimensions of will, of memory, of context and desire that encourage us to define it as 'autobiograpical'. We have seen in this study that the body of Christ as an object of contemplation has entailed just such self-scrutiny. By choosing to focus on the body of Christ in her self-making, she used one of the central resources her culture provided for her; she used it, finally, in the sense that has by now become familiar, to become a member of her collectivity, and to contest the very way those communal boundaries were organized. As a bourgeois woman, then, as a member of the urban elite, she was in precisely the position I have marked out as being a characteristic user of this form of piety: she was part of a class which, just developing its own cultural insignia, might have been a typical candidate for crucifixion piety. The body in her text is thus the body we have become familiar with in this study: open enough to let her in, porous to her and intimate with her; closed enough to make it a special privilege that she should be included.

CONCLUSION

> . . . our task . . . is to study and clarify the resources of
> ambiguity . . . it is in the areas of ambiguity that transform-
> ation takes place; in fact, without such areas, transformation
> would be impossible.
>
> (K. Burke)

Symbolic analysis holds many dangers. Symbols may be used to
short-change or short-circuit historical analysis, for example:
'[T]he temptation is to reduce the historical variety of the forms
of interpretation to what are loosely called symbols or archetypes:
to abstract even these most evidently social forms and to give
them a primarily psychological or metaphysical status.'[1] The lon-
gevity, continuity and persistence of certain symbols may encourage us to fetishize the symbol as the source and origin of meaning
wherein ultimate significance inheres. Cultural criticism, however, understands symbols to be both saturated, laden with context, and manipulable out of that context, freed of it.

> Cultural meaning is both context-laden and context-
> convertible. . . . Symbols are devices in cultural systems
> by which this fact is assured. Thanks to symbols, cultural
> meanings are rich, deep, multivocal, many layered, highly
> wrought, and shared but also rarefiable, subject to abstrac-
> tion, exportable, often communicated; thus not substan-
> tively shared but rather exchanged. Something nonsymbolic
> would be either perfectly context-specific, a reflex of an
> external condition, or absolutely context-free, a given fact,
> an *a priori*. Something symbolic is from different vantages
> perceived as both.[2]

The duplicity that pertains to symbols generally is given particular
edge and focus when considered in relation to the symbol of the
body of Christ in late medieval culture.[3] The context of the
understanding of the dual nature of Christ's body lends it a greater

duplicity than its mere function as symbol alone, for Christ's body was understood as sharing divine with human nature. Its mortality tied it to limits, to finitude, to context; its divinity freed it of that context, made it symbolically mobile. Furthermore, greater accessibility of the body of Christ through the dissemination of texts in the vernacular, and the pedagogic initiatives of the clergy also rendered the context of production, reception and consumption of the symbol of Christ's body more mobile.

That duplicity, a quality of the symbol, an especial quality of the symbol of Christ's body, can be ramified still further if we consider the way it points to the fundamental ambiguities of embodiment. For the body's presence is itself dialectical and contradictory, itself the site of reciprocity and exchange; it is where we are affirmed in an ultimate loneliness and uniqueness, and at the same time where our dependency on others, our vulnerability to them, our resistance of them, our inextricability with them are lamented, celebrated, desired and spurned. In the most complex ways imaginable the body is not just a figure for, but the very medium of both our individuality and our sociality.

Through its capacities as symbol, as symbol of the body, and as symbol more particularly of the cultural configuration of Christ's body, the exchanges, interrelationships, contradictions and interconnections between the natural and the social, the hierarchical and the collective, the individual and the social, the sacred and the profane, between the public and the private, the noumenal and the phenomenal, the unified and multiplicitous, the integrated and fractured, and the transcendent and the immanent can be interrogated. Each set of categories, moreover, can be transcoded by another. This book has explored some of the ways in which the image of Christ's body makes meaning through these interrelationships.

It is impossible to understand the uses of this central image and icon in the texts under analysis without an appreciation of the resources of ambiguity at the disposal of the symbol. What, then, are the resources of ambiguity? What is the necessary link between ambiguity and transformation? I have described the way in which the symbolizing process involves a movement across a classificatory system, thus problematizing a region where language intersects with the world.[4] Either because the referent of the symbol does not have a classificatory system (leading to its drive towards symbolic formulation in the first place), or because

113

the symbol contravenes the existing available taxonomies, a symbol may call both the describing language and the world itself into question.[5] That is why, as Adi Ophir says, one can *only* speak symbolically about Christ.[6] And that is also why the symbolic utterances that circulate around the symbol of Christ's body are the densest site of signification. It is because that symbol violates the classificatory lines of the system (and therefore the order upheld through those divisions and definitions) that contests for new configurations of meaning obsessively locate themselves here. But it is for this reason too, that violent hierarchies may be reinscribed, as symbolic utterances paradoxically, through the very act of boundary-crossing, reveal where the lines of the system are in the very act of rudely violating them.[7]

I have spent much time in this argument stressing the local and immanent configurations of the symbol of Christ's body, but the symbol itself cannot be appreciated without understanding the extreme tensions of ideal and real, of transcendent and immanent played out in the image. The body of Christ is, as I have argued, where the local, minute realization of embodiment, the necessity of its specific and detailed placing, is blessed by the transcendent at the very same time as it compromises it. It is both an articulation, and a deep-rooted, structuring critique in symbolic terms of such idealism. Perhaps the savage brilliance of the symbolism lies in this specific configuration of the transcendent and the immanent; its genius is not (as in ascetic and dualistic readings of late medieval religious culture) to create the transcendent through simple denial of the immanent, but rather to make of the finite, of the immanent, of the physical and mortal its very source of generative power.

Recent accounts of late medieval affective piety have revised earlier readings of medieval asceticism; they have encouraged us to see the affirmative, even celebratory qualities of a form of religious practice hitherto regarded either with a merely morbid curiosity or with more emphatic distaste. Caroline Walker Bynum and Gail McMurry Gibson in their very different ways, and through treatment of very different material, have recently argued for an understanding of the late Middle Ages as a time when the awesome distance of God blessed the mundane, inhabited the intimate and familiar world of the common and the ordinary. For Gibson, such a sacramental world-view bespeaks a 'growing tendency to see the world saturated with sacramental possibility and meaning and to celebrate it'.[8] The incarnation blesses as well as redeeming fallen humanity: 'The spiritual object of meditation is held earthbound for as long as human ingenuity (and pious curiosity) will permit.'[9] Caroline Walker Bynum has argued that the period between 1200 and 1500 sees the development of a new attitude towards the body, one in which physicality came to be seen as 'less a barrier than an opportunity'.[10] In particular:

> The goal of religious women was thus to realize the opportunity of physicality. They strove not to eradicate body but to merge their own humiliating and painful flesh with that flesh whose agony, espoused by choice was salvation. Luxuriating in Christ's physicality, they found there the lifting up and redemption of their own.[11]

What the incarnation licensed in this view was a full participation in bodiliness. And understanding this, she implies, means understanding the notion that 'no other history in the period of Christianity has placed so positive (and therefore so complex and ambiguous) a value on the bodiliness of Christ's humanity.'[12]

Using the revisionist anthropological readings of Maurice Bloch, I would like to provide an account of what my reading of the symbol of Christ's body can tell us about the nature of late medieval sacramentalism. My reading acknowledges that both the ascetic reading of late medieval culture, and the affirmative and sacramental one have much of interest to tell us about late medieval religious culture. Both readings, however, eschew the ideological configurations and dimensions of their subject, and both underestimate the resources of ambiguity in the symbolic working of Christ's body. It is just such an understanding, I argue, that allows us to see that this symbol works, not in either denying or affirming ways, but fundamentally, and at the same time, through affirmation and denial. And this ambiguous working will also allow us to see how it could be used ideologically, i.e. to mobilize symbolic meanings in the service of power.[13]

Bloch maintains that all symbolic constructions of *authority* involve similar elements. The first element in the symbolic construction of authority is the creation of an ideal and transcendent order which is outside of and superior to the human world – eternal, timeless and infinite. This transcendent authority is created antithetically. It is never described, but simply suggested by reference to everything that it is not. Thus, the construction of an ideal order always involves the exaggeration of all that is finite, earthly and mortal: the limits, constraints of bodiliness – death, physical decay, all that is subject to death – are exaggerated in order to represent the purity and supremacy of a transcendent and infinite order. Second, after the ritual creation of that transcendent order, human authority represents itself as a delegation of that order in this life; it can then claim to be ordering the world through a transcendental model. The third manœuvre, according to Bloch, is to compromise with the model of transcendent order. Such a compromise is necessary, for to refuse or deny the world altogether would be to negate rather than legitimate that world. The symbolism of authority argues Bloch, 'must involve a contradiction which allows for the reintroduction of real existence into what still remains the ideal'.[14] Such a view of the workings of symbolism can help us wed an analysis of power to the analysis of meaning and signification, and help us to see how one works through the other. It does not deny the negative elements of such symbolism (the ascetic reading); but neither does it fail to see the affirming, creative potentialities of such symbolism, though it does see the ideological power of the symbolism as working through an allocation (a projection) of human creativity onto a transcendent order that is then mediated by an authority that can come to represent/mediate it. It uses the cathectic, visceral resources of emotions, and of biology itself, antithetically to construct a timeless, perfect world.

In this way out of flesh itself, out of what is most subject to death, is constructed the very world that can resist and transcend it: out of the immanence of the body is created the very resource of power as it legitimates itself with reference to an eternal, everlasting order.

Rather than either affirming or negating bodiliness, then, the image of Christ as suffering, as embodied, as crucified, as always dying, is the very means by which order and authority are created and recreated. In this operation another fundamental transcoding or exchange of meaning can take place in addition to the many others that we have outlined – an exchange between creativity and power itself. The power of the social group that seeks to legitimate itself by reference to this symbol, then, is held in place by the most viscerally felt emotions, by the creative projections of those who use it, look at it, eat it, gaze upon it, identify with it, love it, and seek to penetrate it or to be enfolded within it.

Such an analysis shows us why Christ's body was such a vital cultural resource for those who sought legitimacy within their culture. Given that it was a major symbol for the legitimation of authority, it also inevitably provided the language, resources and opportunity for the construction of counter-hegemonic meanings. Both its hegemonic and counter-hegemonic force derive from its ambivalence.[15] Such an ambivalence is constitutive, not something that will be resolved at the next ordering, the next attempt at perfection. For it will always invite and entice, seem to make essential that ordering in the act of mucking it up, as it 'brings the outside into the inside . . . poison[ing] the comfort of order with the suspicion of chaos'.[16]

It may finally be worth remarking that in our own classificatory schemes for making sense of the past, we make a decisive separation between pre- and post-reformation history. We will then either read our Middle Ages as a retrospectively understood precursor to the inevitable trajectory of British protestantism, or as an insulated, universal and consensual orthodoxy, an orthodoxy that has in the end to remain merely puzzled by the cultural revolution that overtook it. Such a rigid division will then prevent us from seeing the symbolism surrounding Christ's body, the arena of late medieval crucifixion piety, as the very locus and substance of a historically momentous transference of, and struggle over, sacrality.[17] Holding within itself its own complex mixture of iconoclasm and adoration, the image of Christ's body may then be seen as part and parcel of a symbolic dissemination of its own, historically specific and particular economy of meaning. In arguing that Christ's body is where retrospectively defined catholicity and protestantism play out their tropes and struggle for cultural capital, I have provided an account which explains the existence of *both* as dimensions of a specifically late medieval nexus of signification.

To argue for a materialist reading of the symbol of Christ's body in the culture of late medieval England is to have to come to terms, paradoxically, with its most urgent idealist aspirations. For the aspiration always to exceed, to move beyond, to surpass the contingent and present is precisely what renders unstable the very terms of the always tense relationship between transcendence and immanence momentarily, unhappily, productively and dialectically intertwined in the symbol of Christ's body.

NOTES

INTRODUCTION

1 Clifford Geertz, *The Interpretation of Cultures*, New York, Basic Books, 1973, p. 91.

2 Raymond Williams, *Culture*, Glasgow, Fontana, 1981, p. 13.

3 John Thompson, *Ideology and Modern Culture: Critical Social Theory in the Era of Mass Communication*, Stanford, Stanford University Press, 1990, p. 12. Thompson is rigorous and meticulous in his analysis of the relation between symbolic processes and power, a perspective sometimes erased in the Geertzian framework. Thompson's analysis (his words) 'prizes the concept of ideology away from the search for collectively shared values, redirecting it towards the study of the complex ways in which meaning is mobilized for the maintenance of relations of domination' (p. 8). In this context, see also William Roseberry's discussion of the relation explored (or erased) within two different anthropological understandings of history: history as cultural difference, and history as material social process, and his related criticism of Clifford Geertz, *Anthropologies and Histories: Essays in Culture, History and Political Economy*, New Brunswick and London, Rutgers University Press, 1989, pp. 12–13.

4 For a fuller definition of 'concomitance' and its theological and ecclesiastical foundations, see A. Vacant et al., *Dictionnaire de théologie catholique contenant l'exposé des doctrines de la théologie catholique*, Paris, 1909–50. A fuller account is provided in James McGivern, *Concomitance and Communion: A Study of Eucharistic Doctrine and Practice*, Fribourg, The University Press, 1963. The doctrine is elaborated to counter the Berengarian heresy that the body and blood of Christ were not present in the eucharist, but were only signs of God's spiritual reality. Berengar believed that any understanding of Christ's body and blood as actually presenced in the eucharist would entail the blasphemous notion that little bits of Christ's flesh ('portiuncula carnis Christi') would be crunched up in the jaws of the faithful. See G. Macy, *The Theologies of the Eucharist in the Early Scholastic Period: A Study of the Salvific Function of the Sacrament according to the*

Theologians c. 1080–1220, Oxford, Clarendon Press, 1984, and A. J. MacDonald, *Berengar and the Reform of Sacramental Doctrine*, London, Longmans, Green & Co., 1930. It is perhaps interesting to note here that a doctrine which asserted the unity and universality of the central (and defining) symbol of the ecclesiastical polity was first articulated to counteract schism at the level of doctrine, and articulated in the official church council at Constance in 1415, where a united papacy was restored and the ecclesiology which underpinned it articulated. For a detailed elaboration of eucharistic doctrine and symbolism in relation to ecclesiastical polity, see Miri Rubin, *Corpus Christi: The Eucharist in Late Medieval Culture*, Cambridge, Cambridge University Press, 1991.

5 See Caroline Walker Bynum, *Holy Feast and Holy Fast: The Religious Significance of Food to Medieval Women*, Berkeley, University of California Press, 1987, pp. 50–3, my chapter 2, and article, 'Ritual, Church and Theatre: Medieval Dramas of the Sacramental Body' in *Culture and History 1350–1600: Essays on English Communities, Identities and Writing*, ed. David Aers, Brighton, Harvester Press, 1992, especially n. 85.

6 The phrase 'imagined communities' is coined by Benedict Anderson who uses it 'in an anthropological spirit' to define the nation as an 'imagined political community'. He goes on to explain that the nation is 'imagined because the members of even the smallest nation will never know most of their fellow members, meet them, or even hear of them, yet in the minds of each lives the image of their communion'. In stressing the importance of the 'imagined', Anderson is at pains to point out that it is the creative and inventive qualities of the word that he wishes to convey, rather than their possible signification as 'fabricated' or 'false'. What follows from this observation is that 'communities are to be distinguished, not by their falsity/genuineness, but by the style in which they are imagined.' See Benedict Anderson, *Imagined Communities: Reflections on the Origin and Spread of Nationalism*, London, Verso, 1983, p. 15. For an essay that uses this terminology in ways which have implications for the present study see, Peter Womack, 'Imagining Communities: Theatres and the English Nation in the Sixteenth Century', in *Culture and History 1350–1600: Essays on English Communities, Identities and Writing*, ed. David Aers, Brighton, Harvester Press, 1992 pp. 91–145.

7 The terms 'inner difference' and 'self-contestation' are used by Dominick LaCapra in his *Rethinking Intellectual History: Texts, Contexts, Language*, Ithaca, Cornell University Press, 1983, p. 18. For LaCapra's rethinking of the notion of 'context' to render it 'less a shibboleth or a passe-partout and more a limited, critical concept in historical research' (p. 16), see his first chapter, 'Rethinking Intellectual History and Reading Texts', pp. 23–71. For a very useful analysis of the interrelation of symbol and community see Anthony Cohen, *The Symbolic Construction of Community*, London, Tavistock Publications, 1985, pp. 19–21.

8 Raymond Williams, *Politics and Letters: Interviews with New Left Review*, London, New Left Books, 1979, p. 167. The term 'structure of feeling' was coined by Raymond Williams, and it is for him a vital, although very labile, term in the development of a viable and responsible cultural analysis. He first defines the term in *The Long Revolution*, Harmondsworth, Pelican, 1961, p. 64: 'The term I would suggest is *structure of feeling*: it is as firm and delicate as "structure" suggests, yet it operates in the most delicate parts of our activity. In one sense, this structure of feeling is the culture of a period: it is the particular living result of all the elements in the general organization.' In a much later formulation in *Marxism and Literature*, Oxford, Oxford University Press, 1977, pp. 130–2, Williams articulates and develops the concept in relation to the tension between received interpretation and practical experience, where the term 'feeling' is chosen precisely because it is less formal than 'world-view' or 'ideology' and can speak to 'social experiences in solution'. Such experiences are, as he says on p. 134, 'at the very edge of semantic availability'. Thus 'structures of feeling' are 'social experiences in solution': they are a 'cultural hypothesis, actually derived from attempts to understand such elements and their connections in a generation or period, and needing always to be returned, interactively, to such evidence' (*Marxism and Literature*, p. 133). Significantly, the term is used in the chapter entitled 'Structures of Feeling' to attempt to break the conceptual separation of individual and society, a separation which Williams links to the reification of the very categories 'culture' and 'society'. If, he argues, 'culture' and 'society' are 'expressed in a habitual past tense' (p. 128), if indeed, 'the strongest barrier to the recognition of human cultural activity is this immediate and regular conversion of experience into finished products' (p. 128), then we urgently need a term which will *not* describe the social and cultural as radically depersonalized. For an excellent and reflexive discussion of the development of the concept of 'structure of feeling', see the interview with Raymond Williams on *The Long Revolution* in *Politics and Letters*, pp. 156–74.

9 Cohen, p. 21.

10 Jean Comaroff and John Comaroff, *Of Revelation and Revolution: Christianity, Colonialism and Consciousness in South Africa*, Chicago, University of Chicago Press, 1991, p. 29.

11 See Gerald Sider, *Culture and Class in Anthropology and History: A Newfoundland Illustration*, Cambridge, Cambridge University Press, 1986, pp. 4–8, for an examination of the way the anthropological concept of culture is frequently 'a-historical, non-processual and totalizing'. Because it is so often understood as all-inclusive, culture has to be conceptualized as either autonomous and independent, or merely dependent, superstructural. Consequently, 'our task is to see culture not only with its own dynamic and volatile paradoxes, disjunctions and contradictions but also in the specific ways culture both takes from and gives to social relations shape, form and meaning (and meaninglessness, etc.) – to see it as an active force in

history' (p. 7). See also Eric Wolf, *Europe and the People Without History*, Berkeley, University of California Press, 1982, p. 19, for the need to develop 'a new theory of cultural forms' in order to 'understand more precisely (how) cultural forms work to mediate social relationships among particular populations' (p. 19).

12 James Marrow, *Passion Iconography in Northern Europe in the Late Middle Ages and Early Renaissance: A Study of the Transformation of Sacred Metaphor into Descriptive Narrative*, Kortrijk, Belgium, Van Ghemmert Pub. Co., 1979.

13 Peter Brown, *The Body and Society: Men, Women and Sexual Renunciation in Early Christianity*, New York, Columbia University Press, 1988.

14 Caroline Walker Bynum, *Holy Feast and Holy Fast: The Religious Significance of Food to Medieval Women*, Berkeley and Los Angeles, University of California Press, 1987.

15 Miri Rubin, *Corpus Christi: The Eucharist in Late Medieval Culture*, Cambridge, Cambridge University Press, 1991. This book unfortunately came out too late for me to benefit from it in this study. It does, however, provide a discussion of the eucharist as a concerted construction of a pan-European clerical hegemony from the periods *c.* 1000 to the early fifteenth century, and as such presents a sympathetic frame for my own more specific study. Peter Travis has also explored the social configuration of Christ's body in some late medieval dramas in his two articles, 'The Social Body of the Dramatic Christ in Medieval England', *Early Drama to 1600*, *Acta*, 1985, 13, pp. 17–36, and 'The Semiotics of Christ's Body in the Cycles' in *Approaches to Teaching Medieval Drama*, ed. Richard Emmerson, New York, M.L.A., 1990. Karma Lochrie's book, *Margery Kempe and Translations of the Flesh*, Philadelphia, University of Pennsylvania Press, 1991, is now available, once again too late for me to benefit from it in this study.

16 Harold Kane, ed., *The Prickynge of Love*, Salzburg, Institut für Anglistik und Amerkanistik, 1983.

17 Lawrence Powell, ed., *Mirrour of the Blessyd Lyf of Jesu Christ*, Oxford, Henry Frowde, 1908.

18 Sanford Meech and Hope Emily Allen, eds, *The Book of Margery Kempe*, Early English Text Society no. 212, Oxford, Oxford University Press, 1940.

19 Clarissa Atkinson discusses the issue and ascription of autobiography in *Mystic and Pilgrim: The Book and the World of Margery Kempe*, Ithaca and London, Cornell University Press, 1983, pp. 21–37. See also Stephen Medcalf's comments in *The Later Middle Ages*, ed. Stephen Medcalf, London, Methuen & Co., 1981, p. 113, and Barry Windeatt, ed., *The Book of Margery Kempe*, Harmondsworth, Penguin, 1985, p. 9 and p. 11, where the book is described as 'too autobiographical'. See my 'Problems of Authority in Late Medieval English Mysticism: Language, Agency and Authority in *The Book of Margery Kempe*', *Exemplaria*, 1992, vol. 4, no. 1, pp. 171–99, for a discussion of the problematic category of 'mystical autobiography'.

20 Thompson, p. 12.

21 Geertz, p. 90. Geertz's full definition runs as follows: 'a *religion* is (1) a system of symbols which acts to (2) establish powerful, pervasive, and long-lasting moods and motivations in men by (3) formulating conceptions of a general order of existence and (4) clothing these conceptions with such an aura of factuality that (5) the moods and motivations seem uniquely realistic.'

22 The shift in recent historical investigation from religion as a set of ideas to religion as a cultural process is described by one historian as follows: '. . . an earlier essentialist religious frame of reference, in which religion was seen to constitute some kind of universal and self-explanatory essence or enclosed realm, has been slowly giving way to an integration of behaviour traditionally termed "religious" with other forms of social and cultural practice' (Charles Zika, 'Hosts, Processions and Pilgrimage: Controlling the Sacred in Fifteenth-Century Germany', *Past and Present*, 1988, no. 118, p. 26). For an understanding of the Gramscian notion of 'hegemony' see Antonio Gramsci, *Selections from the Prison Notebooks*, ed. Q. Hoare and G. Nowell Smith, New York, International Publishers, 1971. The elucidation and discussion of the concept of hegemony remains a vital issue in cultural studies because it may be considered the dominant form in which power is entailed in culture. For a nuanced discussion of the competitive valency of the terms 'culture', 'ideology' and 'hegemony,' see Comaroff and Comaroff, pp. 19–27, and Raymond Williams, *Marxism and Literature*, p. 110.

23 I am here paraphrasing Pierre Bourdieu, *Outline of a Theory of Practice*, Cambridge Studies in Social Anthropology, Cambridge, Cambridge University Press, 1977, p. 114.

24 Geertz, p. 14: 'Understanding a people's culture exposes their normalness without reducing their particularity. . . . It renders them accessible: setting them in the frame of their own banalities, it dissolves their opacity.'

1 THE TRANSCENDENT AND THE HISTORICAL:
Inventing the disourse of mysticism

1 Freidrich Nietzsche, *The Anti-Christ* in *Twilight of the Gods / The Anti-Christ*, trans. R. J. Hollingdale, Harmondsworth, Penguin, 1968, p. 120.

2 Edward Said, 'Opponents, Audiences, Constituencies and Community' in *Postmodern Culture*, ed. Hal Foster, London and Sydney, Pluto Press, 1983, pp. 145–6.

3 'I am that I am. . . . I am that hath sent me to you' (Exodus 3.14). Quoted also in Michel de Certeau, 'Mystic Speech' in *Heterologies: Discourse on the Other*, Manchester, Manchester University Press, 1986, p. 250, n. 105.

4 William James, *The Varieties of Religious Experience*, New York, 1902, p. 404.

5 Ernst Troeltsch, *The Social Teaching of the Christian Churches*, London and New York, Macmillan, 1931, repr. 1956, vol. 2, p. 791.

6 G. van der Leeuw, *Religion in Essence and Manifestation: A Study in Phenomenology*, trans. J. E. Turner, London, Allen & Unwin, 1938, p. 680, quoted in the French publication in Frits Staal, *Exploring Mysticism*, Harmondsworth, Penguin, 1975, p. 13.

7 Evelyn Underhill, 'Medieval Mysticism' in *Cambridge Medieval History*, vol. 7, Cambridge, Cambridge University Press, 1949, p. 779.

8 Troeltsch, p. 735.

9 For these classic works see Evelyn Underhill, *The Mystic Way: A Psychological Study in Christian Origins*, London and Toronto, J. M. Dent, 1913; *Practical Mysticism: A Little Book for Normal People*, London, J. M. Dent, 1914; *Man and the Supernatural*, New York, E. P. Dutton & Co., 1931; W. T. Stace, *Mysticism and Philosophy*, London, Macmillan, 1960; Rudolf Otto, *Mysticiam East and West*, New York, Macmillan, 1932; R. C. Zaehner, *Mysticism Sacred and Profane*, Oxford, Clarendon Press, 1957; Rufus Jones, *Studies in Mystical Religion*, London, Macmillan, 1923.

10 Robert M. Gimello, 'Mysticism in Its Contexts' in *Mysticism and Religious Traditions*, ed. Steven Katz, Oxford and New York, Oxford University Press, 1983, p. 86, n. 1. And see William Inge's comment in *Mysticism in Religion*, Chicago, University of Chicago Press, 1948, p. 29, 'The objection that mysticism is a religion for the elite must be faced. . . . Berdyaeff, a disillusioned communist, is not afraid to face it. The quantitative majority, he says, has always oppressed the qualitative authority, that which is composed of holy spiritual individuals. History works out in favour of the average man and of the collective. It is for such that dogma and cult have been adapted. . . . Christianity, a religion which is not of this world, suffers humiliation in the world for the sake of the general mass of humanity. The whole tragedy of spiritual humanity lies in that fact.' In the next paragraph the slippage from 'mysticism' to Christianity *per se* is even more arrogantly apparent: 'Christianity gives us a new type of aristocracy. It is utterly opposed to the notion that we can reach the truth by counting heads.' Rufus Jones gives us a different political angle, most clearly expressed in his William Belden lectures delivered at Harvard, *Mysticism and Democracy in the English Commonwealth*, Cambridge, Mass., Harvard University Press, 1932. Here, however, a different elite (the Quakers) are the vanguard of the democratic principle itself.

11 Gimello, p. 86.

12 Steven Katz, 'Editor's Introduction', to *Mysticism and Philosophical Analysis*, Oxford, Oxford University Press, 1978, p. 1.

13 'Anomie' is in many ways the core Durkheimian concept. LaCapra, in his intellectual history of Durkheim, gives a useful definition of Durkheim's 'anomie' which relates the concept to social forms and representational ones: 'In his core concept of anomie, Durkheim

referred to the social and cultural – perhaps what one might call existential – position of man possessed of (and frequently by) symbolism but devoid of substantively limiting norms and meaningful paradigms which give a viably coherent order to experience. Anomic disorientation, confusion, and anxiety were basic causes of breakdown and of new creation in society' *Emile Durkheim: Sociologist and Philosopher*, Chicago and London, University of Chicago Press, 1972, pp. 12–13).

14 Durkheim located this 'infinity sickness' in several aspects of modern culture, for example in romanticism, which tried to erase the distinction of subject and object through its redefinition and resacralization of the aesthetic. See LaCapra, *Durkheim*, p. 162.

15 Evelyn Underhill, *Mysticism: A Study in the Nature and Development of Man's Spiritual Consciousness*, New York, E. P Dutton & Co., 1930, p. xiv.

16 Evelyn Underhill, *Practical Mysticism*, London, J. M. Dent, 1914, p. 4.

17 William Ralph Inge, *Christian Mysticism*, London, Methuen & Co., 1899; reprint edn, London, 1921, p. 5.

18 Regina Bechtler, 'The Mystic and the Church in the Writings of Evelyn Underhill', Ph.D. dissertation, Fordham University, 1979, p. 15. See also Daniel Eliot Bassuk, 'The Secularization of Mysticism – An Analysis and Critique of the Mystical in Rufus Jones and Martin Buber', Ph.D. dissertation, Drew University, 1974, p. 11, where he lists the following participants in the 'mystical revival': Starbuck, Leuba, Coe, Boisen, Pratt, Royce and Bennet in America; in England along with Underhill and Inge, Herman and von Hugel; in France, Bastide, Murisier, Recejac, Boutroux, Delacroix, Poulain, Bremond, Marechal, Bergson; in Germany, Otto, Heiler, Schweitzer; and in Scotland, Hughes. It is possible that von Hugel's work, *The Mystical Element in Religion*, should be excluded from this analysis of the mystical revival. Von Hugel's study consists in an examination of the life of Catharine of Genoa, and is concerned to place mysticism in relation to what von Hugel calls 'historical-institutional elements'. I am indebted to Fritz Bauerschmidt for discussion on this point.

19 John Hoyle, 'Beyond the Sex-Economy of Mysticism: Some Observations on the Communism of the Imagination with reference to Winstanley and Traherne', in *1642: Literature and Power in the Seventeenth Century*, ed. F. Barker, J. Bernstein, J. Coombes, P. Hulme, J. Stone, J. Stratton, University of Essex, 1981, p. 239.

20. This is a sociological commonplace, a nostalgic paradigm which depends on a particular view of the relationship between religion and society, a view which assumes the 'decline' of religious forms. Such a view is heavily contested in critical sociology. For a preliminary mapping of the debates see *Culture and Society: Contemporary Debates*, ed. Jeffrey C. Alexander and Steven Seidman, Cambridge, Cambridge University Press, 1990, pp. 217–74.

21 Max Weber quoting Dowden in *The Protestant Ethic and the Spirit of Capitalism*, New York, Scribner, 1958, pp. 104–5.

22 *From Max Weber: Essays in Sociology*, trans. and ed., and with an introduction by H. H. Gerth and R. Wright Mills, Oxford, Oxford University Press, 1958, p. 155.

23 LaCapra, p. 180.

24 Carl A. Keller, 'Mystical Literature' in *Mysticism and Philosophical Analysis*, ed. Katz, p. 96.

25 Paul Szarmach, 'Introduction' to *An Introduction to the Medieval Mystics of Europe*, ed. Paul Szarmach, Albany, State University of New York Press, 1984, p. 2. It is not, it should be clear, however, an *arbitrary* construct. There may well be a homology between medieval 'mysticism' and its modern construction which has to do, precisely, with the crisis of cultural transmission in both periods.

26 OED. Needless to say, the medieval usage in the Latinate tradition was catered for by the use of the term 'mystica theologia', a term which is not, however, coincident with 'mysticism'. 'Contemplatio' or 'contemplation' were often used and were preferred by both Aquinas and Bonaventura to 'mystica theologia'. A full analysis of the etymology of the word in relation to its social history would have to see it differentially positioned in relation to the changing understanding of religion in the English Enlightenment. See Wilfrid Cantwell Smith, *The Meaning and End of Religion: A New Approach to the Religious Traditions of Mankind*, New York, The Macmillan Company, 1962; Peter Harrison, *'Religion' and the Religions in the English Enlightenment*, Cambridge, Cambridge University Press, 1990.

27 Troeltsch, p. 743.

28 ibid., p. 747.

29 ibid., p. 739.

30 Steven Ozment, *Mysticism and Dissent*, New Haven, Yale University Press, 1973, p. 1.

31 Perhaps Marx's formulation on religion in the introduction to *Critique of Hegel's Philosophy of Right*, Cambridge, Cambridge University Press, 1970, p. 131, develops this dialectical complexity most coherently: 'The wretchedness of religion is at once an expression of and a protest against a real wretchedness. Religion is the sigh of the oppressed creture, the heart of a heartless world and the soul of soulless conditions. It is the opium of the people. . . . Thus, the critique of religion is the critique in embryo of the vale of tears of which religion is the halo.' Marx here insists on the inseparability of religion and society whose disjunction is the premise of the mystical revival.

32 For example Steven T. Katz comments that the mystics 'had knowledge by acquaintance, what their communities taught as knowledge by description. They had existential knowledge of what their co-religionists knew only through propositions' ('The "Conservative" Character of Mysticism' in *Mysticism and Religious Traditions*, Oxford, Oxford University Press, 1983, p. 21).

33 Steven Katz, 'Language, Epistemology, and Mysticism' in *Mysticism and Philosophical Analysis*, Oxford, Oxford University Press, 1978, p. 30.

34 It is not part of my argument here historically to fix the origins of modernity – rather to argue that what 'modernity' does to any era conceived as pre-modern will partly have a mythological function, and this remains true however the phenomenon is periodized. Any historical narrative that insists, for example, on defining 'modernity' as crisis, or instability will need to posit the period preceding the focus of its interest as placidly stable. Blumenberg and Lowith argue the theme of modernity in relation to the Middle Ages in Hans Blumenberg, *The Legitimacy of the Modern Age*, trans. Robert M. Wallace, Cambridge, Mass., MIT Press, 1983, esp. pp. 457–596; Karl Lowith, *Meaning in History: The Theological Presuppositions of History*, Chicago, University of Chicago Press, 1949. For comments relevant to my concerns here on Blumenberg's extrapolations, see Guiseppe Mazzotta, 'Antiquity and the New Arts in Petrarch' in *The New Medievalism*, ed. Marina Brownlee, Kevin Brownlee and Stephen Nichols, Baltimore, Johns Hopkins University Press, p. 47: 'Blumenberg never stops to consider "modernity" as a theoretical, persistently present construct that posits a break from tradition, only to discover that modernity is forever inscribed in the archives of the past. Nor does he probe the self-evident aporia of any historicist philosophy which affirms the ceaseless mobility of the historical process and yet must arrest history's flow in order to impart new direction to it.'

35 See Theodor W. Adorno and Max Horkheimer, *Dialectic of Enlightenment*, New York, Herder & Herder, 1972; reprint edn, London, Verso, 1979, for the most haunting and relentless exploration of this view.

36 In Adorno and Horkheimer's brutal phrase: 'The disenchantment of the world is the extirpation of animism' (ibid., p. 5).

37 Michel de Certeau, 'Mystic Speech' in *Heterologies*, Manchester, Manchester University Press, 1986, p. 82.

38 ibid., p. 86. Such instability and fragmentation of forms of reference are as evident in the late fourteenth century as they are in the early twentieth century; hence the homology subliminally located in the constant referencing of the mystical revivalists to medieval forms of practice.

39 ibid., p. 87.

40 Robert M. Gimello, 'Mysticism in its Contexts' in *Mysticism and Religious Traditions*, p. 62.

41 See, for example, William Inge: 'There have been two schools of mysticism, one of which distrusts and rejects the affirmations of ordinary consciousness, while the other welcomes the visible as a partial manifestation of the spiritual' (*Mysticism in Religion*, p. 26). The negative mode is usually represented by *The Cloud of Unknowing* (see below), and in the writings of the fourteenth-century Dominican German mystics – Eckhart, Tauler and Suso. The writings of the

positive mystical way are usually represented by Richard Rolle and Margery Kempe. There are several writers who fit uneasily into either of these categories, most obviously Walter Hilton and Julian of Norwich. There are critics of such a dichotomy. See, for example, Steven Ozment, 'Mysticism, Nominalism and Dissent' in *The Pursuit of Holiness in Late Medieval and Renaissance Religion*, ed. C. Trinkaus and H. A. Oberman, Leiden, Brill, 1984, pp. 67–92. See also the discussion of Jean Gerson's versions of contemplation in D. Catharine Brown, *Pastor and Laity in the Theology of Jean Gerson*, Cambridge, Cambridge University Press, 1987, pp. 171–208. The alternative classification suggested by John Hirsh, 'The Experience of God: A New Classification of Certain Late Medieval Affective Texts', *Chaucer Review* 1976, 11, pp. 11–21, proposes that we dispense with the term 'mystical' and substitute the classification 'devotional' or 'affective'.

42 '& þerfore beware þat þou conceyue not bodely þat þat is mente goostly, þof al it be spokyn in bodely wordes, as ben þees: UP or DOUN, IN or OUTE, BEHIND or BEFORE, ON O SIDE or ON OÞER. For þof al þat a þing be neuer so goostly in it-self, neuerþerles ȝit ȝif it schal be spoken of, siþen it so is þat speche is a bodeley werk wrouȝt wiþ þe tonge, þe whiche is an instrument of þe body, it behoueþ alweis be spoken in bodely wordes. But what þerof? Schal it þerfore be taken & conceyuid bodely? Nay, it bot goostly' (*The Cloud of Unknowing and the Book of Privy Counselling*, ed. Phyllis Hodgson, EETS o.s. 218, Oxford, Oxford University Press, 1944, p. 114). The translation in the main body of my text is from Clifton Wolters, *The Cloud of Unknowing and Other Works*, Harmondsworth, Penguin, first published 1961, reprint edn, 1978, p. 136. For an analysis of the *Cloud* author's use of 'bodily' language see John Burrow, 'Fantasy and Language in *The Cloud of Unknowing*', *Essays in Criticism*, 1977, vol. 27, pp. 283–98. The Pseudo-Dionysus was probably a sixth-century Syrian ecclesiast, a Christian Neoplatonist. His extant works – *De divinis nominibus, De mystica theologia, De coelesti hierarchia, De ecclesiatica hierarchia*, and some letters – are printed in Migne, *Patrologia Graeca* vols 3, 4 (Paris, 1857). According to P. G. Thery in *Etudes dionysiennes*, Paris 1932, these works probably became known in the West in the mid-eighth century. The most important later translators and commentators were Erigena, Hugh of St Victor, Albertus Magnus and Thomas Aquinas, amongst others. For the influence of the Pseudo-Dionysus on *The Cloud of Unknowing*, see Hodgson, p. lviii.

43 David Knowles, *The Religious Orders in England*, 3 vols, Cambridge, Cambridge University Press, 1948–9, vol. 2, pp. 222–3, quoted and commented on in Clarissa Atkinson, *Margery Kempe: Mystic and Pilgrim*, Ithaca, Cornell University Press, 1983, p. 204. See also my comments and analysis of this distinction in 'A Very Material Mysticism: The Medieval Mysticism of Margery Kempe' in *Medieval Literature: History, Criticism and Ideology*, ed. David Aers, Brighton, Harvester Press, 1986. The widespread vilification of Margery

Kempe reveals the kind of investment going on in the establishment of these boundaries (see chapter 4 below).

44 Hilda Graef, *The Light and the Rainbow*, London, Longmans, 1959, p. 242.

45 'La familiaritas médiévale se teinta d'une certaine féminitié' (*Dictionnaire de Spiritualité*, in the entry under 'Humanité du Christe', p. 1065).

46 Bechtler, p. 299.

47 Review of *The Book of Margery Kempe, The Spectator*, 16 October 1936. For examples of further startled reviews which indicate the extent to which contemporary understandings of religious experience, nurtured by the 'mystical revival', had taken hold, see John Hirsh, 'Margery Kempe' in *Middle English Prose: A Critical Guide to Major Authors and Genres*, ed. A. S. G. Edwards, New Brunswick, Rutgers University Press, 1984, pp. 109–10.

48 For Lee Patterson's analysis of exegetical traditions of criticism in medieval studies, see *Negotiating the Past: The Historical Understanding of Medieval Literature*, Madison, University of Wisconsin Press, 1987, especially chapter 1. Although other aspects of 'medievalism' have been investigated, for example in Alice Chandler, *A Dream of Order: The Medieval Ideal in Nineteenth Century English Literature*, 1971, and Mark Girouard, *The Return to Camelot: Chivalry and the English Gentleman*, New Haven, Yale University Press, 1981, the specifically religious interests of medievalism have not been subject to a great deal of historiographical analysis. An exception is Kevin L. Morris, *The Image of the Middle Ages in Romantic and Victorian Literature*, London, Croom Helm, 1984.

49 Johan Huizinga, *The Waning of the Middle Ages: A Study of the Forms of Life, Thought and Art in France and the Netherlands in the Fourteenth and Fifteenth Centuries*, Harmondsworth, Penguin, 1955, p. 152. First edn 1924.

50 ibid., p. 153.

51 ibid., p. 153.

52 'Spirituality', as André Vauchez points out, is a nineteenth-century concept. See his *La Spiritualité du moyen âge occidental VIIIe-XIIe siècles*, Paris, Presses Universitaires de France, 1975, p. 5. See also Caroline Walker Bynum's comments in her *Jesus as Mother: Studies in the Spirituality of the High Middle Ages*, Berkeley and Los Angeles, University of California Press, 1982, pp. 3–8. It is Peter Heath's contention that it is the very victory of the protestant reformation that has led to the denigration of the religious practices connected with medieval catholicism. In an article on late medieval urban piety in Hull where he attempts to account for the relative lack of research on late medieval popular religion, he says: 'An even more potent explanation may be the very success of the English Reformation and of Protestant and Erasmian propaganda, which together have largely discouraged extended investigation into the doomed pieties and practices of the orthodox. English medievalists and Reformation scholars alike have tended to approach later medieval religion with Wycliffite

and Lollard denouncements and survival in the forefronts of their minds.' See his article, 'Urban Piety in the Later Middle Ages: the Evidence of Hull Wills' in *The Church, Politics and Patronage in the Fifteenth Century*, ed. R. B. Dobson, Gloucester, P. Sutton, 1984, p. 209. For an excellent account of the recent 'reorientation of the reformation' see Robert Scribner, 'Religion, Society and Culture: Reorienting the Reformation' in *History Workshop*, 1982, nos. 13–16. Amongst British historians, attitudes towards late medieval religious practice and its relation to the reformation is still highly contested. C. Haigh in his *Reformation and Resistance in Tudor Lancashire* (Cambridge, Cambridge University Press, 1987), J. Scarisbrick in his *The Reformation and the English People* (Oxford, Blackwell, 1984), and Norman Tanner in his study of late medieval Norwich, *The Church in Late Medieval Norwich 1370–1532* (Toronto, Pontifical Institute for Medieval Studies, 1984) contend that catholicism was extremely viable at the end of the Middle Ages against Geoffrey Elton in his *Reform and Reformation: England 1509–58* (London, Arnold, 1977) and A. G. Dickens in his *The English Reformation* (London, Batsford, 1964), who argue that anti-catholicism and anti-clericalism were widespread. See Robert Whiting's *The Blind Devotion of the People: Popular Religion and the English Reformation* (Cambridge, Cambridge University Press, 1989) for a recent study.

53 Michel de Certeau, p. 82.

54 But if readers prefer I am happy to supply Gimello's who has a similar anxiety about definition: ' "Mystical writings" are thus texts which discuss the path towards realization of the ultimate knowledge which each particular religion has to offer, and which contain statements about the nature of such knowledge' ('Mystical Literature', p. 77).

55 The terms, 'individualistic subjectivism' and 'monologic utterance' are explored in the chapter on 'Verbal Interaction' in *Marxism and the Philosophy of Language* by V. N. Volosinov, Cambridge, Mass., and London, Harvard University Press, 1973, pp. 83–98 and elsewhere in this important book.

56 Volosinov, p. 84.

57 A reference to Rufus Jones' *The Flowering of Mysticism: The Friends of God in the Fourteenth Century*, New York, Macmillan, 1939, whose chapter 12 describes the 'flowering of mysticism' in England in the fourteenth century. Needless to say Jones finds his explanation for this flowering in the effervescence of the human spirit.

58 Michel de Certeau, pp. 92–3. I deal with this issue at greater length in my article, 'Problems of Authority in Late Medieval English Mysticism: Language, Agency and Authority in *The Book of Margery Kempe*'. *Exemplaria*, 1992, vol. 4(1), pp. 171–99. To put it in more theological language, orthodox understandings of mysticism see it as producing a perfect coincidence between the natural and the revealed. And yet its very existence points, rather, to a disjunction between the two.

59 It is interesting in this respect that Gerson, one of the most influential

of late medieval writers on contemplation, defines the mystical, frequently in terms of its dangers and its unauthorized practices. Furthermore, in his writings he frequently evinced a dislike of 'mixed liquid' metaphors or images which worked in similar ways to dissolve distinctions and boundaries between transcendent and immanent, created and uncreated. D. Catharine Brown talks of the fear he displays towards the following images which he discusses in *Jean Gerson: oeuvres complètes*, ed. P. Glorieux, 10 vols, Paris, 1960–73, vol. 3, pp. 286–7: a drop of water losing its essence in a bottle of wine; food that is converted into bodily nourishment, burning iron that seems to be totally fire; eucharistic transformation, vaporized air, etc., see D. Catharine Brown, pp. 202–3.

60 Walter Hilton debates Richard Rolle's experiences of the fiery love of God, for example; see Michael Sargent, 'Contemporary Criticism of Richard Rolle', *Analecta Carthusiana*, 1981, vol. 55(1), pp. 160–205. See also John Phillips, *The Reformation of Images: Destruction of Art in England, 1535–1660*, Berkeley, University of California Press, 1973; Margaret Aston, *Lollards and Reformers: Images and Literacy in Late Medieval Religion*, London, Hambledon Press, 1984; and my chapters 2 and 3 below.

2 CHRIST'S BODY AND THE IMAGING OF SOCIAL ORDER

1 V. A. Kolvé, *The Play Called Corpus Christi*, Stanford, Stanford University Press, 1966, p. 31 and n. 86, p. 282. Kolvé is quoting from W. W. Greg, *The Trial and Flagellation With Other Studies in the Chester Cycle*, Oxford, Oxford University Press, 1935, p. 159. Much of the empirical information put together for the Records of Early English Drama project had necessitated a revision of Kolvé's formalist thesis.

2 Recent historians of the reformation period have decisively reoriented it by reconsidering the role and function of 'religious practice' rather than doctrinal theology. Their consideration is obviously crucial for thinking about the transition from what have conventionally been termed the medieval and renaissance periods. For an illuminating introduction to the literature, see Bob Scribner's review articles, 'Interpreting Religion in Early Modern Europe', *European Studies Review*, 1983, vol. 13, pp. 89–105 and 'Religion, Society and Culture: Reorientating the Reformation', *History Workshop*, 1982, nos. 13–16, pp. 2–22. And see also the bibliographical articles in *Reformation Europe: A Guide to Research*, ed. Steven Ozment, St Louis, Center for Reformation Research, 1982, especially Natalie Zemon Davies' article, 'From "Popular Religion" to Religious Cultures', pp. 321–41, and Francis Oakley's article, 'Religious and Ecclesiastical Life on the Eve of the Reformation', pp. 5–32. See Guy Swanson, *Religion and Regime: A Sociological Account of the Reformation*, Ann

Arbor, University of Michigan Press, 1967, for an analysis of the reformation in terms of changing understandings of immanence.

3 Elaine Scarry, in her excellent and moving book, *The Body in Pain: The Making and Unmaking of the World*, Oxford, Oxford University Press, 1985, writes in a section entitled 'The Transformation of Body into Voice': 'A large part of the mime of power emerges out of the opposition of body and voice,' and she continues, 'for power is in its fraudulent as in its legitimate claims always based on distance from the body' (pp. 45–6). One section of her book constitutes an analysis of the Old Testament, and here she says: 'in the Hebraic scriptures the relationship between the people and their imagined object (God) is repeatedly represented as a relation between a deeply embodied suffering human being and a wholly *disembodied* (i.e. immune from pain) principle of creating, mediated by the recurring image of a colossal weapon that traverses the space between them' (p. 173). Of course in the late medieval understanding of the Trinity, it is precisely the embodiedness of Christ that allows God still to figure as absent. In this context, see Julian of Norwich's complex contemplation of Trinitarian theology, in her comments in *A Book of Showings*, ed. Edmund Colledge and James Walsh, part 2, (long text), Toronto, Pontifical Institute of Medieval Studies, 1978, p. 588: 'And oure sensuallyte is only in the seconde person, Crist Jhesu, in whom is the fader and the holy gost; and in hym and by hym we be myghtly takyn out of hell and oute of the wrechydnesse in erth, and wurschpfully brought up to hevyn, and blyssydfully onyd to oure substannce, encresyd in rychesse and nobly by all the vertu of Crist and by the grace and werkyng of the holy gost.'

4 I am using 'mentality' in a loose sense here, rather than in the sense given to it in *Annales* historiography. For this usage, see Christopher Lloyd, *Explanation in Social History*, Oxford, Blackwell, 1986, p. 243.

5 For further details on Despenser's crushing of the Peasants' Revolt in East Anglia, see the *Chronicon Henrici Knighton* II, pp. 140–1, excerpted and translated by R. B. Dobson in his *The Peasants' Revolt of 1381*, London, Macmillan, 1970, pp. 237–8. But for a cautionary note, see J. L. Bolton, *The Medieval English Economy 1150–1500*, London, Dent, 1980, pp. 215–16, where he says, 'The stories of ruthless suppression contained in the Chronicles are largely unjustified. A quite remarkable degree of clemency was shown which allowed villeinage in England to die a protracted but quiet death.' For an extraordinary incident indicating the extent to which Christ's body in the eucharistic sense was part of a linguistic currency of revolt, see Rosamond Faith's article, ' "The Great Rumour" of 1377 and Peasant Ideology' in *The English Rising of 1381*, ed. R. H. Hilton and T. H. Aston, Cambridge, Cambridge University Press, 1984, p. 66, where she makes reference to a dispute between the abbey of St Albans and some of its tenants. The previous abbot had confiscated millstones from the tenants' illegal handmills and had them cemented into the abbey floor. Faith quotes Walsingham's account

of a break-in, in 1381, into the abbey cloisters where the millstones were pulled up: 'They took the stones outside and handed them over to the commons, breaking them into little pieces and giving a piece to each person, just as the consecrated bread is customarily broken and distributed in the parish churches on Sundays, so that the people, seeing these pieces, would know themselves to be avenged against the abbey in that cause' (*Gesta abbatum monasterii Sancti Albani, a Thomas Walsingham . . . compilata*, 3 vols, London, Rolls Ser., 1867–9, iii, p. 309 and see below n. 49). For a discussion of the appropriation of eucharistic symbolism in this struggle see Steven Justice, *The Literature of 1381*, forthcoming.

6 See for example John Bossy's comment here, 'In 1400 Christ's sufferings were the theme of a pullulation of passionate or macabre fictions, which it took a century or so to reduce to the relative order of the Stations of the Cross and the Sorrowful Mysteries of the Rosary' (*Christianity in the West 1400–1700*, Oxford, Oxford University Press, 1985, p. 7). Of course any 'repetition' is never entirely that. The context of its utterance, the participants in the representation render its meaning different in different contexts. As Allon White puts it in his essay, 'Bakhtin, Sociolinguistics, and Deconstruction' in *The Theory of Reading*, ed. Frank Gloversmith, Brighton, Harvester, 1984, p. 126, 'Each and every time it is uttered, a word is recontextualized, pulled in a slightly different direction, imbued with a different inflection.' The point is worth labouring because of the way repetition is often invoked in conventional textual criticism. As Margaret Miles puts it: 'The systematic study of historical ideas proceeds by "freeing" a theological or a philosophical statement from its position within a particular discourse so that it can be recognized as the identical concept in a new discursive structure' (*Image as Insight: Visual Understanding in Western Christianity and Secular Culture*, Boston, Beacon Press, 1985, p. 26). The exemplary instances of the uses of Christ's body in this chapter should make it clear that its mere repetition hardly homogenizes those uses.

7 *Heresy Trials in the Diocese of Norwich 1428–31*, ed. Norman P. Tanner, Royal Historical Society, Camden 4th series, vol. 20, London, RHS, 1977, pp. 44–5. And for details of these trials see John A. F. Thomson, *The Later Lollards 1414–1520*, Oxford, Oxford University Press, 1965, pp. 122–3. For two excellent articles on women Lollards see Claire Cross, 'Great Reasoners in Scripture: The Activities of Women Lollards 1380–1530' in *Medieval Women*, ed. Derek Baker, Oxford, Blackwell, 1978, pp. 359–80 (Baxter is cited on p. 363), and Margaret Aston's chapter, 'Lollard Women Priests?' in her book, *Lollards and Reformers: Images and Literacy in Late Medieval Religion*, London, Hambledon Press, 1984, pp. 49–71.

8 These examples are given by Margaret Aston in her essay, 'Wyclif and the Vernacular', *Studies in Church History*, Subsidia 5, Oxford, Blackwell, 1987, p. 292, and n. 29, where she cites numerous other examples in addition to show the Lollard reaction to conventional eucharistic doctrine.

9 For Baxter's evidence to this effect in her trial, see Tanner, p. 44:
' " . . . et si vos affectatis videre veram crucem Christi ego volo
monstare eam tibi hic in domo tua propria." Et ista iurata asseruit
se libenter videre velle veram crucem Christi. Et prefata Margeria
dixit, "vide" et tunc extendebat brachia sua in longum, dicens isti
iurate, "hec est vera crux Christi, et istam crucem tu debes et potes
videre et adorare omni die hic in domo tua propria, et adeo tu in
vanum laboras quando vadis ad ecclesias ad adorandas sive orandas
aliquas ymagines vel cruces mortuas." ' For another example, see
Bishop Buckingham's accusation of Anne Palmer and six other Nor-
thampton Lollards: 'Item, that it suffices every Christian to serve
God's commandments in his chamber or to worship God secretly
in the field, without paying heed to public prayers in a material
building, lest conforming to the pharisees he is accounted a hypo-
crite; neither is the material church building held among them as
holy church, but rather every such materially built house is called
by them, "caym" castle.' Quoted by Margaret Aston, in 'Caim's
Castles: Poverty, Politics and Disendowment' in *The Church, Politics
and Patronage*, ed. R. B. Dobson, Gloucester, A. Sutton, 1984, p. 48.

10 *The Book of Margery Kempe*, ed. Hope Emily Allen and Sanford
Meech, EETS o.s. 212, Oxford, Oxford University Press, 1940,
p. 23. Kempe is accused of Lollardy in Canterbury, Bristol, Leicester, York, Hull and London, although it is plain that her religiosity
is very different from Baxter's. See below, chapter 4, for a detailed
reading of *The Book of Margery Kempe*.

11 *Jack Upland, Friar Daw's Reply and Upland's Rejoinder*, ed. P. L.
Heyworth, Oxford, Oxford University Press, 1968, pp. 74–5. Exact
authors of these texts are unknown. 'Jack Upland' is, of course, an
assumed persona, and *Jack Upland* is found in two manuscripts.
Upland's Rejoinder is written in the margins of *Friar Daw's Reply*,
both found in Boleian MS Digby 41 (see Heyworth, p. 2).
Heyworth dates *Upland* no earlier than 1390, and posits 1419–20, as
the probably date of *Daw's Reply* (pp. 17–19).

12 Such a view is an utterly conventional deployment of the image of
the body politic, here used to preserve the specific position of the
friar, who, as the proliferating anti-mendicant satire suggests, is an
anomalous figure in estates theory because he neither *works* (like a
labourer) nor *owns* land (like the monastic and secular lords). The
threat implicit in Upland's Rejoinder (see below) is, then, to non-
working religious. For a recent excellent analysis of the role of the
friar in late medieval anti-clericalism, see Wendy Scase's *'Piers
Plowman' and the New Anti-Clericalism*, Cambridge, Cambridge University Press, 1989.

13 See Heyworth, p. 103.

14 For the 'Twelve Conclusions of the Lollards', which give a good
introductory precis of Lollard doctrine, see Anne Hudson, *Selections
From English Wycliffite Writings*, Cambridge, Cambridge University
Press, 1978, pp. 24–9. And for Lollard polemic against images and

pilgrimages, miracle plays, and teachings on the eucharist, see pp. 83–9, 97–104 and 110–15.

15 Rodney Hilton in *Class Conflict and the Crisis of Feudalism*, London, Hambledon Press, 1985, talks about the 'intense social preoccupation of the contemporary literature. . . . the ploughman becomes a disturbing figure – and not simply because he rather than the knight now appears as mankind's guide to salvation' (p. 248). And again, 'the ploughman who was found to be so disturbing *cannot* be clearly separated from the ploughman who was exalted as the embodiment of social and even theological virtue' (p. 249). See, for example, *Pierce the Ploughman's Creed*, EETS o.s. 30, 1867, edited by Skeat, where the ploughman can teach the creed better than any of the orders of monks or friars. In addition, see Hilton's comparative comments on the figures of ploughman and labourer in 'The Social Structure of the Village' in *The English Peasantry in the Later Middle Ages*, Oxford, Clarendon Press, 1965, p. 21.

16 The Ordinance of Labour (1349) was expanded in the Statute of 1351. For details see Bertha Putnam, *The Enforcement of the Statute of Labourers*, New York, Columbia University Press, 1908. J. L. Bolton, in *The Medieval English Economy*, London, Dent, 1980, p. 237, talks of the tension of post-plague England in the following terms: 'So the bonds of manorial discipline were broken: customary tenants could not be forced to stay on the manor or work for the lord.'

17 Jean Comaroff explores some of the theoretical problems and possibilities that pertain to the 'signifying practice' of bodies social and natural in *Body of Power, Spirit of Resistance: The Culture and History of a South African People*, Chicago, University of Chicago Press, 1985, pp. 6–7.

18 Leonard Barkan, *Nature's Work of Art: The Human Body as Image of the World*, New Haven, Yale University Press, 1975, p. 65, from Aristotle's *Politics*. For an account of late medieval models of social description, including those that use the notion of the body, and the central role of the dissemination of the Aristotelian model (after 1260) in the development of a corporate and contractual view, see Paul Strohm, *Social Chaucer*, Cambridge, Mass., Harvard University Press, 1989, pp. 2–3, 145–51 and 222–3.

19 John of Salisbury develops the most commonly known model in his *Polycraticus*, ed. Clemens Webb, Oxford, Clarendon Press, 1909.

20 See for example Marsilius of Padua (who influenced Wyclif) in the *Defensor pacis*, Dictio II, XXII, 5, ed. C. W. Previte-Orton, Cambridge, The University Press, 1928, p. 345: 'Unde omnes apostolos, prophetas, doctores reliquosque fideles dicit constituere corpus Christi, quod est ecclesia tamquam reliqua membra; neminem autem sicut caput nisi solum Christum.' ('And hence he says that all the apostles, prophets, teachers, and other believers constitute the "body of Christ", which is the church as meaning the other members; but no one is the "head" except Christ alone.') The 'he' referred to here is of course St Paul. Quoted in Gerhart Ladner's essay, 'Medieval

Thought on Church and State' in his *Images and Ideas in the Middle Ages: Selected Studies in History and Art*, Rome, Edizioni di Storia e Letteratura, 1983, vol 2, pp. 454–5.

21 Barkan, p. 88.

22 Quoted in Barkan, p. 82, from a fifteenth-century poem, 'The Descryving of Mannes Membres' in *Twenty-Six Political and Other Poems*, ed. J. Kail, EETS o.s. 124, London, K. Paul, Trench, Trubner & Co., 1904, pp. 123–4.

23 My italics. Mary Douglas, *Natural Symbols: Explorations in Cosmology*, Barrie & Rockliff, 1970; reprint edn, Harmondsworth, Penguin, 1973, p. 101. The entire chapter from which this and the following quotations are excerpted, 'The Two Bodies', makes for fascinating reading.

24 Mikhail Bakhtin, *Rabelais and His World*, MIT, 1968; reprint edn, Bloomington, Indiana University Press, 1984. 'In grotesque realism, therefore, the bodily element is deeply positive. It is presented not in a private, egotistic form, severed from the other spheres of life, but as something universal, representing all the people. As such it is opposed to severance from the material and bodily roots of the world, it makes no pretence to renunciation of the earthy, or independence of the earth and the body. We repeat: the body and bodily life have here a cosmic and at the same time an all-people's character; this is not the body and its physiology in the modern sense of these words, because it is not individualized. The material bodily principle is contained not in the biological individual, not in the bourgeois ego, but in the people, a people who are continually growing and renewed. This is why all that is bodily becomes grandiose, exaggerated, immeasurable' (p. 19).

25 Douglas, p. 98.

26 Douglas, p. 93. She goes on: 'The physical experience of the body, always modified by the social categories through which it is known, sustains a particular view of society. There is a continual exchange of meanings between the two kinds of bodily experience so that each reinforces the categories of the other. As a result of this interaction the body itself is a highly restricted medium of expression. The forms it adopts in movement and repose express social pressures in manifold ways. The care that is given to it, in grooming, feeding and therapy, the theories about what it needs in the way of sleep and exercise, about the stages it should go through, the pains it can stand, its span of life, all the cultural categories in which it is perceived, must correlate closely with the categories in which society is seen in so far as these also draw upon the same culturally processed idea of the body.'

27 The notion of 'three bodies' is developed in Margaret Lock and Nancy Scheper-Hughes' article, 'A Critical-Interpretive Approach in Medical Anthropology: Rituals and Routines of Discipline and Dissent' in *Medical Anthropology: A Handbook of Theory and Method*, ed. Thomas M. Johnson and Carolyn F. Sargent, New York, Greenwood Press, 1990, pp. 50–1. Lock and Scheper-Hughes are

consciously elaborating on Mary Douglas' 'Two Bodies' and John O'Neill's *Five Bodies: The Human Shape of Modern Society*, Ithaca, Cornell Univeristy Press, 1985. Peter Travis marshals O'Neill's categories for his own argument in 'The Social Body of the Dramatic Christ in Medieval England' in *Early Drama to 1600*, ed. Albert Tricomi, *Acta*, 1985, vol. 13, p. 18.

28 Peter Stallybrass and Allon White, *The Politics and Poetics of Transgression*, London, Methuen, 1986, p. 192.

29 Comaroff, pp. 8–9. Such an analysis enables the vital linking of symbolic construction and historical transition.

30 Quoted in Brian Tierney, *The Crisis of Church and State 1050–1300*, Englewood Cliffs, N.J., Prentice-Hall, Inc. 1964, p. 188. Tierney comments on p. 172: 'The struggle between Pope Boniface VIII and King Philip the Fair of France was the first medieval conflict of church and state which can properly be described as a dispute over national sovereignty.' For further discussion of the notion of Corpus Christi as disputed symbol between 'spiritual oneness' over 'secular multiplicity', see 'The Corporate Idea in the Middle Ages', *Review of Politics*, 1947, vol. 9, pp. 423–52.

31 Stallybrass and White, p. 194.

32 Ernst Kantorowicz, *The King's Two Bodies*, Princeton, Princeton University Press, 1957, p. 196. See also Henri de Lubac, *Corpus mysticum: l'eucharistie et l'église au moyen âge*, Paris, Aubier, 1959.

33 Kantorowicz, p. 196.

34 ibid., p. 197.

35 'Una vera est fidelium universalis ecclesia, extra quam nunnus omnino salvatus. In qua idem ipse sacerdos, et sacrificium Jesus Christus; cujus corpus et sanguis in sacramento altaris sub speciebus panis et vini veraciter continentur; transubstantiatis, pane in corpus, et vino in sanguinem, potestate Divina. . . . Et hoc utique sacramentum nemo potest conficere, nisi sacerdos, qui fuerit rite ordinatus secundum claves ecclesiae', *Concilium Laterensae*, IV, chapter 1, Mansi, vol. 22, col. 982, quoted in Jeremy Cohen, *The Friars and the Jews: The Evolution of Medieval Anti-Judaism*, Ithaca and London, Cornell University Press, 1982, p. 251.

36 Nancy Jay, 'Sacrifice as Remedy for Having Been Born of Woman' in *Immaculate and Powerful: The Female in Sacred Image and Social Reality*, ed. Clarissa Atkinson, Constance Buchanan and Margaret Miles, Boston, Beacon Press, 1985, p. 300.

37 Robert Moore, *The Formation of a Persecuting Society*, Oxford, Blackwell, 1987.

38 Cohen, p. 254.

39 The term 'laicization' in convincingly deployed by J. R. Strayer in his article, 'The Laicization of French and English Society in the Thirteenth Century', *Speculum*, 1940, vol 15, pp. 76–85. He describes laicization as 'the development of a society in which primary allegiance is given to lay governments, in which final decisions regarding social objectives are made by lay governments, in which the church is merely a private society with no public powers or

duties' (p. 76). I am using the term here to refer more specifically to the relationship between clergy and populace, and to the popularization of conventual and monastic models of piety outside the monasteries, and anchorites' cells, but the connections between the two uses are evidently there for example in the temporal theories of John Wyclif. For an examination of the religious experiences of the laity see André Vauchez, *Les Laïcs au moyen âge: pratiques et expériences religieuses*, Paris, Editions du Cerf, 1987.

40 Margaret Aston makes the point that it was common, and not 'disrespectful in itself' to refer to the eucharistic bread as 'Christ in a cake'. See her article, 'Wyclif and the Vernacular', *Studies in Church History*, Subsidia 5, Oxford, Blackwell, 1987, p. 288, n. 20. See also *Legends of the Holy Rood*, ed. R. Morris, EETS o.s. 46, 1871, p. 211: 'His fleissh fedith more and lesse/And fendith us from feendis fere;/ The kirnell sprang at Christemasse/That now is crist in a cake clere/The preest drynketh blesyd bere,/Goddis blood in sacrament./ Almyghty God omnipotent,/Hys blessyd body hath sent/To fede hys freendys here.' Kolvé comments in his *The Play Called Corpus Christi*, that the 'Sacrament of the Altar was often spoken of as a kind of banquet which had its beginning on Christmas Day'.

41 The feast was unaugurated by the Bishop of Liège in 1246, and declared a feast for the entire church in 1264 by Pope Urban IV. It was introduced in England in 1318. See Dennis Steel Devlin, 'Corpus Christi: A Study in Medieval Eucharistic Theory, Devotion and Practice', Ph.D. dissertation, University of Chicago, 1975, p. 4; Clifford Davidson, 'Thomas Aquinas, the Feast of Corpus Christi and the English Cycle Plays', *Michigan Academician*, 1974, vol. 7, pp. 103–10; Miri Rubin's chapter, 'A Feast is Born' in her *Corpus Christi: The Eucharist in Late Medieval Culture*, Cambridge, Cambridge University Press, 1991, pp. 164–212.

42 On functionalist social theory generally, see Charles Taylor's excellent essay, 'Understanding and Ethnocentrism' in *Philosophy and Social Science: Philosophical Papers*, vol. 2, Cambridge, Cambridge University Press, 1985, especially p. 122: 'Let us say that there is some truth in the claim that religions generally contribute to social integration; and that we can establish this. The question still arises of the significance of this finding. How much can we explain of the actual shape of the religious practice in this society by this functional theory?' I take very seriously Taylor's claim elsewhere in the same essay: 'Interpretative social science cannot by-pass the agent's self-understanding' (p. 118). Functionalist accounts are very much concerned with the way communities define themselves as such. For a fascinating account of the historiographical usage of the term 'community' see the article by E. J. Calhoun, 'Community: Toward a Variable Conceptualization for Comparative Research', *Social History*, January 1980, vol. 5, pt 1, pp. 105–27, especially p. 106, where Calhoun makes the point that the term 'community' is invariably invoked to 'describe that way of life held inviolable from the immemorial past, but always just on the point of vanishing'. He

points out that the term becomes current during the dramatic changes in the late eighteenth and nineteenth centuries and is governed by a 'contraposition of ideas of country and city'. In a sense the etymology of the term has certain striking parallels with the shift located in my first chapter, where 'mysticism' comes to stand for a 'vanishing' religion.

43 Mervyn James, 'Ritual, Drama and Social Body in the Late Medieval English Town', *Past and Present*, 1983, no. 98, pp. 3–29.

44 ibid., p. 4.

45 ibid., p. 4.

46 Charles Phythian Adams, 'Ceremony and the Citizen: The Communal Year at Coventry 1450–1550' in *Crisis and Order in English Towns 1500–1700: Essays in Urban History*, ed. Peter Clark and Paul Slack, Toronto, University of Toronto Press, 1972, p. 59.

47 The phrase 'continuous political fissure' is taken from R. B. Dobson's article, 'The Risings in York, Beverley and Scarborough, 1380–1381', in *The English Rising of 1381*, ed. R. H. Hilton and T. H. Aston, Cambridge, Cambridge University Press, 1984: see esp. pp. 139–42. For late medieval town life see especially Charles Phythian Adams' essay, 'Urban Decay in Late Medieval England' in *Towns in Societies: Essays in Economic History and Historical Sociology*, ed. Philip Abrams and E. A. Wrigley, Cambridge, Cambridge University Press, 1978, pp. 159–87.

48 Alan H. Nelson, *The Medieval English Stage: Corpus Christi Pageants and Plays*, Chicago and London, University of Chicago Press, 1974, pp. 13 and 223, n. 38. The quotation is from the Newcastle upon Tyne Archives Office, MS Enrolment Book IV, fol. 56ᵛ. Nelson comments that although the ordinance is dated 1536, it may refer to disorders mentioned in the Coopers' Ordinance of 1426. Nelson also refers to a Corpus Christi procession of 1399 in Chester, giving rise to 'a horrifying fracas between the masters and journeymen of the Weavers and Fullers, which took place in front of St Peter's Church at the intersection of the four major streets of the city' (see p. 154).

49 James, p. 11: 'The cultic terminology, then, with its overflow into secular usage, provides an apt commentary on the aspect of the feast in which social wholeness was the central emphasis. This aspect received proper visual expression in the nature of the procession, which was itself the wholeness of the urban social body, gathered in unity and concord to venerate the Corpus Christi, itself a central symbol of social wholeness, and joined in this by the massed crowds through which it moved.'

50 Bossy talks of the transfer of the 'socially integrative powers of the host away from the mass as such and into the feast of Corpus Christi, and by way of that feast to the rituals of monarchy and of secular community'. See John Bossy, 'The Mass as a Social Institution 1200–1700', *Past and Present*, 1983, no. 100, pp. 29–61. Both Bossy and James rely on a Durkheimian account of rite. Such an

understanding is criticized by Steven Lukes in his article, 'Political Ritual and Social Integration', *Sociology*, 1975, vol. 9, pp. 289–308.

51 James, p. 6.

52 ibid., p. 6.

53 See Raymond Firth, *Symbols Public and Private*, Ithaca, Cornell University Press, 1973, p. 425, where he makes the point, 'The doctrine of the Eucharist is then a statement about power and the source of power. It is an assertion that the symbol is not merely about power, but in its inner substance is power. Propositions of this kind are not capable of proof or disproof. But they have sociological implications, including those of defining group allegiance.'

54 Excerpted from Walsingham's *Historia Anglicana* II, 8–13 in *The Peasants' Revolt of 1381*, ed. R. B. Dobson, London, Macmillan, 1970, p. 367. And see Gordon Leff, *Heresy in the Later Middle Ages*, Manchester, Manchester University Press, 1967, p. 561, for a discussion of the connection between Lollardy and sedition. And of course Margaret Aston's article of that name, 'Lollardy and Sedition 1381–1431' in her *Lollards and Reformers*, pp. 1–49. And see also Robert Kett's reference to the holy blood which perhaps exemplifies most clearly the potential results of the democratization of eucharistic symbolism: 'We pray that all bonds men may be made ffre for god made all ffre wᵗ his precious blode sheddyng' quoted in Rodney Hilton, *Bond Men Made Free: Medieval Peasant Movements and the English Rising of 1381*, London, Methuen, 1973, p. 8, from a petition by Robert Kett and his followers, at Mousehold Heath outside Norwich, 1549, and printed in *Kett's Rebellion in Norfolk: Being a History of the Great Civic Commotion that Occurred at the time of the Reformation in the Reign of Edward VI*, by F. W. Russell, 1859, p. 51. Hilton makes the following comment: 'This clause, though late in date, epitomizes the chief desire of rebellious serfs throughout medieval Europe.'

55 Aston, 'Wyclif and the Vernacular', p. 291. And see J. I. Catto's excellent discussion in his 'John Wyclif and the Cult of the Eucharist', *Studies in Church History*, Subsidia 4, Oxford, Blackwell, 1985, p. 269: 'The crisis of Wyclif's career came with striking rapidity after he broadcast, in his "Confessio" or public statement in the Oxford schools on 10 May 1381, his opinion that the presence of the body of Christ in the eucharist was figurative, "sacramental," or in some sense, to anyone not acquainted with the terms of his own mental world, less than real.' Catto goes on to make the vital point that to answer the question as to why this debate should generate such violent, protracted and heated commentary, 'we shall have to consider the religion of his time not as theory but as practice: the cult of the eucharist both within and outside the mass, both the miracle of transubstantiation and the celebration of Corpus Christi' (p. 270).

56 Leff, p. 557

57 Charles Zika, 'Hosts, Processions and Pilgrimages: Controlling the

Sacred in Fifteenth-Century Germany', *Past and Present*, 1988, no. 118, p. 30.

58 See, for example, Dom Gregory Dix, *The Shape of the Liturgy*, London, Dacre Press, 1945, pp. 599–600: 'The old corporate worship of the eucharist is declining into a mere focus for the subjective devotion of each separate worshipper in the isolation of his own mind and it is the latter which is beginning to seem to him more important than the corporate act. The part of the individual layman in that corporate action had long ago been reduced from "doing" to "seeing" and "hearing." Now he is even beginning to think that over much "seeing" (ceremonial) and "hearing" (music) are detrimental to proper "thinking" and "feeling". While the catholic doctrines of the priesthood and the conversion of the elements were retained, the remnants of the corporate action still provided an objective centre which was identical for all present. But it needed only a continuation of the shift of emphasis for the eucharistic action to come to be regarded as a mere *occasion for* or accompaniment to the individual's subjective thought and emotion.' And again Theodor Klauser, *A Short History of the Liturgy*, Oxford, Oxford University Press, 1969, p. 97: '. . . the liturgy which was once and always should be the common act of priest and people, became now exclusively a priestly duty. The people were still present, but they devoted themselves during the sacred action to non-liturgical, subjective, pious exercises.' In this connection see John Bossy's comment on some of the extant liturgical history in his 'The Mass as a Social Institution', where he notes the 'liturgist's concern to reveal the ideal Christian community existing somewhere in the past, or the apologist's interest in the theological or practical abuses thought to have affected the mass in the Middle Ages' (p. 30). Finally, an account of late medieval fervour over the sight of the elevated host is given in E. Dumoutet, *Le Désir de voir l'hoste et les origines de la dévotion au saint-sacrement*, Paris, Beauchesnes, 1926.

59 Caroline Walker Bynum, *Holy Feast and Holy Fast*, Berkeley, University of California Press, 1987, p. 57.

60 Dom Gregory Dix, *The Shape of the Liturgy*, pp. 599–600.

61 Printed in *Tracts on the Mass*, ed. J. Wickham Legg for the Henry Bradshaw Society, vol. 27, London, 1904, pp. 19–29. And for a commentary on Langforde's work in the context of liturgical history, see Dix, pp. 605–8. Dix's commentary makes the point that the devotional exercises which Langforde suggests accompany the eucharistic action, but are not included within it: '. . . the liturgical action, performed exclusively by the priest and server, proceeds in front of the layman in complete detachment from him' (p. 607).

62 Catto, p. 286.

63 Zika, p. 58.

64 For example, see *Middle English Sermons*, ed. W. Ross, EETS o.s. 209, 1938, p. 128: 'It is enough to thee to believe as Holy Churche teacheth thee and let the clerks alone with the argument.' The prohibition is here in direct relation to lay arguments over the

meaning of the sacrament. See Janet Coleman, *Medieval Readers and Writers 1350–1400*, London, Hutchinson, 1981, especially chapter 2, 'Vernacular Literacy and Lay Education', pp. 18–58.

65 See Aston, 'Devotional Literacy' in *Lollards and Reformers*, and her 'Wyclif and the Vernacular'. Following the Fourth Lateran of 1215, frequent synodal constitutions of the English bishops during the thirteenth and fourteenth centuries developed programmes of religious instruction for the laity. Provisions for *clerical* education were part and parcel of such provisions. Manuals written in the vernacular for the clergy include such texts as *Speculum sacerdotale*, ed. Edward H. Weatherly, EETS o.s. 200, London, Oxford University Press, 1936; *Myrc's Duties of a Parish Priest*, ed. Edward Peacock, EETS o.s. 31, 1868, rpt, London, Kegan, Trench, Trubner & Co., 1902; *Robert of Brunne's Handlyng Synne*, ed. F. J. Furnivall, EETS o.s. 119, London, Kegan Paul, Trench, Trubner & Co., 1901, which devotes some thousand lines to a discussion of the sacrament of the altar; *The Lay Folk's Catechism*, ed. Thomas F. Simmons and Henry E. Nolloth, EETS o.s. 118, London, Kegan Paul, Trench, Trubner & Co., 1901, a text in numerous manuscripts composed by Jon Gatryge and based on a loose expansion of Thoresby's catechism (see *Lay Folk's Catechism*, p. 1), and such texts as the 'De festo corporis cristi' contained in the Vernon MS. 195, and addressed to 'ȝe lewede Men' as a means of encouraging participation in the feast of Corpus Christi; *Minor Poems of the Vernon MS.* ed. Carl Horstmann, EETS o.s. 98, London, Kegan Paul, Trench, Trubner & Co., 1892, pp. 168–97. See also Robert R. Raymo's chapter 'Works of Religious and Philosophical Instruction' in Albert Hartung, *A Manual of the Writings of Middle English 1050–1500* vol. 7, 1986. For a full survey of the vernacular literature associated with the dissemination of eucharistic practice see Michèle Theresa Priscandero, 'Middle English Eucharistic Verse: Its Imagery, Symbolism and Typology', Ph.D. dissertation, St John's University, New York, 1975; and Sister Loretta McGarry, 'The Holy Eucharist in Middle English Homiletic and Devotional Verse', Ph.D. dissertation, Catholic University of Washington, 1936.

66 Aston, *Lollards and Reformers*, p. 132, where she comments, 'For lay people to prove themselves capable of theology, direct auditors of God, was to change the world.'

67 Aston in her chapter, 'Devotional Literacy' in *Lollards and Reformers*, p. 132, puts it like this: 'How could Christ himself have dictated to St. Bridget the rule of the Order of St. Saviour to be followed at Vadstena? Since it was in *Swedish* was not this inherently improbable?' And see Eric Colledge, 'Epistola solitarii ad reges: Alphonse of Pecha as Organizer of Birgittine and Urbanist Propaganda', *Medieval Studies*, 1956, vol. 28, p. 43.

68 See Allon White's article, 'Bakhtin, Sociolinguistics and Deconstruction' in F. Gloversmith, ed., *The Theory of Reading*, Brighton, Harvester, 1984, pp. 142–3.

69 M. Bakhtin, *The Dialogic Imagination*, ed. M. Holquist, trans, C.

Emerson and M. Holquist, Austin, University of Texas, 1981, p. 271.

70 *Dialogic Imagination*, p. 62, and see also p. 271.

71 ibid., pp. 68 and 293.

72 *Lanterne of Light* ed. L. M. Swinburn, EETS o.s. 151, London, Kegan Paul, Trench, Trubner & Co., 1917, pp. 84–5. The *Lanterne of Light* is an early fifteenth-century Lollard tract.

73 Roy M. Haines, ' "Wilde Wittes and Wilfulness": John Swetstock's Attack on Those "Poyswunmongeres", the Lollards', *Studies in Church History*, Subsidia 8, 1972, p. 149.

74 For a discussion of the relationship between agency and structure in social theory, see Antony Giddens, *The Constitution of Society: Outline of the Theory of Structuration*, Cambridge, Polity Press, 1984.

75 John O'Neill, *Five Bodies: The Human Shape of Modern Society*, Ithaca, Cornell University Press, 1985, p. 22.

76 For a fuller analysis of some of these texts, see chapter 3, where I also examine the analytic force of the concept of 'internalization' in relation to this literature.

77 'The Abbey of the Holy Ghost' in *Middle English Religious Prose* ed., N. F. Blake, London, Arnold, 1972, pp. 88–103. This piece is also available in Horstmann's *Yorkshire Writers* vol. 1, London, Swan Sonnenschein & Co., 1895. This is a translation of a French prose tract, *Abbaye du Saint Esprit*, and dates from the mid-fourteenth century. D. P. Consacro interprets it as a treatise on the mixed life addressed to men and women who cannot enter a religious community. See Consacro, 'A Critical Edition of The Abbey of the Holy Ghost from All Known Extant Eng MSS with Introduction, Notes, and Glossary', Ph.D. dissertation, Fordham University, 1971. See Raymo, p. 2340.

78 The Lambeth Constitutions are printed in D. Wilkins, *Concilia Magnae Brittaniae et Hibernas* vol. 3, London, 1737, p. 306.

79 *Meditations on the Life of Christ*, trans. Isa Ragusa and Rosalie Green, Princeton, Princeton University Press, 1961, p. 5.

80 Ragusa and Green, p. 2.

81 John Huizinga, *The Waning of the Middle Ages*, Harmondsworth, Penguin, 1924, p. 200.

82 Bossy, p. 59. It should perhaps be noted here that Bossy is not altogether free himself from a nostalgia for 'the polyphonic mysteries of the mass' (his words on p. 61). See for example p. 59, where he asserts that there is indeed a 'unity seeking motive in late medieval Catholicism' which 'ought not to be written off as the imposition of priests and patricians'.

83 Leff, p. 31.

84 Norbert Elias, *The Civilizing Process*, New York, Pantheon Books, 1978, p. 24. He goes on: 'In order to pass beyond this dead end of sociology and the social sciences in general it is necessary to make clear the inadequacy of both conceptions, that of the individual outside society and equally that of the society outside individuals. This is difficult as long as the encapsulation of the self within itself

serves as the untested basis of the image of the individual, and as long as, in conjunction with this, the concepts, "individual" and "society" are understood as if they related to unchanging states.'

85 Maurice Merleau Ponty, *Phenomenology of Perception*, London, Routledge & Kegan Paul, 1962 p. 146.

86 See especially his *Discipline and Punish: The Birth of the Prison*, Harmondsworth, Penguin, 1977.

87 Bryan Turner, *The Body and Society: Explorations in Social Theory*, Oxford, Blackwell, 1984, p. 39.

88 Turner, p. 41.

3 'DYVERSE IMAGINACIOUNS OF CRYSTES LYF': Subjectivity, embodiment and crucifixion piety

1 The phrase 'dyverse ymaginaciouns of Cristes lyf' is from Nicholas Love's *Mirrour of the Blessyd Lyf of Jesu Christ*, ed. Lawrence Powell, London, Henry Frowde, 1908, p. 9.

2 The 'mixed life' comes to denote the kind of devotional life for those who wished to lead lives of contemplation and yet had to remain 'active' in the world. Walter Hilton is one of the major exponents of this life. See *Walter Hilton's Mixed Life*, edited from Lambeth Palace MS 472 by S. J. Ogilvie Thomson, Saltzburg, 1986, pp. 89–113, and below. For an analysis of the audience for whom texts on the 'mixed life' were addressed, see S. S. Hussey, 'The Audience for Middle English Mystics' in *De cella in seculum*, ed, Michael G. Sargent, Cambridge, D. S. Brewer, 1989, pp. 109–22, and Wolfgang Riehle, *The Middle English Mystics*, London, Routledge & Kegan Paul Ltd, 1981, pp. 13–23.

3 See Harold Kane, ed., *The Prickynge of Love*, Salzburg, Institut für Anglistik und Amerikanistik, 1983, and for the *Mirrour* see Powell. Clare Kirchberger has edited a modern English version of *The Prickynge* from the Vernon MS and Bodley 480: see *The Goad of Love: An Unpublished Translation of the* Stimulus amoris *Formerly Attributed to St Bonaventura*, Oxford, Oxford University Press, 1957. For further details on the popularity, exemplarity and availability of these texts, see below.

4 'What is the son of Man but the name of the assumed flesh?' (Bernard Abbot of Clairvaux, *De gradibus humilitatis*, trans. George Bosworth Burch, Cambridge, Mass., Harvard University Press, 1940, pp. 140–1).

5 James Marrow, *Passion Iconography in Northern European Art in the Late Middle Ages and Early Renaissance: A Study of the Transformation of Sacred Metaphor into Descriptive Narrative*, Ars Neerlandica, Studies in the History of Art of the Low Countries, Brussels, Van Ghemmert Pub. Co., 1979, p. 1.

6 Galatians 2.19–20. For the Pauline and early Christian contexts of *imitatio* see Peter Brown, *The Body and Society: Men, Women and*

143

Sexual Renunciation in Early Christianity, New York, Columbia University Press, 1988, pp. 33–65.

7 *Cur Deus homo* can be found in F. S. Schmitt, ed., *S. Anselmi: opera omnia*, 6 vols, Edinburgh, Nelson, 1946, vol. 2, and in translation in *St Anselm: Basic Writings*, trans. S. N. Deane and introduced by Charles Hartshorne, La Salle, Open Court Publishing Co., 1903; reprint edn, 1962, pp. 177–288. The purpose of *Cur Deus homo* is to show that the incarnation is a necessary fact of Christian theology, and the only possible means of man's redemption. As Theresa Coletti notes: '. . . it is the sharing of human flesh between man and God that makes the sacrifice meaningful' in 'Spirituality and Devotional Images: The Staging of the Hegge Cycle', Ph.D. dissertation, University of Rochester, 1975, p. 38. For an analysis of the argument see R. W. Southern, *Saint Anselm and His Biographer: A Study of Monastic Life and Thought 1059–1130*, Cambridge, Cambridge University Press, 1963, pp. 77–121 and for a discussion of the Anselmian theory of atonement in relation to discourses of the self and the sacrament of confession see Linda Georgianna, *The Solitary Self: Individuality in the Ancrene Wisse*, Cambridge, Mass., Harvard University Press, 1981, pp. 91–3.

8 'Dicunt autem Scriptura: "Sicut anima rationalis et caro unus homo, ita Deus et homo unus est Christus." Videte similitudinem. Bene dico anima et caro est homo et iterum bene dico homo est persona. Et rursum bene dico homo est persona. Et rursum bene dico anima et caro est una persona' (Hugh of St Victor, *De sacramentis Christianae fidei*, PL 176: 405A; quoted in Coletti, p. 41; translation in *On the Sacraments of the Christian Faith* by Roy J. Deferrari, Medieval Academy of America, Cambridge, Mass., Crimson Printing Company, 1951, p. 242). See also Gerhard B. Ladner, *Ad imaginem Dei: The Image of Man in Medieval Art*, Latrobe, Pa., Archabbey Press, 1965, pp. 53–8 for a discussion of the influence of Hugh of St Victor in the development of the 'new psychology' of the high Middle Ages. The analogy of the relation between body and soul and the human and divine natures of Christ, though it seems to originate with Hugh of St Victor, is also found amongst the Cistercian writings of Aelred of Rievaulx and Alcher of Clairvaux (see Ladner, p. 59).

9 'Corpus sensu ascendit, spiritus sensualite descendit' (Hugh of St Victor, *De unione corporis et spiritus* PL 177: 285A).

10 'Quoniam igitur prius est ascendere quam descendere in scala Iacob, primum gradum ascensionis collocemus in imo, ponendo totum istum mundum sensibilem nobis tanquam speculum, per quod transeamus ad Deum, opificem summum, ut simis veri Hebraei transeuntes de Aegypto ad terram Patribus repromissimam' (Bonaventura, *Itinerarium mentis in Deum*, Texte de Quarrachi, ed. Henry Dumery, Paris, J. Vrin, 1960, pp. 34–5). Coletti refers to the *Itinerarium* as the definitive statement about such an 'exemplarist understanding of creation' (p. 46).

11 E. de Bruyne, *L'Esthetique du moyen âge*, Louvain, 1949, p. 93, quoted in M. D. Chenu, *Nature, Man and Society in the Twelfth*

Century: Essays on New Theological Perspectives in the Latin West, selected, ed. and trans. by Jerome Taylor and Lester Little, Chicago, University of Chicago Press, 1968, p. 134.

12 'Omnis figura tanto evidentius veritatem demonstrat, quantoper dissimilem similitudinem figurat se esse et non veritatem probat, atque nostrum animum in hoc magis dissimiles similitudines ad veritatem reducint, quo ipsum in sola similitudine manere non permittent' (*In apocal*, i, PL 196: 689).

13 'Fateor, domine, et gratias ego, quia creasti in me hanc imaginem tuam, ut tui memor te cogitem, te amem. Sed sic est abolita attritione vitiorum, sic est offuscata fumo peccatorum, ut non possit facere ad quod facta est, nisi tu renoves et reformes eam' (*St Anselm's Proslogion*, with translation, introduction and philosophical commentary by M. J. Charlesworth, Oxford, Clarendon Press, 1965, p. 114).

14 Chenu, p. xviii.

15 Chenu, p. 123, Chenu goes on to elaborate the particular conception of symbolism understood here: 'The symbol was the means by which one could approach mystery; it was homogeneous with mystery and not a simple epistemological sign more or less conventional in character.' Such a view indicates how central the concept of *anagoge* was: the truth of thing lay not in their own being, but rather in the way their being reflected God. In Chenu's interpretation all reality is lent a religious character by this way of seeing – 'a preference for *meaning* which expressed the religious character of things, over *explanation* which limited itself to the intrinsic causes of phenomenon' (p. 124).

16 'Verum nos vivimus quidem post corpus: sed ad ea quibus beate vivitur, nullus nobis accessus patet, nisi per corpus. Senserat hoc qui dicebat: *Invisibilia Dei . . . per ea quae facta sunt intellecta conspiciuntur* (Rom. 1.20), Ipsa siquidem quae facta sunt, id est corporalia et visibilia ista, nonnisi per corporis instrumentum sensa, in nostram notitiam veniunt. Habet igitur necessarium corpus spiritualis creatura quae nos sumus, sine quo nimarum nequaquam illam scientiam assequitur, quam solam accepit gradum ad ea, de quorum fit cognitione beata.' See Sermo V, *Cantica canticorum: Eighty Six Sermons on the Song of Solomon*, translated, edited and introduced by S. J. Eales, London, Elliot Stock, 1895, and *Sancti Bernardi, opera omnia*.

17 'Quia carnales sumus, et de carnis concupiscentia nascimur, necesse est ut cupiditas vel amor noster a carne incipiat' (*De diligendo Deo* in *Sancti Bernardi, opera omnia*, vol. 3, ed. J. Leclerq et al., Rome, Editions Cisterciennes, 1958–).

18 Introduction to *De gradibus humilitatis*, p. 69.

19 Friedrich Nietszche, *The Anti-Christ*, Harmondsworth, Penguin, 1968, p. 133.

20 The phrase 'radical reflexivity' is taken from Charles Taylor, *Sources of the Self: The Making of the Modern Identity*, Cambridge, Mass., Harvard University Press, 1989, p. 131, where it is used in a discussion of Augustine.

21 *De gradibus*, p. 147. And, indeed, to know yourself as an embodied, corporeal subject.

22 See Jean Leclerq, *Monks and Love in Twelfth-Century France: Psycho-Historical Essays*, Oxford, Oxford University Press, 1979, chapter 2, 'New Recruitment–New Psychology', pp. 8–26.

23 Talal Asad, 'On Ritual and Discipline in Medieval Christian Monasticism', *Economy and Society*, 1987, vol. 16, pt 2, p. 173.

24 Asad, p. 173.

25 ibid., p. 175.

26 See *City of God*, Book 14, chapter 6 for one version of the Augustinian 'will'.

27 My italics, Asad, p. 184.

28 Asad, p. 175.

29 'Talis est quisque, qualis ejus dilectio est. Terram diligis? Terram eris. Deum diligis? quid dicam, Deus eris.' Quoted by Taylor, p. 128.

30 See chapter 2 for a discussion of James.

31 This line is from a lyric recorded in a collection of materials for preaching assembled *c.* 1372 by John of Grimestone, a Norfolk Franciscan friar. The poem is printed as no. 71 in Carleton Brown, ed., *Religious Lyrics of the Fourteenth Century*, Oxford, Oxford University Press, 1952.

32 The phrase 'strategies of profanation' is coined by Peter Travis in his *Dramatic Design in the Chester Cycle*, Chicago, University of Chicago Press, 1982, p. 23. Travis locates 'the full artistic development' of such strategies in the Corpus Christi plays.

33 For discussion of Franciscanism see John Moorman, *A History of the Franciscan Order: From its Origins to the Year 1517*, Oxford, Clarendon Press, 1968; John Fleming, *An Introduction to the Franciscan Order*, Chicago, Franciscan Herald Press, 1977; David Jeffrey, *The Early English Lyric and Franciscan Spirituality*, Lincoln, University of Nebraska Press, 1971; Denise Despres, *Ghostly Sights: Visual Meditation in Late Medieval Literature*, Norman, Pilgrim Books, 1989; Lester Little, *Religious Poverty and the Profit Economy in Medieval Europe*, Ithaca, Cornell University Press, 1978. For a discussion of the influence of Franciscans in the circulation of medieval devotional writings in English see Michael Sargent, 'Bonaventura English: A Survey of the Middle English Prose Translations of Early Franciscan Literature', *Analecta Cartusiana*, 1984, vol. 106, pp. 145–76.

34 This is not to deny the intense relationship between scholasticism and spirituality amongst the fraternal orders, or the association of the most spurious forms of 'glosing' with friars in the anti-mendicant satire of the late Middle Ages. Franciscan exegesis stressed the 'literal' before the other scriptural senses. A distinction needs to be made between the devotion to apostolic simplicity outlined by Francis and the full-scale institutionalization of the order after his death. That distinction informed the persistent charges of hypocrisy that surrounded the friars more surely and systematically than nearly any other religious 'type'.

35 In PL 182 cols 1133–42, PL 184 cols 741–68, PL 159 cols 272–90, and PL 94 cols 561–8 respectively. For a discussion of these works see Marrow, p. 11. All of these texts, though written variously in the first and third person, encourage a response that collapses past and present time; the reader is urged to imagine him/herself present at the events described. No longer merely descriptive or representational, these narrative sequences require an intense form of participation which changes the structures of identity at play.

36 See Michael Sargent, 'Bonaventura English' and Elizabeth Salter, *Nicholas Love's 'Myrrour of the Blessyd Lyf of Jesu Christ'*, *Analecta Cartusiana*, 1974, vol. 10, Salzburg, Institut für Englische Sprache und Literatur, and 'The Manuscripts of Nicholas Love's "Myrrour of the Blessyd Lyf of Jesu Christ" and Related Texts' in *Middle English Prose: Essays on Bibliographical Problems*, ed. A. S. G. Edwards and Derek Pearsall, New York, Garland, 1981, pp. 115–27.

37 A distinction needs to be made here between the kinds of work generated by the reforms of Twelfth Lateran, and effected in England most influentially by John Pecham, Franciscan friar and Archbishop of Canterbury after the Lambeth constitutions of 1281, and by John Thoresby, Archbishop of York from 1353 to 1373, who was an active encourager of reform in the diocese of York, and the genre of the *Life of Christ* reviewed by Salter. The two categories certainly overlap in terms of their pedagogic function, but address their readers in very different ways: the former is more hortatory and instructional, the latter moving between the pedagogic and the far more labile area of participation, 'theatre' and identification. For the texts and mechanisms of dissemination sponsored by reforms of 1215 see Leonard E. Boyle, 'The Fourth Lateran Council and Manuals of Popular Theology' in *The Popular Literature of Medieval England*, ed. Thomas J. Heffernan, Knoxville, University of Tennessee Press, 1985, pp. 30–44; Judith Shaw, 'The Influence of Canonical and Episcopal Reform on Popular Books of Instruction' in Heffernan, pp. 44–61; G. H. Russell, 'Vernacular Instruction of the Laity in the Later Middle Ages in England: Some Texts and Notes', *Journal of Religious History*, 1962–3, vol. 2, pp. 98–119. For the reforms associated with the figure of Thoresby see Jonathan Hughes, *Pastors and Visionaries: Religion and Secular Life in Late Medieval Yorkshire*, Cambridge, Boydell Press, 1988. For a discussion of the genre of medieval Lives of Christ, see Salter's *Nicholas Love's 'Myrrour'*, pp. 55–119.

38 See Salter, *Nicholas Love's 'Myrrour'*, p. 95. Salter categorizes the English Lives of Christ written between 1150 and 1500 in five groups allocated according to their techniques of organization of the 'material' of Christ's life. The first group consists in those Lives which are purely informative, and which contain very few meditative additions. The second group consists of material composed of sections of biblical narrative with commentary and interpretation. This group contains works which are much more homiletic than devotional, or emotional in tone and detail. The third group simi-

larly contains paraphrases of biblical text, but differs from the second group in its considerably less systematic arrangement of material. Narrative and dramatic themes are combined, but in a very 'dramatic' way, deploying many of the methods of secular romance. Salter's fourth group, consisting in works written in most cases before the end of the fourteenth century, constitutes a distinct change in emphasis. As Salter puts it: 'They contain, in varying degree, a vernacular expression of the vein of affective meditation on the Humanity of Christ which runs in Latin literature from the time of Anselm onwards' (p. 98). This group, which includes Love's version of the *Meditationes*, is not simply didactic, but contains meditative material, and tends to abjure allegorical interpretative techniques for the realistic detail which will most excite compassion and love. Exegesis is less important for this group than affective response, and those elements of Christ's life most suitable for this purpose are selected, expanded and glossed. In this group she includes six Lives: the *Southern Passion*, ed. B. D. Brown, EETS o.s. 169, 1927; Love's *Mirrour*, ed. Powell; the prose life in Trinity College Cambridge MS B. 2. 18 (unedited, see Salter p. 10 for description); the *Speculum devotorum* (unedited, found in Cambridge University Library MS Gg. 1. 6 and in a MS in the Foyle Collection at Beeleigh Abbey, Maldon; the *Fruyt of Redempcyon* (printed by Winkyn de Worde in 1532); Walter Kennedy's *Passioun of Christ*, ed. J. Schipper, Vienna, 1901. For Salter's discussion, see pp. 97–8. These six works draw on the Cistercian and Franciscan spiritual traditions, as well as the bible and patristic literature. For the popularity of twelfth-century devotional texts in the later Middle Ages, see Giles Constable, 'Twelfth-Century Spirituality and the Late Middle Ages' in *Medieval and Renaissance Studies*, ed. O. B. Hardison, Chapel Hill, University of North Carolina Press, 1971, pp. 27–60.

39 Ogilvie-Thomson, pp. 89–103.
40 See Hussey, p. 113.
41 I am very grateful to Michael Sargent for providing me with a copy of the paper from which this quotation was taken. The paper, 'Contemplative Piety and Popular Piety in Late Medieval England', was read by Sargent at the New Chaucer Society meetings in Vancouver in August 1988. For further consideration of the expansion of audience for vernacular piety in the late Middle Ages see Hilary M. Carey, 'Devout Literate Laypeople and the Pursuit of the Mixed Life in Later Medieval England', *Journal of Religious History*, 1986–7, vol. 14, pp. 361–81. Vincent Gillespie has written about the production of religious books in the period 1375–1475 as 'responses to and catalysts of, the rapidly developing interest in and market for vernacular guides to godliness' in 'Vernacular Books of Religion' in *Book Production and Publishing in Britain 1375–1475*, eds. Jeremy Griffiths and Derek Pearsall, Cambridge, Cambridge University Press, 1989, p. 317. For a further exploration of passion imagery in late medieval vernacular writings in terms of the growing incidence of address to a lay audience see Gillespie's 'Strange Images of Death:

The Passion in Later Medieval English Devotional Writings' in *Zeit, Tod und Ewigkeit in der Renaissance Literatur, Analecta Cartusiana*, 1987, vol. 117, pp. 111–57. Also see the thesis of A. I. Doyle for the role of the clergy in the circulation of theological writings in the later middle Ages, 'A Survey of the Origins and Circulation of Theological Writings in England in the Fourteenth, Fifteenth and Sixteenth centuries', Ph.D. dissertation, Cambridge University, 1953.

42 Emile Durkheim, *The Elementary Forms of the Religious Life*, trans. Joseph Ward Swain, London, Allen & Unwin, 1915, p. 40. For the value of Durkheimian analysis of religious/symbolic form see the essays on social change and sacralization in *Durkheimian Sociology: Cultural Studies*, ed. Jeffrey C. Alexander, Cambridge, Cambridge University Press, 1988, pp. 23–91, and *Culture and Society: Contemporary Debates*, ed. Jeffrey C. Alexander and Steven Seidman, Cambridge, Cambridge University Press, 1990, pp. 17–21 and 147–63.

43 Roger Callois, *Man and the Sacred*, Illinois, Free Press of Glencoe, 1959, p. 23. For Callois, this (Durkheimian) understanding of sacred-profane relations constructs *ritual* as the primary regulator of the transformation of sacred-profane relations. Acts of consecration and deconsecration establish the proper and improper contact of the spheres. This fundamental ambiguity in the category of the sacred is also commented on by Mircea Eliade: 'The ambivalence of the sacred is not only in the psychological order (in that it attracts and repels), but also in the order of values; the sacred is at once "sacred" and "defiled" ', *Patterns in Comparative Religion*, 1958, pp. 14–15. For further comments about the place of ambiguity in religious ritual and symbolism, see below and conclusion.

44 'Any structure of ideas is vulnerable at its margins' (*Natural Symbols*, pp. 121 and 161: 'The danger which is risked by boundary transgression is power.')

45 Peter Stallybrass makes a similar point in a revisionist reading of the Mary Douglas passage quoted above: 'For if the boundaries are indeed vulnerable, they also suggest possible metamorphoses: transgressions of bodily boundaries map transformations of the psychic economy, of spatial division, and of the hierarchies of the social formation' in his article 'Boundary and Transgression: Body, Text, Language', *Stanford French Review*, 1990, vol. 14, p. 16.

46 In discussing the nature of profanation, Paul Boissac has recently made a distinction that is useful for our analysis. He specifies that profanation 'is not so much the breaking of a rule made explicit in a legal code as the exposure of the rule of rules, the principle or principles that are so fundamental for the holding together of the regulative system that they cannot be formulated' (*By Means of Performance: Intercultural Studies of Theatre and Ritual*, ed. Richard Schnechner and Willie Appel, Cambridge, Cambridge University Press, 1990, p. 197). In Boissac's view, it is the nature of the rules transgressed, rather than the quality of the transgressions that distinguishes profanation from simple rule-breaking. 'It is as if the cultural

system with all the prescriptive and prohibitive rules which form its body were actually relying on a few crucial but unformulable rules, some sort of culturally tacit axioms or silent dogmas from which all other rules are derived and justified but which are themselves undemonstrable, unjustifiable and ultimately impotent' (p. 197). Profanation would then constitute a specific class of actions which question these tacit principles through the 'selective transgression of some of the rules derived from them' (p. 199).

47 For a survey of the devotion to Christ's wounds in the late Middle Ages, see L. Gougaud's article; 'La Mesure de la plaie côtée', *Revue d'Histoire Ecclésiastique*, 1924, vol. 20, p. 223, and his book, *Dévotions et pratiques ascétiques au moyen âge*, Paris, Collection Pax, 1925, and Douglas Gray's group of short articles in *Notes and Queries*, 1963, vol. 208, pp. 50–1, 82–9, 127–34, 163–8, which discuss numerous examples from unedited British manuscripts. For a discussion of the establishment of the Mass of the Five Wounds, see R. W. Pfaff, *New Liturgical Feasts in Late Medieval England*, Oxford, Clarendon Press, 1970. Douglas Gray discusses devotion to the wounds and the theme of the passion in the medieval English religious lyric in his *Themes and Images in the Medieval Religious Lyric*, London, Routledge & Kegan Paul, 1972, especially pp. 122–46.

48 Salter, p. 129.

49 *Stimulus amoris Fr. Iacobi Mediolanensis: canticum pauperis Fr. Iannis Peckham*, Bibliotheca Franciscana Ascetica Medii Aevi, iv, Quaracchi, Collegio S. Bonaventura, 1905.

50 The short text is published in the Quaracchi edition. The long text is presented under the authorship of Bonaventura in the Peltier edition of his works, *S. Bonaventura: opera omnia*, xii, Paris, 1868 and see Sargent, 'Bonaventura English', p. 158.

51 Sargent, p. 159. Harold Kane has edited the version of *The Prickynge* from BL MS Harley 2254. See Harold Kane, ed., *The Prickynge of Love*, Salzburg Studies in English Literature: Elizabethan and Renaissance Studies 91:10, Salzburg, 1983. The following quotations from *The Prickynge* are taken from his edition, cited henceforth as Kane. Clare Kirchberger has produced a modernization of *The Prickynge* based on the text in the Vernon MS, with comparison to Bodley 480. The Latin version is extant in 221 known manuscripts as full text, and 147 other manuscripts in fragmentary form according to the Quaracchi editors (Kirchberger, p. 18). Kirchberger ascribes the translation to Walter Hilton, an ascription that has since been contested. For a discussion of the question of authorship see Sargent, 'Bonaventura English', p. 161.

52 Kane, p. 2.

53 ibid., p. 3.

54 ibid., pp. 5–6.

55 ibid., p. 6.

56 ibid., p. 10.

57 ibid., p. 10.

58 ibid., p. 12.

59 ibid., p. 8.
60 ibid., p. 6.
61 ibid., p. 9.
62 ibid., p. 9–10. Anselm evolves the notion (especially in his prayers and meditations) that Christ had given redemptive birth to mankind in a death that was itself an act of labour. The 'maternal' aspects of Christ's love are most extensively and systematically developed by Julian of Norwich in her *Shewings*, ed. Eric Colledge and James Walsh, Toronto, Institute of Pontifical Studies, 1978. See also Caroline Walker Bynum's *Jesus as Mother: Studies in the Spirituality of the High Middle Ages*, Berkeley, University of California Press, 1982.
63 Riehle, p. 46.
64 Kane, p. 13.
65 ibid., p. 7.
66 ibid., pp. 15–16.
67 ibid., pp. 14–15.
68 ibid., p. 33.
69 ibid., p. 10.
70 Roberto da Matta, 'Carnival in Multiple Planes' in *Rite, Drama, Festival, Spectacle: Rehearsals Towards a Theory of Cultural Performance*, ed. John J. MacAloon, Philadelphia, Institute for the Study of Human Issues, 1984, p. 214.
71 da Matta, p. 214.
72 The title of Gail Gibson's recent book, *The Theater of Devotion: East Anglian Drama and Society in the Late Middle Ages*, Chicago, University of Chicago Press, 1989, bears eloquent testimony to the complex relations between devotional theatre and 'theatrical' devotion. Michael O'Connell has explored the relations between theatrical representation and what has come to be understood as 'sacramentality' in a recent paper delivered at the Seventh Citadel conference on Medieval and Renaissance Literature in Charleston, March 1991, entitled 'God's Body: Incarnation, Physical Embodiment, and the Legacy of Biblical Theater in the Sixteenth Century'. I am very grateful to Michael O'Connell for sending me his work in progress. It is interesting to see the tensions around 'theatricality' being acted out around the stigmata of St Francis. Francis' stigmata are simultaneously signs of his humility and likeness to Christ and of his special merit as a chosen vehicle of grace, and there is much discussion in the *Legenda majora* about how, when and whether these signs of hidden grace should be made public: 'When he realized that he could not conceal the stigmata which had been imprinted so plainly on his body from his intimate companions, he was thrown into an agony of doubt; he was afraid to make God's secret publicly known, and did not know whether he should say what he had seen, or keep it quiet' (*St. Francis of Assisi: Writings and Early Biographies: English Omnibus of the Sources for the Life of St Francis*, ed. Marion Habig, Chicago, Franciscan Herald Press, 1983, p. 731). For an account of his intensely theatricalized death, wherein he shows himself to be master of symbolic form, see pp. 737–41. John Moorman

notes that 'St. Francis was one of the greatest actors the world has ever known' (Habig, p. 1815).

73 See above, n. 30.

74 Mary Douglas, *Purity and Danger: An Analysis of the Concepts of Pollution and Taboo*, London, Routledge & Kegan Paul, 1966, p. 4.

75 Dider Anzieu, *The Skin Ego*, New Haven, Yale University Press, 1989, p. 3.

76 'Meditations on the Passion', in *English Writings of Richard Rolle. Hermit of Hampole*, ed. Hope Emily Allen, Oxford, Oxford University Press, 1931; reprint edn, Gloucester, Alan Sutton, 1988, pp. 34–6.

77 *Orationes ad membra Christi* in *Opera omnia* V, pp. 204–8, cited in Sixten Ringbom, *Icon and Narrative: The Rise of the Dramatic Closeup in Fifteenth Century Devotional Painting*, Doornspijk, The Netherlands, Davaco, 1984, p. 49.

78 The poem is edited in two versions in *Legends of the Holy Rood: Symbols of the Passion and Cross Poems*, EETS o.s. 46, London, N. Trubner & Co., 1871, pp. 170–96. The Middle English 'Charters of Christ' image Christ's body itself as the parchment upon which a deed is written, with pens imaged as the scourges used by Jews. These works turn on the notion of a charter drawn up like a legal document in which Christ grants mankind title to heaven. Here the wound in the side is often imaged as the seal of the deed. For an examination of this genre, see Mary Caroline Spalding, 'The Middle English Charters of Christ', Ph.D. dissertation, Bryn Mawr, 1914.

79 Part 7 of the *Ancrene Wisse*, for example, displays Christ's body like an armoured knight who has his shield (body) pierced for love of his lady. See Geoffrey Shepherd, ed., *Ancrene Wisse: Parts Six and Seven*, Manchester, Manchester University Press, 1972. And see Rosemary Woolf, 'The Theme of Christ the Lover-Knight in Medieval English Literature', *Review of English Studies*, 1962, n.s. 13, pp. 1–16.

80 *The Politics and Poetics of Transgression*, London, Methuen, 1986, p. 58. Stallybrass and White are working with a model of inversion derived from Barbara Babcock: ' "Symbolic inversion" may be broadly defined as any act of expressive behaviour which inverts, contradicts, abrogates, or in some fashion presents an alternative to commonly held cultural codes, values and norms be they linguistic, literary or artistic, religious, social and political' (*The Reversible World: Symbolic Inversion in Art and Society*, Ithaca, Cornell University Press, 1978, p. 14). Stallybrass and White use the term 'hybridization' rather than mere inversion, with its suggestion of binary reversal, to imply a 'boundary phenomenon . . . in which self and other become enmeshed in an inclusive, heterogeneous, dangerously unstable zone' (p. 193).

81 See Margaret Aston, 'Wyclif and Vernacular', *Studies in Church History*, Subsidia 5, Oxford, Blackwell, 1987; Anne Hudson, 'Lollardy: The English Heresy' in *Religion and National Identity*, ed. Stuart

Mews, *Studies in Church History* vol. 18, Oxford, Blackwell, 1982, pp. 261–83.

82 Kirchberger, p. 30.

83 ibid., p. 26.

84 The issue of the dividing line between a meditational exploration of 'likeness' and deification or identity with God was at issue in the controversies over Eckhardt's writings, and Marguerite Porete, burnt for heresy in Paris. If Christ's body, as I have been arguing in this chapter, is where the very divisions of high and low can be obliterated, it is also where they can be violently and hierarchically reimposed.

85 Sargent describes it as the 'most popular major devotional or mystical text' and says that the role played by the *Meditationes* in the European vernaculars 'does indeed say something of the character of later medieval English spirituality' ('Bonaventura English', p. 151).

86 Salter, p. 103. Salter notes at least twenty-two manuscript copies of the whole, and ten containing the passion material alone. The first complete translation was Nicholas Love's (Salter, p. 45).

87 Sargent, 'Contemplative Literature', p. 7. Salter notes forty-seven manuscripts containing the *Mirrour*. For a full analysis see Salter, chapter 1, 'The Manuscripts and Printed Editions of the "Myrrour" ', pp. 1–22. Sargent more recently notes forty-nine complete manuscripts, ten extracts and fragments, and two composite texts (see his 'Contemplative Literature', p. 9). A. I. Doyle notes a pattern of increasing lay and secular ownership of the *Mirrour* (Salter, p. 16). This is reinforced by Sargent's recent research.

88 Arundel's certificate of approval notes that the translation is 'ad fidelium edificationem et hereticorum sive Lollardorum confutationem'. This note of approbation precedes most of the versions of Love's translations in the extant manuscripts. Cited by Salter, p. 2.

89 The figure of Richard Rolle was controversial amongst those of a contemplative persuasion. Carthusians, as major disseminators of devotional writing, certainly disagreed about its advisability for the purposes of spiritual instruction. See Michael Sargent, 'The Transmission by the English Carthusians of some Late Medieval Spiritual Writings', *Journal of Ecclesiastical History*, 1976, vol. 27, pp. 225–40 and Sargent, 'Contemporary Criticism of Richard Rolle', *Analecta Cartusiana*, 1981, vol. 55, pt 1, pp. 160–205.

90 Powell, p. 8.

91 ibid., pp. 8–9.

92 ibid., p. 24.

93 ibid., p. 25.

94 In the original *Meditationes*, the passion section is arranged according to the canonical hours. For comparison see other Middle English versions of the *Meditationes* such as the Thornton manuscript's 'Privity of the Passion', printed in Horstmann, ed., *Yorkshire Writers: Richard of Hampole and His Followers*, Swan Sonnenschein & Co., London, 1895, vol. 1, pp. 198–218, and the 'Medytacyuns of the Soper of oure lorde Ihesu' in J. R. Cowper, ed., EETS o.s. 60,

London, 1885, pp. 1–24. For a recent analysis of the relationship between liturgy and meditation in late medieval mystical writings see Marion Glasscoe, 'Time of Passion: Latent Relationships between Liturgy and Meditation in two Middle English Mystics' in *Langland, the Mystics and the Medieval English Religious Tradition: Essays in Honour of S. S. Hussey*, ed. Helen Phillips, Cambridge, D. S. Brewer, 1990, pp. 141–61.

95 Powell, pp. 12–13.

96 The phrase 'mastery of the mystery' was the title of a paper given by Miri Rubin at the New Chaucer Society meetings at Vancouver in August 1988.

97 Powell, p. 9.

98 ibid., p. 10.

99 ibid., p. 10.

100 *Everyman*, l. 739, *Everyman and Medieval Miracle Plays* ed. A. C. Cawley, London, J. M. Dent, 1977, p. 228.

101 Powell, p. 301.

102 Sargent, 'Contemplative Literature', p. 8. The treatise on the euchar-ist derives from the Middle English version of Henry Suso's *Horologium sapientiae, The Seven Poyntes of True Love and Everlasting Wisdom*, probably, according to Roger Lovatt, in circulation in England by the mid 1370s. The *Horologium sapientiae* has been edited by C. Horstmann from MS Douce 114, *Anglia*, 1887, vol. 10, pp. 323–89. For the circulation of the text in England, see Eric Colledge, *Dominican Studies*, 1953, vol. 6, pp. 77–89, and Roger Lovatt, 'The Imitation of Christ in Late Medieval England', *Transactions of the Royal Historical Society* 5th series, 1968, vol. 18, pp. 97–121 and 'Henry Suso and the Medieval Mystical Tradition in England' in *The Medieval Mystical Tradition in England*, Exeter, 1982, pp. 47–62.

103 Powell, p. 204.

104 ibid., p. 204.

105 ibid., p. 208.

106 ibid., p. 323.

107 ibid., p. 324.

108 See Rossell Hope Robbins, 'Levation Prayers in Middle English Verse', *Modern Philology*, 1942, vol 40, pp. 131–46. 'Levation' pray-ers were poems to be recited by the laity after the consecration of the host at elevation. Since no translation of the mass was available, paraliturgical prayers were provided for the laity for appropriate moments of the mass. Many of these prayers were used in private reading. Thomas F. Simmons has edited four manuscripts of the lay folk's mass book in *The Lay Folk's Mass Book*, EETS o.s. 71, London, Trubner & Co., 1879.

109 See Loretta McGarry, 'The Holy Eucharist in Middle English Homi-letic and Devotional Verse', Ph.D. dissertation, Catholic University of America. Washington, 1936, p. 180.

110 Taken from 'The Examination of Sir John Oldcastle' in *Fifteenth-Century Verse and Prose*, ed., and with an introduction by Alfred W. Pollard, New York, E. P. Dutton & Co., 1903, p. 187. The trial

exists in one manuscript along with the trial of William Thorpe. Pollard edits his version from the printed one of 1530. For details on the general procedure of the examination of Lollards and the episcopal registers on which such historical evidence is based see Anne Hudson, 'The Examination of Lollards', *Bulletin of the Institute of Historical Research*, 1973, vol. 46, pp. 145–59.

111 Victor Turner, *Process, Performance and Pilgrimage: A Study in Comparative Symbology*, New Delhi, Concept Publishing Co., 1979, p. 147.

112 Turner, *Process*, p. 147.

113 ibid., p. 147.

114 For further detail about the context surrounding the trial see Peter McNiven, *Heresy and Politics in the Reign of Henry IV: The Burning of John Badby*, Cambridge, Boydell Press, 1987, pp. 223–5.

115 Pollard, p. 187.

116 James Gairdner's account in *Lollardy and the Reformation in England: An Historical Survey*, London, Macmillan & Co., 1908, p. 77.

117 ibid., p. 93.

118 Peter Heath, *Church and Realm, 1272–1461: Conflict and Collaboration in an Age of Crisis*, London, Fontana, 1988, p. 278.

119 ibid., p. 269.

120 'Religious Change under Henry V' in *Henry V: The Practice of Kingship*, ed. G. L. Harriss, Oxford, Oxford University Press, 1985, p. 97.

121 Jonathan Hughes, *Pastors and Visionaries: Religion and Secular Life in Late Medieval Yorkshire*, Cambridge, Boydell Press, 1988, p. 365.

122 Chichele issued an order after Agincourt that a feast day should be inaugurated to honour 'England's patron saint' on 23 April (see Hughes, p. 364, Catto, p. 107, and Pfaff, *New Liturgical Feasts*).

123 Catto, p. 115.

124 Salter, p. 24.

125 Heath, p. 273, and see Dom David Knowles, *The Religious Orders in England* vol. 2, Cambridge, Cambridge University Press, 1955, p. 175.

126 Catto, p. 111.

127 See Lovatt and Sargent for Carthusians as major transmitters of devotional literature.

128 Gairdner, p. 85.

129 Arundel, who had sworn on the body of Christ that Richard II would not be deposed, was complicit in using his ecclesiastical authority to 'de-authorize Richard II' and establish Henry IV in his place. See McNiven, p. 68. For a discussion of the role of popular religious cults in combating the Lancastrian dynasty, see J. W. McKenna, 'Popular Canonization as Political Propaganda: The Cult of Archbishop Scrope', *Speculum*, 1970, vol. 45, pp. 608–23.

130 For details of Henry V's religious observances see *Gesta Henrici Quinti*, ed., F. Taylor and J. S. Roskell, Oxford, 1975, p. 155.

131 Christ's body underpins the sacramental system by functioning as the central sacrament – the eucharist – and the only one that is

definitionally attached to clerical power, and by providing in the theory of incarnation and redemption the doctrinal support for sacramental symbols.

132 Gibson, p. 6.

133 Peter Travis, 'The Social Body of the Dramatic Christ in Medieval England', *Early Drama to 1600*, *Acta*, 1985, vol. 13, p. 33.

4 THE USES OF CORPUS CHRISTI AND *THE BOOK OF MARGERY KEMPE*

1 *The Book of Margery Kempe*, ed. Sanford Meech and Hope Emily Allen, EETS o.s. 212, Oxford, Oxford University Press, 1940, p. 86. Henceforth cited as Kempe.

2 Ute Stargardt for example makes the following comments: 'Her consistent inability to differentiate between metaphor and actual experience appears with most embarrassing clarity in her descriptions of her soul's marriage to the Godhead.' See her essay, 'The Beguines of Belgium, the Dominican Nuns of Germany, and Margery Kempe' in *The Popular Literature of Medieval England*, ed. Thomas J. Heffernan, Knoxville, University of Tennessee Press, 1985, p. 300. Wolfgang Riehle makes a similar point: 'She is no longer capable of separating the sensual from the spiritual' (*The Middle English Mystics*, London, Routledge, Kegan & Paul, 1981, p. 11). Stephen Medcalf calls Kempe's reading of the spiritual in material terms a 'misplaced concreteness' in his essay in *The Later Middle Ages*, London, Methuen, 1981, p. 110. In Evelyn Underhill's view, it is such 'misplaced concreteness' that embarrasses the category of mysticism itself. Her review of the book upon its discovery expresses the thought that it is 'disconcerting to the students of medieval mysticism' (*The Spectator*, 16 October 1936, p. 642). There is also a spirited 'defence' of Margery Kempe as in E. I. Watkins' essay, 'In Defence of Margery Kempe' in *Poets and Mystics*, London, Sheed & Ward, 1953. For an essay surveying the extraordinary focus on the personality of Kempe see Roberta Bux Bosse, 'Margery Kempe's Tarnished Reputation: a Reassessment', *Fourteenth Century English Mystics Newsletter*, 1979, vol. 5, pt 1, pp. 9–19. See also David Aers, 'The Making of Margery Kempe: Individual and Community' in *Community, Gender and Individual Identity: English Writing 1360–1430*, ed. D. Aers, London, Routledge, 1988, pp. 73–116 and my 'A Very Material Mysticism: The Medieval Mysticism of Margery Kempe' in *Medieval Literature: Criticism, History, Ideology*, ed. D. Aers, Brighton, Harvester, 1986, pp. 34–57.

3 The influence of Love is ubiquitous, but see especially Kempe's meditations in chapters 78–83 (Kempe, pp. 184–202). For the scribe's familiarity with the *Prickynge*, see Kempe, p. 153.

4 Kempe, p. 132.

5 ibid., p. xxxii.

6 ibid., p. xlvi. And see Henry Plomer, *Wynkyn de Worde and his*

Contemporaries from the Death of Caxton to 1535, London, Grafton & Co., 1925, pp. 41–63.

7 In this connection see Karma Lochrie's article, '*The Book of Margery Kempe*: The Marginal Woman's Quest for Literary Authority', *Journal of Medieval and Renaissance Studies*, 1986, vol. 16, pt 1, pp. 33–55.

8 The 'discernment of spirits' was the procedure whereby authentic revelations were distinguished from false ones. For a discussion roughly contemporary with Margery Kempe, see *The Chastising of God's Children and the Treatise of Perfection of the Sons of God* ed. Joyce Bazire and E. Colledge, Oxford, Blackwell, 1957, pp. 173–82, which deals with the tokens by which good spirits may be distinguished from bad ones. One such sign is 'whether he submitteth hym or his visions loweli to the doom of his goostli fadir, or of other discreet and sad goostli lyuers, for drede of illusion, or ellis kepith hem priuey and shewith hem not, but stondith to his owne examyneng, and to his owne doom'. Christ gives Margery five 'tokyns' that are the signs of her special grace (see Kempe, p. 183). The issue of the discernment of spirits was at stake in the discussions over the canonization of Birgitta, a notable influence on Margery Kempe. The anxiety about women's revelations is discussed in relation to the 'discernment of spirits' by Jean Gerson. Gerson's 'De probatione spiritum' was written during the Council of Constance against the claims put forward on behalf of St Birgitta (see Eric Colledge, '*Epistola solitarii ad reges*: Alphonse of Pecha as Organizer of Birgittine and Urbanist Propaganda,' *Medieval Studies*, 1956, vol. 18, p. 43. Adam Easton, monk of Norwich, and later cardinal, writes a defence of St Birgitta, *Defensorium S. Birgittae* addressed to Boniface IX. The text can be found in three manuscripts: Bodleian MS Hamilton 7, Oxford University, folios 229–48; Lincoln Cathedral MS, 114, folios 23^v to 53^v and Universitätbibliothek Uppsala MS, c518 folios 248–73. For a discussion of Easton's defence see James A. Schmidtke, ' "Saving" by Faint Praise: St Birgitta of Sweden, Adam Easton and Medieval Antifeminism', *American Benedictine Review*, 1982, vol. 33, pt 2, pp. 149–61. Margery's Carmelite confessor, Alan of Lynn, made indexes to Birgitta's *Revelations*. See Kempe, pp. 259 and 268, Goodman, p. 353 for a discussion of 'orthodox' local clerical interest in revelatory phenomena in the 1410s.

9 Kempe, p. 8.

10 ibid., pp. 18–20.

11 ibid., p. 183.

12 ibid., p. 70.

13 ibid., p. 69.

14 ibid., p. 148.

15 ibid., p. 68.

16 See pp. 89ff.

17 e. g. Kempe, p. 142.

18 For incidents at Bristol, pp. 107–9; for Leicester, p. 111; for York, pp. 120–2, 124–5; and Hull, p. 129.

19 ibid., pp. 29–30.
20 See pp. 96, 108.
21 See Clarissa Atkinson, *Mystic and Pilgrim: The Book and the World of Margery Kempe*, Ithaca, Cornell University Press, p. 114 and see also Sue Ellen Holbrook, 'Order and Coherence in *The Book of Margery Kempe*' in *The Worlds of Medieval Women: Creativity, Influence, Imagination*, ed. Constance H. Berman, Charles W. Connell and Judith Rice Rothschild, Morgantown, West Virginia University Press, 1985, pp. 97–112.
22 See chapter 3.
23 Kempe, pp. 1–2.
24 ibid., p. 23.
25 See Aers, Atkinson, Beckwith, Deborah Ellis, 'Margery Kempe and the Virgin's Hot Caudle', *Essays in Arts and Sciences*, 1985, vol. 14, pt. 3, pp. 1–12; Gail McMurray Gibson, 'St Margery: *The Book of Margery Kempe*' in *Theater of Devotion: East Anglian Drama and Society in the Late Middle Ages*, Chicago, University of Chicago Press, 1989, pp. 47–67; Antony Goodman, 'The Piety of John Brunham's Daughter of Lynn' in *Medieval Women* ed. Derek Baker, Oxford, Blackwell, 1978, pp. 347–59.
26 Goodman, p. 353.
27 ibid., p. 353.
28 Kempe, p. 20.
29 ibid., p. 20.
30 ibid., pp. 48–9.
31 ibid., p. 49.
32 ibid., p. 212. Margery is herself accused of being a marriage-breaker (ibid., p. 133).
33 ibid., p. 25.
34 ibid., p. 81.
35 ibid., p. 18. For further references to the tradition of Jesus as mother see Kari Elizabeth Borresen, 'Christ notre mère, la théologie de Juliennne de Norwich', *Mitteilungen und Forschungsbeitrage der cusanus-Gesellschaft*, 1978, vol. 13, pp. 320–9; Caroline Walker Bynum, *Jesus as Mother: Studies in the Spirituality of the High Middle Ages*, Berkeley, University of California Press, 1982.
36 ibid., p. 31.
37 ibid., p. 31.
38 ibid., p. 90.
39 ibid., p. 30.
40 ibid., p. 17.
41 ibid., p. 206.
42 ibid., p. 50. Hope Emily Allen notes Rolle's usage of the same phrase in Kempe, p. 282, n. 50/32.
43 See Kempe's description of the 'terys of compunccyon, deuocyon, & compassyon' (p. 31). As Allen notes, Julian regarded tears as a sign of holiness, (p. 272), as do all her ecclesiastical supporters. For a recent account of tears in relation to 'feminine spirituality' see Elizabeth Robertson, 'Medieval Medical Views of Women and

158

Female Spirituality' in *Medieval Views of the Body* ed. Linda Lomperis and Sarah Stanbury, forthcoming, University of Pennsylvania Press.

44 *Sarum Missal*, p. 402 and Atkinson, p. 59.

45 Atkinson, p. 59; Kempe, p. 43. No precise equivalent of these words ascribed to Jerome can be found in his writings.

46 See Kempe, pp. 152–4. The Middle English text of Jacques de Vitry's *vita* of Mary of Oignies is edited by Carl Horstmann in *Anglia* 1885, vol. 8, pp. 134–83, which also contains Middle English versions of the lives of Cristina Mirabilis (by Thomas de Cantim-pré), and Elizabeth of Spaldbeck (by Philip de Clarevalle). Douce 114 was written in a Carthusian house in Nottingham, perhaps before the completion of Margery Kempe's book, but it is not clear which version Kempe's priest had available to him. See also Brenda Bolton, '*Vitae matrum*: A Further Aspect of the Frauenfrage' in *Medieval Women*, ed. D. Baker pp. 253–73. For the relation of Kempe's text to these *vitae*, see Stargardt.

47 Kempe, p. 216. See also Aers, p. 78: and for similar 'accounting for the beyond' Jacques Chiffoleau, *La Comptabilité de l'au-delà: les hommes, la mort et la religion dans la région d'Avignon à la fin du moyen-âge*, Rome, Publications de la Sorbonne, 1980.

48 Kempe, p. 69.

49 ibid., p. 36.

50 ibid., p. 151.

51 Denise Despres, *Ghostly Sights: Visual Meditation in Late Medieval Literature*, Norman, Pilgrim Books, 1989, p. 82.

52 See especially, Kempe, pp. 205–6, where Christ himself absolves her from the charge of hypocrisy. Significantly, Christ's statement is made in the context of a discussion of different kinds of devotion – the devotion expressed in saying beads, fasting, and acts of public penance. For a discussion of the repeated attribution of hypocrisy and histrionics in the *Book* by her contemporaries and later critical commentators, see my 'Problems of Authority in Late Medieval English Mysticism: Agency and Authority in *The Book of Margery Kempe*', in *Exemplaria*, 1992, vol. 4, pt. 1, pp. 171–99.

53 Kempe, p. 1.

54 ibid., p. 89.

55 ibid., p. 89.

56 ibid., pp. 89–90.

57 For further exploration of the paradox of 'autobiography' within the context of mystical revelations, see my 'Problems of Authority.'

58 Kempe, p. 17.

59 ibid., p. 89.

60 ibid., p. 216.

61 Cited by F. R. H. du Boulay, *The England of Piers Plowman: William Langland and his Vision of the Fourteenth Century*, Cambridge, D. S. Brewer, 1991, p. 71. This is a common analogy in Lollard writings: see, for example, Ritchie Kendall, *The Drama of Dissent*, Chapel Hill, University of North Carolina Press, 1986, pp. 17ff., where

Kendall discusses the Lollard redefinition of sacramentality as the scriptures.

62 Kempe, p. 107.
63 See Charles Zika, 'Hosts, Procession and Pilgrimage: Controlling the Sacred in Fifteenth-Century Germany', *Past and Present*, 1988, no. 118, pp. 30ff. and see chapter 1.
64 Kempe, p. 107.
65 ibid., p. 36.
66 For an in-depth discussion of the dimensions of eucharistic piety with particular relation to the position of women see Caroline Walker Bynum, *Holy Feast and Holy Fast: The Religious Significance of Food to Medieval Women*, Berkeley, University of California Press, 1987.
67 Kempe, p. 17. For Kempe's eucharistic miracle competitively claimed to be better than the one granted to St Birgitta, see p. 47, and for Margery Kempe's 'saviour' of St Margaret's by means of the sacrament of Christ's body, see, pp. 162–3. Margery's very vocal 'howselyngs' are discussed in the *Book* on p. 139, and elsewhere.
68 See for example Kempe. p. 55: 'The prest whech wrot þis boke for to preuyn þis creaturys felyngys many tymes & dyuers tymes he askyd hir qwestyons-& demawndys of thyngys þat wer for to komyn, un-sekyr & uncerteyn as þat tyme to any creatur what xuld be þe ende, preyng hir, þei sche wer loth & not wylly to do swech thyngys, for to prey to God þerfor & wetyn, whan owyr Lord wold visiten hir wyth deuocyon, what xuld be þe ende, and trewly wyth-owtyn any feynyng tellyn hymhow sche felt, & ellys wold he not gladlych a wretyn þe boke', and pp. 170–1.
69 ibid., p. 142.
70 ibid., p. 17.
71 ibid., p. 23.
72 ibid., p. 34.
73 ibid., p. 109 and see below, p. 107.
74 ibid., p. 161.
75 ibid., p. 158.
76 ibid., p. 158.
77 ibid., p. 25.
78 'Sche was schreuyn sum-tyme twyes or thryes on þe day' (Kempe, p. 12), and see her first chapter when she describes her earlier notion that her own penance, rather than the sacrament of confession will grant her God's mercy, a Lollard heresy. 'For sche was euyr lettyd be hyr enmy, þe Deuel, euyr-mor seyng to hyr whyl sche was in good heele hir nedyd no confessyon but don penawns be hir-self a-loone, & all schuld be for-ȝouyn, for God is mercyful j-now' (p. 7). It is significant for the complex relations between Kempe and the clergy that her first visions of Christ occur in the context of her madness after the birth of her first child; her madness and despair are partially induced by the severity of a particular confessor over a sin she has great difficulty in confessing. Given that the discourse of 'confession' helps provide a language through which subjectivity

is elaborated and formulated, it is interesting to see this moment given such importance in her book by its positioning at the very beginning. For an analysis of the sacrament of confession in the later Middle Ages, see Thomas Tentler, *Sin and Confession on the Eve of the Reformation*, Princeton, Princeton University Press, 1977. For a discussion of the discourse of confession in relation to penitential literature and the kind of subjectivity it evolves, see Lee Patterson, 'Chaucerian Confession: Penitential Literature and the Pardoner', *Medievalia et Humanistica*, 1976, n. s. 7, pp. 153–73.

79 Zika, p. 63.

80 Kempe, pp. 72–3.

81 For Alan of Lynn (*c.* 1348–1428), see ibid., p. 268, n. 22/11–12. He is first introduced into the *Book* on p. 22, and is the most distinguished of Kempe's local supporters; a Doctor of Divinity at Cambridge, a Carmelite and a native of Lynn, he compiled indices for the *Revelationes Brigittae* and the *Prophetiae Brigittae*. Wenslawe is the German priest whom Margery Kempe sees when she is first celebrating mass in the church of St John Lateran; he is her principal confessor in Rome (see Kempe, pp. 82, 83, 85, 91, 97). Southfield is mentioned in the *Book* on p. 41. He is reputed to have had supernatural visitations in which the virgin appeared to him. Spryngolde is referred to as her 'principal confessowr' (p. 169), or as her 'gostly fader' (p. 227). A 'bacheler of lawe' (p. 150), he is the parish priest at St Margaret's. Richard Caister is vicar of St Stephen's in Norwich and appears to have been the object of a local cult (see Kempe. p. 320, and 'Richard of Caister and His Metrical Prayer', *Norfolk Archaeology*, 1910, vol. 17, pp. 221–31). Kempe consults him on p. 38. Kempe also mentions an 'ankyr' whom she visits (p. 103). The other much more well-known figure whom she visits is of course Julian of Norwich (p. 41).

82 Goodman, p. 357.

83 For Kempe's mention of her father, see p. 111. Also see Dorothy M. Owen, *The Making of King's Lynn: A Documentary Survey*, London, Oxford University Press, 1984, pp. 138, 139, 185–7, 197, 215, 324, 388, 392.

84 Henry H. Hillen, *History of the Borough of King's Lynn*, Norwich, East of England Newspaper Co., Ltd, 1907, p. 47. The burgesses were exempt from the payments due to the bishop as lord of the burgh, to which strangers were subject.

85 Hillen, p. 49, and Owen pp. 379–82.

86 Hillen, p. 131. Atkinson mentions the dispute, p. 76.

87 Cited by Hillen, p. 180.

88 Hillen, p. 129.

89 Foxe, *Actes and Monuments*, 1562, vol. 2, p. 807, cited by Hillen, p. 128.

90 Hillen, p. 80.

91 Kempe, p. 9.

92 Aers, p. 76.

93 ibid., p. 75.

94 'Sexual Economics, Chaucer's Wife of Bath and the *Book of Margery Kempe*,' *Minnesota Review*, 1975, n. s. 5, pp. 104–15.

95 Owen, p. 37.

96 Kempe, p. 109.

97 ibid., p. 36.

98 ibid., p. 104.

99 Goodman, p. 357.

100 Kempe, pp. 85–6, 92, 96–7, 102, 105–6, and Goodman, pp. 355–6.

101 Norman Tanner in his *The Church in Late Medieval Norwich 1370–1532*, Toronto, Pontifical Institute for Medieval Studies, 1984, notes that there were béguinages, for example in the vicinity of Norwich; in other words there were communities of lay women.

102 Goodman, p. 356.

103 ibid., p. 357.

104 Gibson, p. 47. See Kempe, pp. 358–9, for a copy of the section of the Account Roll of the Trinity guild of Lynn recording Kempe's entry.

105 See Joshua and Lucy Toulmin Smith, *English Gilds: their Statutes and Customs A.D. 1389*, EETS o.s. 40, London, N. Trubner & Co., 1870; H. F. Westlake, *The Parish Gilds of Medieval England*, London, Macmillan, 1919; Barbara Hanawalt, 'Keepers of the Lights: Late Medieval English Parish Gilds', *Journal of Medieval and Renaissance Studies*, 1984, vol. 14, pt 1, pp. 21–37; Gervase Rosser, 'Communities of Parish and Guild in the Late Middle Ages' in *Parish, Church and People: Local Studies in Lay Religion 1350–1750*, ed. S. J. Wright, London, Hutchinson, 1988, pp. 29–56; William R. Jones, 'English Religious Brotherhoods and Medieval Lay Piety: The Inquiry of 1388–89' *The Historian*, 1973/4, vol. 36, pp. 646–65; Miri Rubin, 'Corpus Christi Fraternities and Late Medieval Lay Piety', *Studies in Church History*, 1986, vol. 23, pp. 97–109; Ben McRee, 'Religious Gilds and Regulation of Behavior in Late Medieval Towns' in *People, Politics and Community* ed., J. Rosenthal and Colin Richmond, pp. 108–21; Clive Burgess, ' "A Fond Thing Vainly Invented": An Essay on Purgatory and Pious motive in Later Medieval England' in Wright, ed., pp. 56–84; Jacques Le Goff, *La Naissance du purgatoire*, Paris, Gallimard, 1981; John Bossy, *Christianity in the West*, Oxford, Oxford University Press, 1985, pp. 45–56; and K. L. Wood-Legh, *Perpetual Chantries*, 1965.

106 The Trinity guild dates from roughly the thirteenth century. Owen reiterates the importance of its commercial and municipal activities adding: 'equally significant, because of its wide membership, were the repeated cries for prayers for its departed membership "according to the fashion of Lynn" by the town bellman, the lavish funerals and soul-masses, attended by all brothers in the town, and marked by lights and torches, by the distribution of bread and shoes to the poor, and of money to priests, the annual masses on Trinity Day and its eve, in the guild chapel within St Margaret's church, and the regular daily celebrations there' (p. 61).

107 ibid., p. 61.

108 Westlake, p. 45; Rosser, p. 40.

109 See Rubin.

110 Westlake, p. 50.

111 See Rubin, Rosser and Hanawalt.

112 Rosser, p. 35.

113 ibid., p. 43.

114 ibid., p. 43.

115 Pamela Graves, 'Social Space in the English Medieval Parish Church', *Economy and Society*, 1989, vol. 18, pt. 3, pp. 299–301. Bourdieu's concept of the *habitus* is developed in his *Outline of a Theory of Practice* trans. R. Nice, Cambridge, Cambridge University Press, 1977, pp. 78ff. Theoretically, it is an attempt to develop an analysis of material culture in such a way that the dangers of objectivism and subjectivism are avoided. Hence, Bourdieu's comments on p. 83: 'If one ignores the dialectical relationship between the objective structures and the cognitive and motivating structures which they produce and which tend to reproduce them, if one forgets that these objective structures are themselves products of historical practices and are constantly reproduced and transformed by historical practices whose productive principle is itself the product of the structures which it consequently tends to reproduce, then one is condemned to reduce the relationship between the different social agencies . . . to the logical formula enabling any one of them to be derived from any other.' The concept of the *habitus* allows for the breakdown of the opposition between symbol and economy, the material and the symbolic, as defined by the divergent traditions of Durkheim and Marx (see Bourdieu, p. 177, and below, pp. 108–9).

116 Graves, p. 299; Bourdieu, p. 89.

117 Bourdieu, p. 90; Graves, p. 309.

118 ibid., p. 307.

119 ibid., p. 307.

120 ibid., p. 313.

121 ibid., pp. 314–15.

122 ibid., pp. 311, 314.

123 Kempe, pp. 58–60. As Owen says: 'It was in defence of the revenue from burials and churching and from personal tithes that they, or more correctly, the prior and convent at Norwich, continued to obstruct the attempts of the congregation of St Nicholas to form a separate parish, and to prevent burial offerings being assigned to the friaries' (p. 27).

124 Kempe, p. 59.

125 Graves, p. 316. The church of St Margaret's itself has a 'dual aspect' (Owen, p. 27) for as well as being a parish church it was 'also the church of a small priory built by the monks of Norwich on its south side'. The monks had considerable property in the town of Lynn; the priory maintained the chancel, apart from the north side where the Trinity guild had its chapel.

126 Rosser, p. 44.

127 Kempe, p. 50.

128 ibid., p. 52.
129 For her eucharistic vision which surpasses Birgitta's, see Kempe, p. 47, and for her competing for God's love with Mary Magdalen, see p. 176.
130 See above, p. 91.
131 Kempe, p. 256.
132 ibid., p. 156.
133 ibid., p. 220.
134 Bourdieu, pp. 176–7.
135 ibid., pp. 177–8.
136 See my chapter 2, and my earlier comments on James and Bossy. Bakhtin has also been an influential source for a kind of organicist populism.
137 Bourdieu, p. 178.
138 The phrase 'symbolic capital' is central to Bourdieu's materialist reading of the symbol. Symbolic capital is 'a transformed and therefore *disguised* form of physical "economic" capital' and 'produces its proper effect inasmuch, and only inasmuch, as it conceals the fact that it originates in "material" forms of capital which are also, in the last analysis, the source of its effects' (p. 183).
139 See, for example, Goodman, pp. 349–50, where he talks about Kempe's 'retentive rather than inventive' mind and her 'mental banality': 'Margery Kempe's mental banality provides some assurance for the reliability of her vivid recollections of incidents and feelings.'
140 Bourdieu, pp. 8–9.

CONCLUSION

1 Raymond Williams, *The Country and the City*, cited in William Roseberry, *Anthropologies and Histories: Essays in Culture, History and Political Economy*, New Brunswick and London, Rutgers University Press, 1989, p. xvi. And see Kathleen Ashley's comments on the tendency to essentialize in symbolic analysis, *Interpreting Cultural Symbols: Saint Anne in Late Medieval Society*, ed. Kathleen Ashley and Pamela Sheingorn, Athens and London, University of Georgia Press, 1990, p. 5.
2 James A. Boon, *Other Tribes, Other Scribes: Symbolic Anthropology in the Comparative Study of Cultures, Histories, Religions and Texts*, Cambridge, Cambridge University Press, 1982, p. 121.
3 Boon describes the 'literal duplicity' of symbols, p. 121.
4 See chapter 3, pp. 45–77. I have been influenced by Adi Ophir, *Plato's Invisible Cities: Discourse and Power in the Republic*, Maryland, Barnes and Noble, 1991, in articulating this theory of symbolic utterance (see p. 41).
5 ibid., p. 41. Ophir phrases it in the following way: 'A symbolic utterance of this sort refers to something a conventional classificatory system cannot capture, and at the same time to the language that

fails to refer; it draws attention precisely to those distinctions in the classificatory system that are blurred by the referred entity' (p. 42).

6 ibid., p. 42.
7 ibid., p. 42.
8 Gibson, p. 6.
9 ibid, p. 6.
10 Bynum, *Holy Feast and Holy Fast*, Berkeley, University of California Press, 1987, p. 194.
11 Bynum, p. 246.
12 Bynum, p. 252. For Bynum's refutation of medieval asceticism see, pp. 217, 218, 245 and 294: 'The extravagant penitential practices of the thirteenth to the fifteenth century, the cultivation of pain and patience, the literalism of *imitatio crucis* are, I have argued, not primarily an attempt to escape from the body. They are not the products of an epistemology or psychology or theology that sees soul struggling against its opposite matter. . . . Rather, late medieval asceticism was an effort to plumb and to realize all the possibilities of the flesh. It was a profound expression of the doctrine of the Incarnation: the doctrine that Christ, by becoming human, saves *all* that the human being is.'
13 My readings here are indebted to the work of Maurice Bloch. See his *Ritual, History and Power*, London, Athlone Press, 1989, *From Blessing to Violence: History and Ideology in the Circumcision Ritual of the Merina of Madagascar*, Cambridge, Cambridge University Press, 1986, and with Jonathan Parry ed., *Death and the Regeneration of Life*, Cambridge, Cambridge University Press, 1982.
14 *Ritual, History and Power*, p. 188.
15 See Jean Comaroff and John Comaroff, *Of Revelation and Revolution: Christianity, Colonialism and Consciousness in South Africa*, Chicago, University of Chicago Press, 1991, p. 29: 'Between the conscious and the unconscious lies the most critical domain of all for historical anthropology. . . . It is the realm of partial recognition, of inchoate awareness, of ambiguous perception, and sometimes, of creative tension; that liminal space of human experience in which people discern acts and facts but cannot or do not order them into narrative descriptions or even into articulate conceptions of the world; in which signs or events are observed, but in a hazy, translucent light; in which individuals or groups know that something is happening to them but find it difficult to put their fingers on quite what it is. It is from this realm, we suggest, that silent signifiers and unmarked practices may rise to the level of explicit consciousness, of ideological assertion, and become the subject of overt political and social contestation – or from which they may recede into the hegemonic, to languish there unremarked for the time being.'
16 Zygmunt Bauman, *Modernity and Ambivalence*, Ithaca, Cornell University Press, 1991, p. 56.
17 Such a transference is obviously not a one-way street.

WORKS CITED

Adorno, Theodor, *Minima moralia*, translated by E. F. N. Jephcott, London, New Left Books, 1974.

Adorno, Theodor and Horkheïmer, Max, *Dialectic of Enlightenment*, translated by John Cumming, London, New Left Books, 1979.

Aers, David, *Community, Gender and Individual Identity: English Writing 1360–1430*, London, Routledge, 1988.

Alexander, J. C., ed., *Durkheimian Sociology: Cultural Studies*, Cambridge, Cambridge University Press, 1988.

Alexander, J. C. and Seidman, Steven, eds, *Culture and Society: Contemporary Debates*, Cambridge, Cambridge University Press, 1990.

Allen, Hope Emily, ed., *English Writings of Richard Rolle*, Oxford, Oxford University Press, 1931; reprint edn, Gloucester, Alan Sutton, 1988.

Allen, Hope Emily and Meech, Sanford, *The Book of Margery Kempe*, Early English Test Society o.s. 212, Oxford, Oxford University Press, 1940.

Anderson, Benedict, *Imagined Communities: Reflections on the Origin and Spread of Nationalism*, London, Verso, 1983.

Anselm, *Basic Writings*, translated by S. N. Deane and introduced by Charles Hartshorne, La Salle, Open Court Publishing Co., 1903; reprint ed., 1962.

—— *S. Anselmi: opera omnia*, 6 vols, edited by F. S. Schmitt, Edinburgh, Nelson, 1946.

—— *Proslogion*, edited by M. J. Charlesworth, Oxford, Clarendon Press, 1965.

Anzieu, Didier, *The Skin Ego*, New Haven, Yale University Press, 1989.

Aristotle, *The Politics*, edited by Stephen Everson, Cambridge, Cambridge University Press, 1988.

Asad, Talal, 'Anthropological Conceptions of Religion: Reflections on Geertz', *Man*, 1983, vol. 18, no. 2, pp. 237–68.

—— 'On Ritual and Discipline in Medieval Christian Monasticism', *Economy and Society*, 1987, vol. 16, pt 2, pp. 159–203.

Ashley, Kathleen and Sheingorn, Pamela, eds, *Interpreting Cultural Symbols: Saint Anne in Late Medieval Society*, Athens and London, University of Georgia Press, 1990.

Aston, Margaret, *Lollards and Reformers: Images and Literacy in Late Medieval Religion*, London, Hambledon Press, 1984.

—— 'Caim's Castles: Poverty, Politics and Disendowment' in *The Church, Politics and Patronage*, edited by Richard Barrie Dobson, New York, A. Sutton, 1984.

—— 'Wyclif and the Vernacular', *Studies in Church History*, Subsidia 5, Oxford, Blackwell, 1987.

Atkinson, Clarissa, *Margery Kempe: Mystic and Pilgrim*, Ithaca, Cornell University Press, 1983.

Babcock, Barbara, *The Reversible World: Symbolic Inversion in Art and Society*, Ithaca, Cornell University Press, 1978.

Baker, Derek, ed., *Medieval Women, Studies in Church History*, Subsidia 1, Oxford, Blackwell, 1978.

Bakhtin, Mikhail, *The Dialogic Imagination*, translated by C. Emerson and M. Holquist, Austin, University of Texas, 1981.

—— *Rabelais and His World*, translated by Helene Iswolsky, MIT, 1968; reprint edn, Bloomington, Indiana University Press, 1984.

Barkan, Leonard, *Nature's Work of Art: The Human Body as Image of the World*, New Haven, Yale University Press, 1975.

Bassuk, Daniel Eliot, 'The Secularization of Mysticism: An Analysis and Critique of the Mystical in Rufus Jones and Martin Buber', Ph.D. dissertation, Drew University, 1974.

Bauman, Zygmunt, *Modernity and Ambivalence*, Ithaca, Cornell University Press, 1991.

Bauml, Franz, 'Varieties and Consequences of Medieval Literacy and Illiteracy', *Speculum*, 1980, vol. 55, pt 2, pp. 237–65.

Bazire, Joyce and Colledge, E., eds, *The Chastising of God's Children and the Treatise of Perfection of the Sons of God*, Oxford, Blackwell, 1957.

Beadle, Richard, ed., *The York Plays*, London, Arnold, 1982.

Bechtler, Regina, 'The Mystic and the Church in the Writings of Evelyn Underhill', Ph.D. dissertation, Fordham University, 1979.

Beckwith, Sarah, 'A Very Material Mysticism: The Medieval Mysticism of Margery Kempe' in *Medieval Literature: History, Criticism and Ideology*, pp. 34–57, edited by David Aers, Brighton, Harvester Press, 1986.

—— 'Problems of Authority in Late Medieval English Mysticism: Language, Agency and Authority in *The Book of Margery Kempe*', *Exemplaria*, 1992, vol. 4, pt 1, pp. 171–99.

—— 'Ritual, Church and Theatre: Medieval Dramas of the Sacramental Body' in *Culture and History 1350–1600: Essays on English Communities, Identities and Writing*, pp. 65–89, edited by David Aers, Brighton, Harvester Press, 1992.

167

Bernard of Clairvaux, *Cantica canticorum: Eighty Six Sermons on the Song of Solomon*, edited and translated by S. J. Eales, London, Eliot Stock, 1895.

—— *De gradibus humilitatis*, translated by George Bosworth Burch, Cambridge, Mass., Harvard University Press, 1941.

—— *De diligendo Deo, Sancti Bernardi, opera omnia*, edited by J. Leclerq *et al.*, Rome, Editionnes Cisterciennes, 1958–.

Bevington, David, *Medieval Drama*, Boston, Houghton Mifflin, 1975.

Blake, N. F., *Middle English Religious Prose*, London, Arnold, 1972.

Bloch, Maurice, *From Blessing to Violence: History and Ideology in the Circumcision Ritual of the Merina of Madagascar*, Cambridge, Cambridge University Press, 1986.

—— *Ritual, History and Power*, London, Athlone Press, 1989.

—— Maurice and Parry, Jonathan, eds, *Death and the Regeneration of Life*, Cambridge, Cambridge University Press, 1982.

Blunt, J. H., *The Myroure of Oure Ladye*, Early English Text Society e.s. 19, London, Kegan Paul, Trench, Trubner & Co., 1873.

Boissac Paul, 'The Profanation of the Sacred in Circus Clown Performance' in *By Means of Performance: Intercultural Studies of Theatre and Ritual*, pp. 194–207, edited by Richard Schnechner and Willa Appel, Cambridge, Cambridge University Press, 1990.

Bolton, Brenda, '*Vitae matrum*: A Further Aspect of the Frauenfrage' in *Medieval Women*, pp. 253–73, edited by Derek Baker, Oxford: Blackwell, 1978.

Bolton, J. L, *The Medieval English Economy 1150–1500*, London, Dent, 1980.

Bonaventura, *Itinéraire de l'esprit vers Dieu*, edited by H. Dumery, texte de Quarrachi, Paris, J. Vrin, 1960.

—— *Opera omnia*, edited by Peltier, Paris, 1968.

Boon, James A., *Other Tribes, Other Scribes: Symbolic Anthropology in the Comparative Study of Cultures, Histories, Religions and Texts*, Cambridge, Cambridge University Press, 1982.

Borreson, Kari Elizabeth, 'Christ notre mère, la théologie de Julienne de Norwich', *Mitteilungen und Forschungsbeitrage der cusanus-Gesellschaft*, 1978, vol. 13, pp. 320–9.

Bosse, Roberta Bux, 'Margery Kempe's Tarnished Reputation: A Reassessment', *Fourteenth Century English Mystics Newsletter*, 1979, vol. 5, pt 1, pp. 9–19.

Bossy, John, 'The Mass as a Social Institution 1200–1700', *Past and Present*, 1983, no. 100, pp. 29–61.

—— *Christianity in the West 1400–1700*, Oxford, Oxford University Press, 1985.

du Boulay, F. R. H., *The England of Piers Plowman: William Langland*

and his Vision of the Fourteenth Century, Cambridge, D. S. Brewer, 1991.

Bourdieu, Pierre, *Outline of a Theory of Practice*, translated by R. Nice, Cambridge, Cambridge University Press, 1977.

Boyle, Leonard E., 'The Fourth Lateran Council and Manuals of Popular Theology' in *The Popular Literature in Medieval England*, pp. 30–44, edited by Thomas J. Heffernan, Knoxville, University of Tennessee Press, 1985.

Brown, B. D., *Southern Passion*, Early English Text Society o.s. 169, London, Humphrey Milford, 1927.

Brown, Carleton, ed., *Religious Lyrics of the Fourteenth Century*, Oxford, Oxford University Press, 1952.

Brown, Peter, *The Body and Society: Men, Women and Sexual Renunciation in Early Christianity*, New York, Columbia University Press, 1988.

Burgess, Clive, ' "A Fond Thing Vainly Invented": An Essay on Purgatory and Pious Motive in Later Medieval England' in *Parish, Church and People: Local Studies in Lay Religion 1350–1750*, pp. 56–84, edited by S. Wright, London, Hutchinson, 1988.

Burrow, John, 'Fantasy and Language in *The Cloud of Unknowing*', *Essays in Criticism*, 1977, vol. 27, pp. 283–98.

Bynum, Caroline Walker, *Jesus as Mother: Studies in the Spirituality of the High Middle Ages*, Berkeley, University of California Press, 1982.

—— *Holy Feast and Holy Fast*, Berkeley, University of California Press, 1987.

Calhoun, C. J., 'Community: Toward a Variable Conceptualization for Comparative Research', *Social History*, 1980, vol. 5, pt 1, pp. 105–27.

Callois, Roger, *Man and the Sacred*, Illinois, Free Press of Glencoe, 1959.

Cantwell Smith, Wilfrid, *The Meaning and End of Religion: A New Approach to the Religious Traditions of Mankind*, New York, Macmillan 1962.

Catto, Jeremy, 'Religious Change under Henry V' in *Henry V: The Practice of Kingship*, pp. 97–117, edited by G. L. Harriss, Oxford, Oxford University Press, 1985.

—— 'John Wyclif and the Cult of the Eucharist', *Studies in Church History*, Subsidia 4, Oxford, Blackwell, 1985.

de Certeau, Michel, *Heterologies*, Manchester, Manchester University Press, 1986.

Chandler, Alice, *A Dream of Order: The Medieval Ideal in Nineteenth-Century England*, New Haven, Yale University Press, 1981.

Chenu, M. D., *Nature, Man and Society in the Twelfth Century: Essays on New Theological Perspectives in the Latin West*, translated by Jerome Taylor and Lester Little, Chicago, University of Chicago Press, 1968.

Chiffoleau, Jacques, *La Comptabilité de l'au–delà: les hommes, la mort et la religion dans la région d'Avignon à la fin du moyen-âge*, Rome, Publications de la Sorbonne, 1980.

Chroust, Anton-Hermann, 'The Corporate Idea in the Middle Ages', *Review of Politics*, 1947, vol. 9, pp. 423–52.

Clanchy, M. T., *From Memory to Written Record: England 1066–1307*, Cambridge, Mass., Harvard University Press, 1979.

Cohen, A. P., *The Symbolic Construction of Community*, London, Tavistock Publications, 1985.

Cohen, Jeremy, *The Friars and the Jews: The Evolution of Medieval Anti-Judaism*, Ithaca and London, Cornell University Press, 1982.

Coleman, Janet, *Medieval Readers and Writers 1350–1400*, London, Hutchinson, 1981.

Coletti, Theresa, *Spirituality and Devotional Images: The Staging of the Hegge Cycle*, Ph.D. dissertation, University of Rochester, 1975.

Colledge, E., 'The *Buchlein der ewige Weisheit* and the *Horologium sapientiae*', *Dominican Studies*, 1953, vol. 6, pp. 77–89.

—— ' "Epistola solitarii ad reges": Alphonse of Pecha as Organizer of Birgittine and Urbanist Propaganda,' *Medieval Studies*, 1956, vol. 18, pp. 19–49.

—— ed., *The Medieval Mystics of England*, New York, Charles Scribner & Sons, 1961.

Colledge, E. and Walsh, J., eds, *A Book of Shewings to the Anchoress Julian of Norwich*, 2 vols, Toronto, Pontifical Institute of Medieval Studies, 1978.

Comaroff, Jean, *Body of Power, Spirit of Resistance: The Culture and History of a South African People*, Chicago and London, University of Chicago Press, 1985.

Comaroff, Jean and Comaroff, John, *Of Revelation and Revolution: Christianity, Colonialism and Consciousness in South Africa*, Chicago, University of Chicago Press, 1991.

Consacro, Peter, 'A Critical Edition of The Abbey of the Holy Ghost from All Known Extant Eng MSS with Introduction, Notes, and Glossary', Ph.D. dissertation, Fordham University, 1971.

Constable, Giles, 'Twelfth-Century Spirituality and the Late Middle Ages' in *Medieval and Renaissance Studies*, pp. 27–60, edited by O. B. Hardison, Chapel Hill, University of North Carolina Press, 1971.

Cowling, Douglas, 'The Liturgical Celebration of Corpus Christi in Medieval York', *Reed Newsletter*, 1976, vol. 1, pt. 2, pp. 5–9.

Cowper, J. R, ed., *Medytacyuns of the Soper of oure Lorde Ihesu*, Early English Text Society o.s. 60, London, 1885.

Cross, Claire, 'Great Reasoners in Scripture: The Activities of Women Lollards 1380–1530' in *Medieval Women*, pp. 359–80, edited by Derek Baker, Oxford, Blackwell, 1978.

Cumming, William Patterson, ed., *Revelations of St. Birgitta*, Early English Text Society o.s. 178, London, Oxford University Press, 1929.

Davidson, Clifford, 'Thomas Aquinas, the Feast of Corpus Christi and the English Cycle Plays', *Michigan Academician*, 1974, vol. 7, pp. 103–10.

Davies, Natalie Zemon, 'From "Popular Religion" to Religious Cultures' in *Reformation Europe: A Guide to Research*, pp. 321–41, edited by Steven Ozment, St Louis, Center for Reformation Research, 1982.

Delaney, Sheila, 'Sexual Economics, Chaucer's Wife of Bath and the *Book of Margery Kempe*', *Minnesota Review*, 1975, n.s. 5, pp. 104–115.

Despres, Denise, *Ghostly Sights: Visual Meditation in Late Medieval Literature*, Norman, Pilgrim Books, 1989.

Devlin, Dennis Steel, 'Corpus Christi: A Study in Medieval Eucharistic Theory, Devotion and Practice', Ph.D. dissertation, University of Chicago, 1975.

Dickens, A. G., *The English Reformation*, New York, Schocken Books, 1964.

Dictionnaire de spiritualité ascétique et mystique doctrine et histoire, edited by Marcel Villier *et al.*, 10 vols, 1937–.

Dictionnaire de théologie catholique contenant l'exposé des doctrines de la théologie catholique, leurs preuves et leur histoire, edited by A. Vacant et al., 15 vols, Paris, 1909–50.

Dix, Dom Gregory, *The Shape of the Liturgy*, London, Dacre Press, 1945.

Dobson, R. B., ed., *The Peasants' Revolt of 1381*, London, Macmillan, 1970.

—— 'The Risings in York, Beverley and Scarborough 1380–81' in *The English Rising of 1381*, pp. 112–42, edited by R. H. Hilton and T. H. Aston, Cambridge, Cambridge University Press, 1984.

Douglas, Mary, *Purity and Danger: An Analysis of the Concepts of Pollution and Taboo*, London, Routledge & Kegan Paul, 1966.

—— *Natural Symbols: Explorations in Cosmology*, Barrie & Rockliff, 1970; reprint edn, Harmondsworth, Penguin, 1973.

Doyle, A. I., 'A Survey of the Origins and Circulation of Theological Writings in English in the Fourteenth, Fifteenth and Sixteenth Centuries with Special Consideration of the Part of the Clergy Therein', Ph.D. dissertation, Cambridge University, 1953.

Dumoutet, E., *Le Désir de voir l'hoste et les origines de la dévotion au saint-sacrement*, Paris, Beauchesnes, 1926.

Durkheim, Emile, *The Elementary Forms of the Religious Life*, translated by Joseph Ward Swain, London, Allen & Unwin, 1915.

Eccles, Mark, ed., *The Macro Plays*, Early English Text Society o.s 262, Oxford, Oxford University Press, 1969.

Edwards, A. S. G., ed., *Middle English Prose: A Critical Guide to Major Authors and Genres*, New Brunswick, Rutgers University Press, 1984.

Eliade, Mircea, *Patterns in Comparative Religion*, New York, Sheed & Ward, 1958.

Elias, Norbert, *The Civilizing Process*, 2 vols, New York, Pantheon Books, 1982.

Ellis, Deborah, 'Margery Kempe and the Virgin's Hot Caudle', *Essays in Arts and Sciences*, 1985, vol. 14, pt 3, pp. 1–12.

Ellis, Roger, ' "Flores ad fabricandum . . . coronam": An Investigation into the Uses of the Revelations of St Bridget of Sweden in Fifteenth-Century England,' *Medium Aevum*, 1982, vol. 51, pt 2, pp. 163–85.

Elton, Geoffrey, *Reform and Reformation: England 1509–58*, London, Arnold, 1977.

Erbe, Theodor., ed., *Mirk's Festiall*, Early English Text Society e.s. 96, London, Kegan Paul, Trench, Trubner & Co., 1905.

Faith, Rosamond, ' "The Great Rumour" of 1377 and Peasant Ideology' in *The English Rising of 1381*, pp. 43–73, edited by R. H. Hilton and T. H. Aston, Cambridge, Cambridge University Press, 1984.

Firth, Raymond, *Symbols Public and Private*, Ithaca, Cornell University Press, 1973.

Flanigan, Clifford, 'Liminality, Carnival and Social Structure: The Case of Late Medieval Biblical Drama' in *Victor Turner and the Construction of Cultural Criticism: Between Literature and Anthropology*, pp. 42–64, edited by Kathleen Ashley, Bloomington and Indianapolis, Indiana University Press, 1990.

Fortescue, Adrian, *The Mass: A Study of the Roman Liturgy*, London, Longman, 1912.

Foucault, Michel, *Discipline and Punish: The Birth of the Prison*, translated by Alan Sheridan, Harmondsworth, Penguin, 1977. First published as *Surveiller et punir: naissance de la prison*, Paris, Editions Gallimard, 1975.

Furnivall, F. J., *Robert of Brunne's Handlyng Synne*, Early English Text Society o.s. 119, London, Kegan Paul, Trench, Trubner & Co., 1901.

—— ed., *Hoccleve: The Minor Poems*, Early English Text Society e.s. 61, London, Kegan Paul, Trench, Trubner & Co., 1892.

Gadamer, Hans Georg, *Truth and Method*, translated and edited by Garrett Barden and John Cumming, New York, Seabury Press, 1975.

Gairdner, James, *Lollardy and the Reformation in England: An Historical Survey*, London, Macmillan & Co., 1908.

Geertz, Clifford, *The Interpretation of Cultures*, New York, Basic Books, 1973.

Georgianna, Linda, *The Solitary Self: Individuality in the Ancrene Wisse*, Cambridge, Mass., Harvard University Press, 1981.

Gibson, Gail McMurray, *The Theater of Devotion: East Anglian Drama and Society in the Late Middle Ages*, Chicago, University of Chicago Press, 1989.

Giddens, Anthony, *The Constitution of Society: Outline of the Theory of Structuration*, Cambridge, Polity Press, 1984.

Gillespie, Vincent, 'Strange Images of Death: The Passion in Later Medieval English Devotional and Mystical Writings' in *Zeit, Tod und Ewigkeit in der Renaissance Literatur*, pp. 111–57, *Analecta Cartusiana*, 1987, no. 117, Salzburg, Institut für Anglistik und Amerikenistik.

—— 'Vernacular Books of Devotion' in *Book Production and Publishing in Britain 1375–1475*, edited by Jeremy Griffiths and Derek Pearsall, Cambridge, Cambridge University Press, 1989.

Gimello, Robert M., 'Mysticism in Its Contexts' in *Mysticism and Religious Traditions*, pp. 61–88, edited by S. Katz, Oxford and New York, Oxford University Press, 1983.

Girouard, Mark, *The Return to Camelot: Chivalry and the English Gentleman*, New Haven, Yale University Press, 1981.

Glasscoe, Marion, 'Time of Passion: Latent Relationships between Liturgy and Meditation in Two Middle English Mystics' in *Langland, the Mystics and the Medieval English Religious Tradition: Essays in Honour of S. S. Hussey*, pp. 141–61, edited by Helen Phillips, Cambridge, D. S. Brewer, 1990.

Goodman, Antony, 'The Piety of John Brunham's Daughter of Lynn' in *Medieval Women*, pp. 347–59, edited by Derek Baker, Oxford, Blackwell, 1978.

Gougaud, L., 'La Mesure de la plaie côtée', *Revue d'Histoire Ecclésiastique*, 1924, vol. 20, pp. 223–7.

—— *Dévotions et pratiques ascétiques au moyen âge*, Paris, Collection Pax, 1927.

Graef, Hilda, *The Light and the Rainbow*, London, Longmans, 1959.

Gramsci, Antonio, *Selections from the Prison Notebooks*, edited by Q. Hoare and G. Nowell Smith, New York, International Publishers, 1971.

Graves, Pamela, 'Social Space in the English Medieval Parish Church', *Economy and Society*, 1989, vol. 18, pt 3, pp. 297–322.

Gray, Douglas, *Themes and Images in the Medieval Religious Lyric*, London, Routledge & Kegan Paul, 1972.

—— 'The Five Wounds of Our Lord', *Notes and Queries*, 1963, vol. 108, pp. 50–1, 82–9, 127–34, 163–8.

Greg, W. W., *The Trial and Flagellation with Other Studies in the Chester Cycle*, Oxford, Malone Society, 1935.

Habig, Marion, ed., *St. Francis of Assisi: Writings and Early Biographies: English Omnibus of the Sources for the Life of St. Francis*, Chicago, Franciscan Herald Press, 1983.

Haigh, C., *Reformation and Resistance in Tudor Lancashire*, Cambridge, Cambridge University Press, 1987.

Haines, Roy, ' "Wilde Wittes and Wilfulness": John Swetstock's Attack on Those "Poyswunmongeres", the Lollards', *Studies in Church History*, Subsidia 8, pp. 143–53, Oxford, Blackwell, 1971.

Hanawalt, Barbara, 'Keepers of the Lights: Late Medieval English Parish Gilds', *Journal of Medieval and Renaissance Studies*, 1984, vol. 14, pt 1, pp. 21–37.

Harrison, Peter, *'Religion' and the Religions in the English Enlightenment*, Cambridge, Cambridge University Press, 1990.

Heath, Peter, 'Urban Piety in the Later Middle Ages: The Evidence of Hull Wills' in *The Church, Politics and Patronage in the Fifteenth Century*, pp. 209–34, edited by R. B. Dobson, Gloucester, Alan Sutton, 1984.

—— *Church and Realm, 1272–1461: Conflict and Collaboration in an Age of Crisis*, London, Fontana, 1988.

Heyworth, P. L., ed., *Friar Daw's Reply and Upland's Rejoinder*, Oxford, Oxford University Press, 1968.

Hillen, Henry J., *History of the Borough of King's Lynn*, Norwich, East of England Newspaper Co., Ltd, 1907.

Hilton, Rodney, *The English Peasantry in the Later Middle Ages*, Oxford, Clarendon Press, 1965.

—— *Bond Men Made Free: Medieval Peasant Movements and the English Rising of 1381*, London, Methuen, 1973.

—— *Class Conflict and the Crisis of Feudalism*, London, Hambledon Press, 1985.

Hirschkop, Ken, 'Bakhtin, Discourse and Democracy', *New Left Review*, 1986, no. 160, pp. 92–113.

Hirschkop, Ken, and Shepherd, David, eds., *Bakhtin and Cultural Theory*, Manchester, Manchester University Press, 1989.

Hirsh, J. C., 'Author and Scribe in *The Book of Margery Kempe*', *Medium Aevum*, 1975, vol. 44, pp. 145–50.

—— 'The Experience of God: A New Classification of Certain Late Medieval Affective Texts', *Chaucer Review*, 1976, vol. 11, pp. 11–21.

Hodgson, Phyllis, ed., *The Cloud of Unknowing and the Book of Privy Counselling*, Early English Text Society o.s. 218, Oxford, Oxford University Press, 1944.

Hodgson, Phyllis and Liegey, G. M., eds, *The Orcherd of Syon*, Early English Text Society o.s. 258, Oxford, Oxford University Press, 1966.

Holbrook, Sue Ellen, 'Order and Coherence in the Book of Margery Kempe' in *The Worlds of Medieval Women: Creativity, Influence, Imagination*, pp. 97–112, edited by Constance H. Berman, Charles W. Connell and Judith Rice Rothschild, Morgantown, West Virginia University Press, 1985.

Horstmann, C., ed., *Prosalegenden: Die Legenden des Ms. Douce 114, Anglia*, 1885, vol. 8, pp. 134–83.

—— ed., *Minor Poems of the Vernon MS.*, Early English Text Society o.s. 98, London, Kegan Paul, Trench, Trubner & Co., 1892.

—— ed., *Yorkshire Writers: Richard of Hampole and his Followers: An English Father to the Church and his Followers*, London, Swan Sonnenschein and Co., 1895.

Howard, D., *Writers and Pilgrims: Medieval Pilgrimage Narratives and their Posterity*, Berkeley, University of California Press, 1980.

Hoyle, John, 'Beyond the Sex-Economy of Mysticism: Some Observations on the Communism of the Imagination with Reference to Winstanley and Traherne' in *1642: Literature and Power in the Seventeenth Century*, edited by F. Barker, J. Bernstein, J. Coombes, P. Hulme, J. Stone, J. Stratton, University of Essex, 1981.

Hudson, Anne, 'The Examination of Lollards', *Bulletin of the Institute of Historical Research*, 1973, vol. 46, pp. 145–59.

—— ed., *Selections from English Wycliffite Writings*, Cambridge, Cambridge University Press, 1978.

—— 'Lollardy: The English Heresy' in *Religion and National Identity*, pp. 261–83, edited by Stuart Mews, *Studies in Church History*, Subsidia 18, Oxford, Blackwell, 1982.

—— *The Premature Reformation: Wycliffite Texts and Lollard History*, Oxford, Clarendon Press, 1988.

Hughes, Jonathan, *Pastors and Visionaries: Religion and Secular Life in Late Medieval Yorkshire*, Cambridge, Boydell Press, 1988.

Huizinga, Johan, *The Waning of the Middle Ages: A Study of the Forms of Life, Thought and Art in France and the Netherlands in the Fourteenth and Fifteenth Century*, Harmondsworth, Penguin, 1955. First published in Holland in 1919.

Hussey, S. S., 'The Audience for Middle English Mystics' in *De cella in seculum*, pp. 109–22, edited by Michael G. Sargent, Cambridge, D. S. Brewer, 1989.

Hutcheon, Linda, *A Poetics of Postmodernism: History, Theory, Fiction*, London, Routledge, 1988.

Inge, William, *Christian Mysticism*, London, Methuen & Co., 1899; reprint ed., London, 1921.

—— *Mysticism in Religion*, Chicago, University of Chicago Press, 1948.

James, Mervyn, 'Ritual, Drama and Social Body in the Late Medieval English Town', *Past and Present*, 1983, no. 98, pp. 3–29.

James, William, *The Varieties of Religious Experience*, New York, 1902.

Jay, Nancy, 'Sacrifice as Remedy for Having Been Born of Woman' in *Immaculate and Powerful: The Female in Sacred Image and Social Reality*, pp. 283–309, edited by Clarissa Atkinson, Constance Buchanan and Margaret Miles, Boston, Beacon Press, 1985; in England, Seabury Press.

Jeffrey, David, *The Early English Lyric and Franciscan Spirituality*, Lincoln, University of Nebraska Press, 1971.

Johnstone, A. F. and Rogerson, Margaret, eds, *Records of Early English Drama: York*, Toronto, University of Toronto Press, 1979.

Jones, Rufus, *Studies in Mystical Religion*, London, Macmillan, 1923.

—— *Mysticism and Democracy in the English Commonwealth*, Cambridge, Mass., Harvard University Press, 1932.

—— *The Flowering of Mysticism: The Friends of God in the Fourteenth Century*, New York, Macmillan, 1939.

Jones, W. R., 'English Religious Brotherhoods and Medieval Lay Piety: The Inquiry of 1388–89', *The Historian*, 1973/4, vol. 36, pp. 646–59.

Kail, J., ed., *Twenty-Six Political and Other Poems*, Early English Text Society o.s. 124, London, K. Paul, Trench, Trubner & Co., 1904.

Kane, Harold, ed., *The Prickynge of Love*, Salzburg, Institut für Anglistik und Amerikanistik, 1983.

Kantorowicz, Ernst, *The King's Two Bodies*, Princeton, Princeton University Press, 1957.

Katz, Steven, ed., *Mysticism and Philosophical Analysis*, Oxford, Oxford University Press, 1978.

—— 'The "Conservative" Character of Mysticism' in *Mysticism and Religious Traditions*, pp. 3–60, edited by Steven Katz, Oxford, Oxford University Press, 1983.

Kendall, Ritchie, *The Drama of Dissent*, Chapel Hill, University of North Carolina Press, 1986.

Kirchberger, Clare, ed., *The Goad of Love*, Oxford, Oxford University Press, 1957.

Klauser, Theodor, *A Short History of the Liturgy*, Oxford, Oxford University Press, 1969.

Knowles, David, *The Religious Orders in England*, 3 vols, Cambridge, Cambridge University Press, 1948–9.

Kolve, V. A., *The Play Called Corpus Christi*, Stanford, Stanford University Press, 1966.

Konrath, W., ed., *William of Shoreham's Poems*, Early English Text Society e.s. 86, London, Kegan Paul, Trench, Trubner & Co., 1902.

Kristensson, G., ed., *John Mirk's Instructions for Parish Priests*, Lund Studies in English, 1974, vol. 49.

LaCapra, Dominick, *Emile Durkheim: Sociologist and Philosopher*, Chicago and London, University of Chicago Press, 1972.

—— *Rethinking Intellectual History: Texts, Contexts, Language*, Ithaca, Cornell University Press, 1983.

Ladner, Gerhart, *Images and Ideas in the Middle Ages: Selected Studies in History and Art*, Rome, Edizioni di Storia e Letteratura, 1983.

Leclerq, Jean, *Monks and Love in Twelfth-Century France: Psycho-Historical Essays*, Oxford, Oxford University Press, 1979.

Leeuw, G. van der, *Religion in Essence and Manifestation: A Study in Phenomenology*, translated by J. E. Turner, London, Allen & Unwin, 1938.

Leff, Gordon, *Heresy in the Later Middle Ages*, Manchester, Manchester University Press, 1967.

Le Goff, Jacques, *La Naissance du purgatoire*, Paris, Gallimard, 1981.

Little, Lester, *Religious Poverty and the Profit Economy in Medieval Europe*, Ithaca, Cornell University Press, 1978.

Lloyd, Christopher, *Explanation in Social History*, Oxford, Blackwell, 1986.

Lochrie, Karma, 'The Book of Margery Kempe: The Marginal Woman's Quest for Literary Authority', *Journal of Medieval and Renaissance Studies*, 1986, vol. 16, pt 1, pp. 33–55.

—— *Margery Kempe and Translations of the Flesh*, Philadelphia, University of Pennsylvania Press, 1991.

Lock, M. and Scheper-Hughes, Nancy, 'A Critical Interpretive Approach in Medieval Anthropology' in *Medical Anthropology: A Handbook of Theory and Method*, pp. 47–72, edited by Thomas M. Johnson and Carolyn F. Sargent, New York, Greenwood Press, 1990.

Lovatt, Roger, 'The Imitation of Christ in Late Medieval England', *Transactions of the Royal Historical Society*, 1968, 5th series, no. 18, pp. 97–121.

—— 'Henry Suso and the Medieval Mystical Tradition in England' in *The Medieval Mystical Tradition in England*, pp. 47–62, edited by Marion Glasscoe, Exeter, 1982.

de Lubac, Henri, *Corpus mysticum: l'eucharistie et l'eglise au moyen-âge*, Paris, Aubier, 1959.

Lukes, Steven, 'Political Ritual and Social Integration', *Sociology*, 1975, vol. 9, pp. 289–308.

McGarry, Sister Loretta, 'The Holy Eucharist in Middle English Homiletic and Devotional Verse', Ph.D. dissertation, Catholic University of Washington, 1936.

McNiven, Peter, *Heresy and Politics in the Reign of Henry IV: The Burning of John Badby*, Cambridge, Boydell Press, 1987.

McRee, Ben, 'Religious Gilds and Regulation of Behavior in Late Medieval Towns' in *People, Politics and Community*, pp. 108–21, edited by J. Rosenthal and Colin Richmond, Gloucester, Alan Sutton, 1987.

Macy, Gary, *The Theologies of the Eucharist in the Early Scholastic Period: A Study of the Salvific Function of the Sacrament according to the Theologians c. 1080–1220*, Oxford, Clarendon Press, 1984.

Marrow, James, *Passion Iconography in Northern European Art in the Late Middle Ages and Early Renaissance: A Study of the Transformation of Sacred Metaphor into Descriptive Narrative*, Ars Neerlandica, Studies in the History of Art of the Low Countries, Kortrijk, Belgium, Van Ghemmert Pub. Co., 1979.

Marsilius of Padua, *Defensor pacis*, edited by C. W. Prévite-Orton, Cambridge, The University Press, 1928.

Marx, Karl, *Critique of Hegel's Philosophy of Right*, Cambridge, Cambridge University Press, 1970.

Medcalf, Stephen, *The Later Middle Ages*, London, Methuen, 1981.

Meech, Sanford and Allen, Hope Emily, eds, *The Book of Margery Kempe*, Early English Text Society o.s. 212, Oxford, Oxford University Press, 1940.

Merleau Ponty, Maurice, *Phenomenology of Perception*, London, Routledge & Paul, 1962.

Miles, Margaret, *Image as Insight: Visual Understanding in Western Christianity and Secular Culture*, Boston, Beacon Press, 1985.

Moore, Robert, *The Formation of a Persecuting Society*, Oxford, Blackwell, 1987.

Moorman, John, *A History of the Franciscan Order: From its Origins to the Year 1517*, Oxford, Clarendon Press, 1968.

Moran, Jo Ann Hoeppner, *The Growth of English Schooling 1340–1548: Learning, Literacy, and Laicization in Pre-Reformation York Diocese*, Princeton, Princeton University Press, 1985.

Morris, Kevin, *The Image of the Middle Ages in Romantic and Victorian Literature*, London, Croom Helm, 1984.

Morris, R., ed., *Legends of the Holy Rood, Symbols of the Passion and Cross Poems*, Early English Text Society o.s. 46, London, N. Trubner & Co., 1871.

Myers, A. R., *English Historical Documents 1327–1485*, London, Eyre & Spottiswoode, 1969.

Nelson, Alan H., *The Medieval English Stage: Corpus Christi Pageants and Plays*, Chicago and London, University of Chicago Press, 1974.

Nicholson, Linda J., *Gender and History: The Limits of Social Theory in the Age of the Family*, New York, Columbia University Press, 1986.

Nietzsche, Friedrich, *The Anti-Christ*, in *Twilight of the Gods / The Anti-Christ*, translated by R. J. Hollingdale, Harmondsworth, Penguin, 1968.

Oakley, Francis, 'Religious and Ecclesiastical Life on the Eve of the Reformation' in *Reformation Europe: A Guide to Research*, pp. 5–32, edited by Steven Ozment, St Louis, Center for Reformation Research, 1982.

Oberman, H. and Trinkaus, C., *The Pursuit of Holiness in Late Medieval and Renaissance Religion*, Leiden, Brill, 1974.

O'Connell, Michael, 'God's Body: Incarnation, Physical Embodiment, and the Legacy of Biblical Theater in the Sixteenth Century', paper given at the Seventh Citadel conference on Medieval and Renaissance Literature in Charleston, March 1991.

Ogilvie-Thomson, S. J., ed., *Walter Hilton's Mixed Life*, Salzburg, Institut für Englische Sprache und Literatur, 1986.

O'Neill, John, *Five Bodies: The Human Shape of Modern Society*, Ithaca, Cornell University Press, 1985.

Ophir, Adi, *Plato's Invisible Cities: Discourse and Power in the Republic*, Maryland, Barnes & Noble, 1991.

Orme, Nicholas, *English Schools in the Middle Ages*, New York, Harper & Row, 1973.

Otto, Rudolf, *Mysticism East and West*, New York, Macmillan, 1932.

Owen, Dorothy, *The Making of King's Lynn: A Documentary Survey*, London, Oxford University Press, 1984.

Ozment, Steven, *Mysticism and Dissent*, New Haven, Yale University Press, 1973.

—— ed., *Reformation Europe: A Guide to Research*, St Louis, Center for Reformation Research, 1982.

Parkes, M. B., 'The Literacy of the Laity' in *Literature and Western Civilization*, pp. 555–78, edited by D. Daiches and A. Thorlby, London, Aldus Books, 1973.

Patterson, Lee, 'Chaucerian Confession: Penitential Literature and the Pardoner', *Medievalia et Humanistica*, 1976, n. s. 7, pp. 153–73.

—— *Negotiating the Past: The Historical Understanding of Medieval Literature*, Madison, University of Wisconsin Press, 1987.

—— 'On the Margin: Postmodernism, Ironic History, and Medieval Studies', *Speculum*, 1990, vol. 65, pp. 87–108.

Peacock, Edward, ed., *John Mirk's Instructions for Parish Priests*, Early English Text Society o.s. 31, 1868; rpt London, Kegan, Trench, Trubner & Co., 1902.

Petroff, Elizabeth Alvida, ed., *Medieval Women's Visionary Literature*, Oxford, Oxford University Press, 1986.

Pfaff, Richard, *New Liturgical Feasts in Later Medieval England*, Oxford, Clarendon Press, 1970.

Phillip, John, *The Reformation of Images: Destruction of Art in England, 1535–1660*, Berkeley, University of Californa Press, 1973.

Phythian Adams, Charles, 'Ceremony and the Citizen: The Communal Year at Coventry 1450–1550' in *Crisis and Order in English Towns 1500–1700: Essays in Urban History*, pp. 57–85, edited by Peter Clark and Paul Slack, Toronto, University of Toronto Press, 1972.

—— 'Urban Decay in Late Medieval England' in *Towns in Societies: Essays in Economic History and Historical Sociology*, pp. 159–87, edited by Philip Abrams and E. A. Wrigley, Cambridge, Cambridge University Press, 1978.

Plomer, Henry R., *Wynkyn de Worde and his Contemporaries from the Death of Caxton to 1535*, London, Grafton & Co., 1925.

Pollard, A., ed., *Fifteenth-Century Verse and Prose*, New York, E. P. Dutton & Co., 1903.

Powell, Lawrence, ed., *Mirrour of the Blessyd Lyf of Jesu Christ*, London, Henry Frowde, 1908.

Priscandero, Michèle Theresa, 'Middle English Eucharistic Verse: Its Imagery, Symbolism and Typology', Ph.D. dissertation, St John's University, New York, 1975.

Quarrachi, *Stimulus amoris Fr. Iacobi Mediolanensis; canticum pauperis Fr. Iannis Peckham*, Bibliotheca Franciscana Ascetica Medii Aevi, 4, Quaracchi, Collegio S. Bonaventura, 1905.

Ragusa, Isa and Green, Rosalie, eds, *Meditations on the Life of Christ*, translated by Isa Ragusa and Rosalie Green, Princeton, Princeton University Press, 1961.

Raymo, Robert R., 'Works of Religious and Philosophical Instruction' in *A Manual of the Writings of Middle English 1050–1500*, pp. 2255–378, compiled by Albert Hartung, vol. 7, Connecticut Academy of Arts and Sciences, Hamden, Conn., Shoestring Press, 1986.

Riehle, Wolfgang, *The Middle English Mystics*, London, Routledge & Kegan Paul Ltd, 1981.

Riley, Denise, *'Am I that Name?' Feminism and the Category of Women in History*, Minneapolis, University of Minnesota Press, 1988.

Ringbom, Sixten, *Icon and Narrative: The Rise of the Dramatic Close-up in Fifteenth-Century Devotional Painting*, Doornspijk, The Netherlands, Davaco, 1984.

Robbins, Rossell Hope, 'Levation Prayers in Middle English Verse', *Modern Philology*, 1942, vol. 40, pp. 131–46.

Robertson, Elizabeth, 'Medieval Medical Views of Women and Female Spirituality' in *Medieval Views of the Body*, edited by Linda Lomperis and Sarah Stanbury, forthcoming, University of Pennsylvania Press.

Roseberry, William, *Anthropologies and Histories: Essays in Culture, History and Political Economy*, New Brunswick and London, Rutgers University Press, 1989.

Ross, W, ed., *Middle English Sermons*, Early English Text Society o.s. 209, London, Oxford University Press, 1938.

Rosser, Gervase, 'Communities of Parish and Guild in the Late Middle Ages' in *Parish, Church and People: Local Studies in Lay Religion 1350–1750*, pp. 29–55, edited by S. J. Wright, London, Hutchinson, 1988.

Rubin, Miri, 'Corpus Christi Fraternities and Late Medieval Lay Piety', *Studies in Church History*, 1986, 23, pp. 97–109.

—— *Corpus Christi: The Eucharist in Late Medieval Culture*, Cambridge, Cambridge University Press, 1991.

Russell, F. W., *Kett's Rebellion in Norfolk: Being a History of the Great Civic Commotion that Occurred at the time of the Reformation in the Reign of Edward VI*, 1859.

Russell, G. H., 'Vernacular Instruction of the Laity in the Later Middle

Ages in England: Some Texts and Notes', *Journal of Religious History*, 1962–3, vol. 2, pp. 98–119.

Said, Edward, 'Opponents, Audiences, Constituencies and Community' in *Postmodern Culture*, pp. 135–59, edited by Hal Foster, London and Sydney, Pluto Press, 1983.

Salter, Elizabeth, *Nicholas Love's 'Myrrour of the Blessyd Lyf of Jesu Christ'*, *Analecta Cartusiana*, vol. 10, Salzburg, Institut für Englische Sprache und Literatur, 1974.

—— 'The Manuscripts of Nicholas Love's *Myrrour of the Blessyd Lyf of Jesu Christ* and Related Texts' in *Middle English Prose: Essays on Bibliographical Problems*, pp. 115–27, edited by A. S. G. Edwards and Derek Pearsall, New York, Garland, 1981.

Sargent, Michael, 'The Transmission by the English Carthusians of Some Late Medieval Spiritual Writings', *Journal of Ecclesiastical History*, 1976, vol. 27, pp. 225–40.

—— 'Contemporary Criticism of Richard Rolle', *Analecta Cartusiana*, 1981, vol. 55, pt 1, pp. 160–205.

—— 'Bonaventura English: A Survey of the Middle English Prose Translations of Early Franciscan Literature', *Analecta Cartusiana*, 1984, vol. 106, pp. 145–76.

—— 'Contemplative Piety and Popular Piety in Late Medieval England', paper read at the New Chaucer Society meetings in Vancouver in August 1988.

Scarisbrick, J., *The Reformation and the English People*, Oxford, Blackwell, 1984.

Scarry, Elaine, *The Body in Pain: The Making and Unmaking of the World*, Oxford, Oxford University Press, 1985.

Scase, Wendy, *'Piers Plowman' and the New Anti-Clericalism*, Cambridge, Cambridge University Press, 1989.

Schmidtke, James A. ' "Saving" by Faint Praise: St. Birgitta of Sweden, Adam Easton and Medieval Antifeminism', *American Benedictine Review*, 1982, vol. 33, pt 2, pp. 149–61.

Scribner, Robert, 'Religion, Society and Culture: Reorienting the Reformation', *History Workshop*, 1982, nos. 13–16, pp. 2–22.

—— 'Interpreting Religion in Early Modern Europe', *European Studies Review*, 1983, vol. 13, pp. 89–105.

Shaw, Judith, 'The Influence of Canonical and Episcopal Reform on Popular Books of Instruction' in *The Popular Literature of Medieval England*, pp. 41–61, edited by Thomas Heffernan, Knoxville, University of Tennessee Press, 1985.

Sheingorn, Pamela, *The Easter Sepulchre in England*, Kalamazoo, Medieval Institute Publications, 1987.

Shepherd, Geoffrey, ed., *Ancrene Wisse: Parts Six and Seven*, Manchester, Manchester University Press, 1972; first issued 1959.

Sider, G., *Culture and Class in Anthropology and History: A Newfoundland Illustration*, Cambridge, Cambridge University Press, 1986.

Simmons, Thomas J. and Nolloth, Henry E., eds, *The Lay Folk's Catechism*, Early English Text Society o.s. 118, London, Kegan Paul, Trench, Trubner & Co., 1901.

Skeat, W. W., *Pierce the Ploughman's Creed*, Early English Text Society o.s. 30, London, N. Trubner & Co., 1867.

Southern, R. W., *Saint Anselm and His Biographer: A Study of Monastic Life and Thought 1059–1130*, Cambridge, Cambridge University Press, 1963.

Spalding, Mary Caroline, 'The Middle English Charters of Christ', Ph.D. dissertation, Bryn Mawr College, 1914.

Staal, Frits, *Exploring Mysticism*, Harmondsworth, Penguin, 1975.

Stace, W. T., *Mysticism and Philosophy*, London, Macmillan, 1960.

Stallybrass, Peter, 'Boundary and Transgression: Body, Text, Language', *Stanford French Review*, 1990, vol. 14, pts 1–2, pp. 9–26.

Stallybrass, Peter and White, Allon, *The Politics and Poetics of Transgression*, London, Methuen, 1986.

Stargardt, Ute, 'The Beguines of Belgium, the Dominican Nuns of Germany, and Margery Kempe' in *The Popular Literature of Medieval England*, pp. 277–313, edited by Thomas J. Heffernan, Knoxville, University of Tennessee Press, 1985.

Stevens, Martin, 'Illusion and Reality in the Medieval Drama', *College English*, 1970–1, vol. 32, pp. 448–64.

Strayer, J. R., 'The Laicization of French and English Society in the Thirteenth Century', *Speculum*, 1940, vol. 15, pp. 76–85.

Swanson, Guy, *Religion and Regime: A Sociological Account of the Reformation*, Ann Arbor, University of Michigan Press, 1967.

Swinburne, L. M., ed., *Lanterne of Light*, Early English Text Society o.s. 151, London, Kegan Paul, Trench, Trubner & Co., 1915.

Szarmach, Paul, ed., *An Introduction to the Medieval Mystics of Europe*, Albany, State University of New York Press, 1984.

Tanner, Norman P, ed., *Heresy Trials in the Diocese of Norwich 1428–31*, Royal Historical Society, Camden, 4th Series, vol. 20, London, 1977.

—— *The Church in Late Medieval Norwich 1370–1532*, Toronto, Pontifical Institute for Medieval Studies, 1984.

Taylor, Charles, *Philosophy and Social Science: Philosophical Papers*, vol. 1, *Human Agency and Language*, Cambridge, Cambridge University Press, 1985.

—— *Sources of the Self: The Making of the Modern Identity*, Cambridge, Mass., Harvard University Press, 1989.

Tentler, Thomas, *Sin and Confession on the Eve of the Reformation*, Princeton, Princeton University Press, 1977.

Thompson, John, *Ideology and Modern Culture: Critical Social Theory in the Era of Mass Communication*, Stanford, Stanford University Press, 1990.

Thomson, John A. F., *The Later Lollards 1414–1520*, Oxford, Oxford University Press, 1965.

Tierney, Brian, *The Crisis of Church and State 1050–1300*, Englewood Cliffs, N. J., Prentice-Hall, Inc., 1964.

Toews, John, 'Intellectual History after the Linguistic Turn: The Autonomy of Meaning and the Irreducibility of Experience', *American Historical Review*, 1987, vol. 92, pp. 879–907.

Toulmin Smith, Joshua and Toulmin Smith, Lucy, *English Gilds: Their Statutes and Customs, A.D. 1389*, Early English Text Society o.s. 40, London, N. Trubner & Co., 1870.

Touraine, Alain, *Return of the Actor: Social Theory in Post-industrial Society*, translated by Myrna Godzich, Minneapolis, University of Minnesota Press, 1988.

Travis, Peter, *Dramatic Design in the Chester Cycle*, Chicago, University of Chicago Press, 1982.

—— 'The Social Body of the Dramatic Christ in Medieval England', *Early Drama to 1600*, Acta, 1985, vol. 13, pp. 17–36.

—— 'The Semiotics of Christ's Body in the English Cycles' in *Approaches to Teaching Medieval Drama*, pp. 67–78, edited by Richard Emmerson, New York, MLA, 1990.

Troeltsch, Ernst, *The Social Teaching of the Christian Churches*, London and New York, Macmillan, 1931; repr. 1956.

Turner, Bryan, *The Body and Society: Explorations in Social Theory*, Oxford, Blackwell, 1984.

Turner, Victor, *Process, Performance and Pilgrimage: A Study in Comparative Symbology*, New Delhi, Concept Publishing Co., 1979.

Underhill, Evelyn, 'Medieval Mysticism' in *Cambridge Medieval History*, vol. 7, pp. 777–812, Cambridge, Cambridge University Press, 1949.

Vauchez, André, *La Spiritualité du moyen âge occidental VIIIe-XIIe siècle*, Paris, Presses Universitaires de France, 1975.

—— *Les Laïcs au moyen âge: pratiques et expériences religieuses*, Paris, Editions du Cerf, 1987.

Volosinov, V. I., *Marxism and the Philosophy of Language*, translated by Ladislaw Matejka, Cambridge, Mass., and London, Harvard University Press, 1973.

Wallace, David, 'Mystics and Followers in Siena and East Anglia: A Study in Taxonomy, Class and Cultural Mediation' in *The Medieval Mystical Tradition in England*, pp. 167–91, edited by Marion Glasscoe, Cambridge, D. S. Brewer, 1984.

Watkins, E. I., *Poets and Mystics*, London, Sheed & Ward, 1953.

Weatherly, Edward. H., ed., *Speculum sacerdotale*, Early English Text Society o.s. 200, London, Oxford University Press, 1936.

Weber, Max, *The Protestant Ethic and the Spirit of Capitalism*, New York, Scribner, 1958.

—— *Essays in Sociology*, translated, edited, and with an introduction by H. H. Gerth and R. Wright Mills, Oxford, Oxford University Press, 1958.

Weimann, Robert, *Shakespeare and the Popular Tradition in the Theater: Studies in the Social Dimension of Dramatic Form and Function*, Baltimore, Johns Hopkins University Press, 1978.

Westlake, H. F., *The Parish Gilds of Medieval England*, London, Macmillan, 1919.

White, Allon, 'The Struggle Over Bakhtin: Fraternal Reply to Robert Young', *Cultural Critique*, 1987/8, vol. 8, pp. 217–41.

—— 'Bakhtin, Sociolinguistics, and Deconstruction' in *The Theory of Reading*, pp. 123–46, edited by Frank Gloversmith, Brighton, Harvester, 1984.

Whiting, Robert, *The Blind Devotion of the People: Popular Religion and the English Reformation*, Cambridge, Cambridge University Press, 1989.

Wickham Legg, J., ed., *Tracts on the Mass*, London, Henry Bradshaw Society, vol. 27, 1904.

Wilkins, D., *Concilia Magnae Brittaniae et Hibernas*, vol. 3, London, 1737.

Williams, R., *The Long Revolution*, Harmondsworth, Pelican, 1961.

—— *Marxism and Literature*, Oxford, Oxford University Press, 1977.

—— *Politics and Letters: Interviews with New Left Review*, London, Verso, 1979.

Wilson, Katharina, ed., *Medieval Women Writers*, Manchester, Manchester University Press, 1984.

Wolf, Eric, *Europe and the People Without History*, Berkeley, University of California Press, 1982.

Womack, Peter, 'Imagining Communities: Theatres and the English Nation in the Sixteenth Century' in *Culture and History 1350–1600: Essays on English Communities, Identities and Writing*, pp. 91–145, edited by David Aers, Brighton, Harvester Press, 1992.

Wood-Legh, K. L., *Perpetual Chantries*, Cambridge, Cambridge University Press, 1965.

Woolf, Rosemary, 'The Theme of Christ the Lover-Knight in Medieval English Literature', *Review of English Studies*, 1962, vol. 13, pp. 1–16.

Young, Karl, *The Drama of the Medieval Church*, 2 vols, Oxford, Clarendon Press, 1933.

Zaehner, R. C., *Mysticism Sacred and Profane*, Oxford, Clarendon Press, 1957.

Zika, Charles, 'Hosts, Processions and Pilgrimages: Controlling the Sacred in Fifteenth-Century Germany', *Past and Present*, 1988, no. 118, pp. 25–64.

INDEX

'Abbey of the Holy Ghost, The' (treatise on the mixed life) 41–2, 142n.

accident and substance, relationship between 3

Adorno, Theodor W. and Max Horkheimer, *Dialectic of Enlightenment* 13, 126n.

Aelred of Rievaulx 144n.

Aers, David: *Medieval Literature: History, Criticism and Ideology* 100, 108, 127n., 158n., 159n.

affective theology 50–2

Alan of Lynn (Margery Kempe's confessor) 97–8, 157n., 161n.

Alcher of Clairvaux 144n.

allegorical exegesis 4

Allen, Hope Emily, on Margery Kempe 107

ambiguity: in category of the sacred 55–6, 149n.; and creative process 117, 165n.

ambivalence, in embodiment of Christ 5, 117

anagogy, concept of 48, 49, 145n.

analogy: of body and society 27–30; rejection of in negative mystical way 14–15; use of in positive mystical way 15–16

Ancrene Wisse 152n.

Angela of Foligno, St 15

anomie, concept of 11, 123–4n.; and literature on mysticism 9–10

Anselm, St.: on Christ giving birth to mankind 150–1n.; encouragement of devotion to Christ's humanity 54; *Cur Deus homo* 47, 143–4n.; *St Anselm's Proslogion* 48, 145n.

anti-clericalism, 25–6, 96, 98, 128–9n., 133n.; *see also* clerical authority: Lollards and Lollardy

art history, and image of Christ's body 4

Arundel, Archbishop 42, 64, 153n.; and deposition of Richard II 155n.; and Margery Kempe 90; and Nicholas Love 75; and trial of Sir John Oldcastle 72

Asad, Talal, 'On Ritual and Discipline in Medieval Christian Monasticism' 50–1, 146n.

ascetism 115, 165n.

assimilation, mysticism as 10

Aston, Margaret: *Lollards and Reformers: Images and Literacy in Late Medieval Religion* 37, 130n., 132n., 140n., 141n.; 'Wyclif and the Vernacular' 35, 132n., 137n., 139n., 140n., 152n.

Atkinson, Clarissa, *Mystic and Pilgrim: The Book and the World of Margery Kempe* 83, 89, 121n., 127n., 157–8n., 161n.

atonement, theory of 144n.